Babies with CVI

Nurturing Visual Abilities and Development in Early Childhood

Babies with CVI

Nurturing Visual Abilities and Development in Early Childhood

Anne McComiskey

APHPress

American Printing House for the Blind

Library of Congress Cataloging-in-Publication Data

Names: McComiskey, Anne V., 1945- author.
Title: Babies with CVI : nurturing visual abilities and development in early childhood / Anne V. McComiskey.
Description: Louisville : APH Press, American Printing House for the Blind, 2021. | Includes bibliographical references and index. | Summary: "Babies with CVI: Nurturing Visual Abilities and Development in Early Childhood is a guide through the history and best practices related to the treatment of CVI in children from birth to 36 months. This book is based on the author's nearly five-decade career working with families in homes and classrooms. Understanding and knowledge about effective interventions to address the visual skills of children with CVI evolved enormously over that period. Babies with CVI reflects that evolution. The book presents specific approaches and strategies that families and visual impairment professionals can use to meet the unique learning needs of a child with CVI. It stresses the importance of early intervention, proper evaluation, and integrating teaching opportunities into the child's daily routine"-- Provided by publisher.
Identifiers: LCCN 2021019220 (print) | LCCN 2021019221 (ebook) | ISBN 9781950723003 (paperback) | ISBN 9781950723010 (epub)
Subjects: LCSH: Pediatric neuroophthalmology. | Vision disorders in children.
Classification: LCC RE48.2.C5 M28 2021 (print) | LCC RE48.2.C5 (ebook) | DDC 618.92/0977--dc23
LC record available at https://lccn.loc.gov/2021019220
LC ebook record available at https://lccn.loc.gov/2021019221

TABLE OF CONTENTS

FOREWORD

It seems like I've known Anne McComiskey all of my professional life. I began working for the American Foundation for the Blind (AFB) in 1982 as the National Consultant in Early Childhood. Anne was a teacher in Atlanta, where she founded the early childhood services program BEGIN for infants and young children at the Center for the Visually Impaired in 1985. At the time, the Individuals with Disabilities Act was still called the Education for All Handicapped Children Act and early intervention services had not yet become part of the law.

I depended on people like Anne to carry out my work at AFB, and she helped in the field test of the first edition of my book *Reach Out and Teach: Helping Your Child who is Visually Impaired Learn and Grow* (Ferrell, 1985). The BEGIN program was one of the few initiatives in the nation that provided comprehensive early intervention services to infants with visual impairment and their families. It joined ground-breaking programs like the Foundation for Blind Children in Arizona and the Blind Babies Foundation in California. *Babies with Cerebral Visual Impairment* is a book I wish I had when I began working with babies and families back in 1975. This kind of work was all so new then—new to me and new to the field. My teacher preparation program focused on teaching school-age children, not working with adults who had never anticipated becoming the parents of children with a disability. I learned from week to week, and from family to family.

Babies with Cerebral Visual Impairment would have shortened my learning period. The book provides strategies for approaching families, making home visits, and having appropriate (and sometimes difficult) conversations. Better yet, Anne gives the reader activities and interventions for working with infants and toddlers with CVI. These activities are designed to help the children develop their visual skills and to increase their learning opportunities. She also takes the reader through a history of CVI and provides valuable resources for families and educators.

Anne and I haven't seen each other often over these last 38 years, but when we do get together, it is like we have never been apart. It's like that with treasured friends and colleagues—time passes, but once reunited, you pick up the conversations and ideas right where you left off. That is what being a professional is all about. This book continues Anne's journey, and mine. It will do the same for you.

Kay Alicyn Ferrell, PhD
Professor of Special Education, *Emerita*
University of Northern Colorado
Broomfield, Colorado
September 30, 2020

ACKNOWLEDGMENTS

It may "take a village" to raise a child, but this book took a much wider community. My best teachers and inspirations continue to be the parents who work so hard to help their babies with CVI, with special thanks to Dawn Burdett and the Burdett family for their inspiration and love. I am grateful to my colleagues who have shared their stories and encouraged and guided me during my work on this book. A big thank you to Dr. Irene Topor, who offered guidance about functional vision and ongoing support, and Dr. Amy K. Hutchinson, pediatric ophthalmologist and professor in Georgia, and a founding member of the Pediatric Cortical Visual Impairment Society, who assisted with several chapters. Amy's knowledge, encouragement, and enthusiasm for the project were critical to the book, especially to the validity of information presented. My thanks go to Dr. Lea Hyvärinen for sharing her knowledge and observations about babies with CVI and the use of corrective lenses. I extend special thanks and appreciation to the American Foundation for the Blind and American Printing House for the Blind and their many wonderful editors for their encouragement, and expertise. I extend my admiration and gratitude to all the dedicated professionals who work with and have written about cortical blindness, cortical visual impairment, neurological visual impairment, and cerebral visual impairment, especially Christine Roman-Lantzy, Gordon Dutton, Amanda Hall Lueck, and Lea Hyvärinen. There is still so much to learn about this complicated condition.

I hope that readers will find my insights, suggestions and information helpful as they work with this unique and special population of babies and their incredible parents and family.

INTRODUCTION

From 1964 to1965, German measles was an epidemic in the United States, leaving thousands of infants with congenital rubella syndrome—a condition that resulted in a variety of birth defects including brain-related visual impairment. Two-year old Cindy, her mother Judy, and I met during this incredible time. All three of us were confused about what to do to help Cindy and to support Judy. I had been a fifth- and sixth-grade teacher at Perkins School for the Blind in Massachusetts before moving to California to start a pilot program for babies of the epidemic. If it weren't insensitive, I would talk about "the halt leading the blind".

The 3-year-olds in the program were more like infants. Some could not crawl, let alone walk. None had toilet training. Several could not eat solid food or use a spoon. They had no language except for screaming or crying. Most didn't like to touch things or to be touched. Few were blind, but none used vision effectively. It was a very strange classroom! I kept wishing that I had been able to start teaching the parents and working with their children when they were babies. It was during this time that I first heard the term *cortical blindness*—a term we started to refer to as "cortical." We teachers did not know or understand much of anything about this unfamiliar diagnosis. The term became a way to explain behaviors and disabilities for which we had no other explanation and very little idea what to do about.

Move the calendar forward about 10 years; medical and educational knowledge had advanced significantly regarding children with brain-related vision loss. One crucial finding gained in that period is that because of the brain's ability to rewire, children with cerebral visual impairment/cortical visual impairment (CVI) could very often develop visual abilities—and *the earlier they start learning to work to develop these abilities, the better.*

Cindy, Judy, and I learned a lot together, but we didn't know most of the critical information about CVI that would be known

.st a decade later. Within 10 years, there was a large amount of
new information and new training available to help professionals
help babies with CVI. Professionals were learning about the
brain and how children with CVI learn. At that time, I worked on
an intra-disciplinary team in an early intervention program. The
knowledge of psychologists, physical and occupational therapists,
speech and language therapists, special educators, and vision
specialists was blended into creating strong plans for families and
their children with special needs. I learned so much about the
importance of touch, music, positioning, movement, and listening.
Combining this new information with what I had learned in my
earlier years about helping babies who were "cortical," made our
efforts more effective—babies started to develop visual abilities
and skills that surprised even me. Furthermore, their parents
became knowledgeable sources of information and support for
other parents.

Yet even with all of the knowledge available today, I continue
to read on the internet and hear about teachers and parents of
children with visual impairments who do not know what to do, and
who do not understand how critical a role timing plays in helping
these babies learn. *Babies with Cerebral Visual Impairment* is
my effort to present easy-to-digest information to parents and
professionals less familiar with the learning needs of babies with
CVI, and to offer suggestions for interventions and strategies to
help these babies learn visual skills and maximize visual learning
opportunities. It is my hope that, with this information, parents
can start to implement some of these easy interventions with their
baby even before there is a formal diagnosis. The days of "take
her home and love her" are over. Action is what these babies need
now to help them become their best selves.

Understanding and knowledge about effective interventions
to address the visual skills of children with CVI has been evolving
for decades. This book reflects that evolution, along with my
decades of experience working in homes and classrooms with
parents and their babies. It is now apparent that very early
initiation of intervention affects outcomes, and that there are

older. The aim of this book is to supplement that information by focusing on a topic that is not as widely covered in literature—that of the visual needs of *babies* with CVI. In addition, since CVI is a condition that affects the whole family, this book also addresses the needs of the parents of babies who have CVI. In addressing these needs, this book will provide information about a baby's visual system and how it relates to CVI, discuss the factors that affect parents' abilities to implement strategies with their babies and to collaborate with professionals about their babies' needs, offer strategies and goals for home organization, and offer suggestions for effective teaching interventions.

I wish you and your students/babies much success.

TERMS USED IN THE BOOK

When discussing CVI, it is not uncommon to hear two different terms for the abbreviation: *cerebral* visual impairment and *cortical* visual impairment. Although the terms are sometimes used interchangeably, they are not synonymous; Cerebral visual impairment is generally considered to be broader in scope and more encompassing of cortical visual impairment. The term *cerebral visual impairment* will be used in this book and is explained in detail in **Chapters 2 and 3**.

Parent refers to those who are primary caregivers of a baby with CVI. *Babies* refer to very young children from birth to three years of age. *Infant* refers to babies in their first year of life.

effective approaches and specific strategies and activities that help babies with CVI learn to build visual skills and increase learning opportunities. It is also apparent that there are several important factors for professionals to consider when planning goals and interventions for babies with CVI. First, the student is a *baby* whose unique learning needs significantly affect interactions and interventions. The student is uniquely connected to his or her parents, whose knowledge about CVI and understanding of effective approaches is an important factor in a baby's progress. Second, the student is *visually impaired,* and the needs and approaches in working with a baby who is visually impaired must not be overlooked. And third, this student has *cerebral visual impairment,* and the needs and approaches in working with a baby with CVI must not be confused as being identical to the needs of children who have an ocular visual impairment. My experience with the importance of these factors is what motivated this book.

EARLY VISUAL DEVELOPMENT GUIDE

This book introduces the Early Visual Development Guide, a planning tool designed to help readers track the visual milestones that indicate a baby's progress in learning early visual skills and behaviors, specifically visual alerting, visual engagement, and the integration of vision with other developmental skills—the three main levels outlined in the guide. The guide provides activities and tips to help babies progress in these skill areas. When the early visual skills presented in the guide are accomplished, a baby with CVI can be considered to have alerted his or her vision to enable the child to begin to develop more advanced visual skills. A baby who has progressed through the three levels of the guide is visually ready to move on to the visual motor and visual perceptual skills identified in other resources for visual development, such as the CVI Range (Roman-Lantzy, 2018) and the Oregon Project for Preschool Children Who Are Blind or Visually Impaired (Anderson, Boigon, Davis, & DeWaard, 2007).

Much of the available information about children with CVI discusses the needs of children who are preschool aged or

CHAPTER 1

Supporting Parents of Babies with Cerebral Visual Impairment

Teachers of children with cerebral visual impairment (CVI) have a dual teaching focus. On the one hand, they are focused on the developmental and visual skills of children. On the other hand, they are also focused on educating and supporting parents of children with CVI. This secondary function is no less important because the success of young children to reach developmental goals and increase visual ability is directly related to their parents' knowledge of CVI, as well as to parents' readiness and ability to implement interventions. This book provides information for professionals working with babies newly diagnosed with CVI, as well as for parents who need information and emotional support to help their babies reach important goals. This book also aims to provide information to help parents and professionals build partnerships and move together through processes that will help a baby with CVI achieve goals leading to improved visual skills and physical, intellectual, and social development.

Figure 1.1 outlines steps to building partnerships from the professional's point of view and identifies steps to help achieve these goals. The steps in this process correspond to chapters in this book. Each step is discussed in more detail in the following chapters. Building a relationship with the baby and the family **(Chapter 1)** is a vital first step in laying a foundation of support. The next step is to increase the family's knowledge base about vision and CVI **(Chapters 2 and 3)**, including what actions parents can take to help their baby develop visual skills. The third step is to organize a home team and build a home file of pertinent information about the baby's visual skills **(Chapter 4)**. From there, the home team creates a home action plan **(Chapter 4)**. This plan outlines the structure of the baby's overall education, listing specific goals to help that particular child increase vision

Figure 1.1
From Building Partnerships to Achieving Goals

Achieve goals leading to
increased visual abilities

Implement activities and strategies

Create a home action plan

Organize home team and gather
information about a baby's skills

Increase family's knowledge about
CVI and interventions

Build a relationship with the baby
and the family

Note. This arrow graphic shows six steps in the process from building relationships with a baby and their family to achieving goals leading to increased visual abilities.

and development. Finally, Developing Visual Skills/Interventions **(Chapter 5)** and the Early Visual Development Guide **(Chapter 6)** identify activities and strategies that will help a baby reach the goals outlined in the home action plan. These six steps share one aim: to increase the family's ability to help their baby with CVI maximize his or her visual abilities and development.

Many parents report that the support and information they received from their child's teacher within the first years after their baby was diagnosed with CVI enabled them to feel hope and regain the strength and energy to help their baby. A teacher of children with visual impairments can provide support by helping parents in these four ways:

- To understand that early intervention plays an important role to help improve their baby's vision and development

- To realize that the grief that follows a significant medical diagnosis may affect their emotions, behaviors, and energy, and can also make bonding with a baby who has a visual impairment especially challenging

- To learn about CVI and important strategies that can help a baby's development

- To build productive relationships with professionals such as teachers and medical doctors

EARLY INTERVENTION

Parents whose babies have just been diagnosed with CVI typically feel distraught. Their self-confidence might be shaken, which may cause them to feel that they are not ready to help their baby. After being given a diagnosis of CVI, parents may wonder what facts they need to know, what strategies they need to learn, and what sources they can access for answers. Feelings of stress and confusion may make otherwise intelligent people suddenly unable to grasp important information about how to help their baby. A teacher of children with visual impairments can support parents during this difficult time by explaining the importance of

Learning that their child has been diagnosed with CVI can be very distressing to many parents. A teacher of children with visual impairments can help by meeting with the family during this difficult time to offer emotional support, explain the importance of early interventions, and answer the family's questions.

early intervention services and how their child will benefit from specific interventions (Chen, 2014a).

Early intervention is a multifaceted process when addressing any disability. It involves multiple steps and requires different professionals working together as a team (see **Sidebar 1.1**) along with a child's family (Pogrund, 2002b). It is the process of providing services, education, and support to children under 3 years of age who are deemed to have an established condition, or who are evaluated and diagnosed with a disability or delay that may affect their development or impede their education. Early intervention programs and services emphasize natural environments, such as home and community settings, and are more effective if started immediately after a disability or delay has been identified. Early intervention services are outlined in Part C of the Individuals with Disabilities Education Improvement Act (IDEA 2004), a U.S.

Early Intervention Team Members

The early intervention process includes assessment and planning to meet the unique needs of each child and their family. A team is part of the service delivery model for young children (Correa, Fazzi, & Pogrund, 2002; Fazzi & Klein, 2002; Pogrund, 2002b). In addition to essential professionals, any individuals who the parents consider supportive, informative, and helpful can also serve as team members.

Team members can include:

- The parents or primary caregivers who know the child best and can ideally serve as the leaders of their baby's team
- A teacher of children with visual impairments who specializes in teaching children who are blind or visually impaired, specifically those with CVI
- An orientation and mobility (O&M) specialist who can help instruct the child to move safely in his or her environment
- An assistive technology specialist who can guide the team in selecting appropriate assistive technology for the child
- A physical therapist who can use therapeutic exercises to improve function and mobility
- An occupational therapist who can work on promoting activities of daily living
- A speech and language therapist or pathologist who can address difficulties with speech, language, and concept development.
- An early interventionist who specializes in working with infants and preschoolers

(continued)

- A specialist on multiple disabilities if the baby has other disabilities in addition to CVI

- A nurse who can help evaluate medical issues and needs

- A social worker or family counselor who can offer guidance as well as psychological and emotional support

- A family advocate who can work with the family to ensure they receive appropriate services and support

- Any family members or friends who can offer emotional or other support

federal law that governs how states and public agencies provide early intervention, special education, and related services to children with disabilities. Private individuals and agencies are yet another source of early intervention services.

Professionals and individuals who work in education understand one important fact: High-quality learning experiences provided early enough will build a foundation for a child's success in school and in life. While early education is helpful for all children, it is especially important for infants and toddlers with disabilities. Children with disabilities need access to high-quality early intervention services that will help prepare them for a successful transition to preschool and kindergarten.

A baby with CVI frequently has other needs in addition to visual difficulties because he or she may have a variety of other conditions that may or may not be related to the brain injury that caused the CVI. During this early diagnostic period, it is understandable that parents will want to be aware of all the issues that may affect their baby's health and development. As a result, parents may direct much of their energy toward seeking out additional appointments, diagnostic testing, and therapies.

However, during this hectic time, it is unlikely that parents have had the opportunity to learn about brain plasticity, or the capacity of the brain to reorganize itself as it develops (Catteneo & Merabet, 2015). While the brain remains plastic throughout a person's life, the most critical period of brain plasticity occurs during infancy and early childhood, which makes timing an important factor in a baby's visual development (Roman-Lantzy, 2018; brain plasticity and early development are discussed further in **Chapter 3**). It is important that parents understand that early experiences along with appropriate, specific interventions and strategies can affect the developing brain and enhance a baby's visual skills and overall development. Doctors and other professionals, as well as government agencies, understand the critical importance of early intervention and should be able to connect parents to appropriate early intervention programs where families can find the support and guidance that they need (see also **Appendix B, Resources**).

UNDERSTANDING GRIEF

Parents whose baby has recently been diagnosed with a disability such as CVI may experience grief. It is an unlearned, spontaneous process (Moses, 1987). Grief can have a major impact on both the lives and decisions of parents of a child with disabilities. After receiving a diagnosis, parents have reported confusion about the changes they notice in their feelings, behavior, and energy. Some parents may mistakenly interpret these natural grief responses as a sign that they will be unable to care for or love their baby with CVI. A teacher of children with visual impairments can support families by helping them understand that these feelings are normal, and that grief affects people in predictable ways. Parents are typically relieved and encouraged when they learn that their grief is an expected, spontaneous reaction and it does not indicate that they are unable to love and care for their baby. Publications such as *On Grief and Grieving* (Kübler-Ross & Kessler, 2005) and *The Impact of Childhood Disability: The Parent's Struggle* (Moses, 1987) provide valuable insights about the experience of grief to both parents and professionals. The experience of grieving includes several stages consisting of different emotions. Recent studies show that these stages do not occur in a predictable order. Instead, different grief emotions will appear, disappear, and reappear at different times, and may be triggered by different events (Fazzi et al., 2002).

THE STAGES OF GRIEF

The grief experience table (**Table 1.1**) lists the stages of grief that the author has directly observed in parents of babies with visual impairments. The table also identifies several behaviors and reactions parents commonly exhibit during each stage and suggest actions professionals can take to support families during these difficult times. *Listening* and *providing attachment interventions* are suggested for each stage. Both are uniquely beneficial in supporting parents and in helping to increase their ability to attach with their baby.

Shock

Parents who have just learned that their baby has CVI are typically numb and in shock. Initially they may feel as though they are watching events unfold from outside of their own bodies. They may be easily distracted, unfocused, forgetful, and fatigued. The most important support professionals can provide to parents who are in shock is to listen to how the parents describe their feelings and reactions to their baby's diagnosis. During an early home visit, in addition to listening, professionals must be prepared to provide brief and clear answers to parents' questions. They will also need to provide information about visual impairment, an overview of how CVI relates to brain plasticity, and an explanation about the stages of the grief process. During this early visit, professionals might also introduce an early visual skill intervention (as detailed in **Chapter 6**) to help parents feel empowered to help their child. This book provides succinct information related to visual impairment in general, and CVI in particular, that can serve as a helpful reference during early meetings with parents (see **Appendix C**).

Table 1.1
Grief Experience Table

Stage/Emotion	Behavior(s)	Support
Shock	• Numb	• LISTEN
		• Explain the grief process
	• Distracted	
	• Forgetful	• Offer brief, clear answers to questions
	• Unfocused	• Suggest baby massage activity to increase parent-baby attachment
		• Suggest visual skill building intervention
		• Refer to other resources and groups
	• Feeling "out of body"	
	• Exhausted	• Suggest participation in parent-child music class
	• Low affect	
Sadness / Depression	• Crying or feeling depressed	• LISTEN
	• Low or negative affect	• Refer to other professionals, information websites, support groups, or another mentor parent supporter
	• Exhausted	• Suggest parent-baby attachment interventions
	• May become sick	• Suggest music or movement class to increase relaxation and attachment
	• Has trouble sleeping	

(continued)

Table 1.1 (continued)

Stage/ Emotion	Behavior(s)	Support
Denial	• Difficulty focusing • Sleeping excessively to escape sadness • Working excessively to escape sadness • Defensive • Downplays seriousness of diagnosis • Belief that a higher power will "fix" the issue • Insists that doctors are incorrect about diagnosis • Belief that situation is consequence of past actions.	• LISTEN • Relate positive observations
Anxiety	• Anxious about possibility of other revelations about baby's health • Worried about the baby • Is quiet, timid, overly attentive • Controlling	• Offer support referrals • Suggest parent-baby attachment interventions • LISTEN • Suggest chest-to-chest relaxation • Introduce to parent mentor • Suggest parent-baby attachment interventions
Guilt	• Preoccupied with future • Obsessive • Ignores other children	• LISTEN • Provide support activities, including activities that include siblings

Table 1.1 (continued)

Stage/ Emotion	Behavior(s)	Support
	• Feels "deserving" of present situation	• Suggest parent-baby attachment interventions
		• Provide referrals as appropriate
Resentment/ Anger	• Is curt, rude or angry	• LISTEN
	• Places blame on others	• Avoid difficult discussions
	• Litigious	
	• Questions spiritual beliefs	
	• Experiences partner discord	
Bargaining	• Excessive focus on behaving ethically	• LISTEN
	• Obsessively researches child's condition	• Refer to support sources, appropriate websites, and programs
	• Volunteers	
Acceptance	• Behaves more calmly	• LISTEN
	• Is ready to listen	• Explain that emotions from previous stages of grief may reappear, but now with diminished intensity
	• Interest in participating in interventions	
	• Demonstrates closer attachment with baby	

Note. This table identifies several behaviors often associated with various stages of grief and suggests interventions that have proven to be particularly helpful to parents during each stage.

Sadness and Depression

Feelings of sadness and depression typically follow shock. Parents may switch from emotionally demonstrative behaviors (such as crying) to displaying emotional flatness, and low or negative affect. They may become exhausted or physically ill, have difficulty focusing, or experience trouble sleeping. Alternatively, they may sleep or work in excess in order to avoid confronting their feelings. Feelings of sadness may resurface later on occasions such as their child's birthday, when additional health issues are diagnosed, at the introduction of new adaptive equipment, or upon hearing insensitive comments from others. At the first family meeting, professionals can suggest a simple activity to help parents engage or bond with their baby. A massage activity, such as the one listed in **Appendix A**, can help sad or depressed parents feel closer to their baby while also providing important sensory contact. This contact can be positive for both the baby and the parent (Chen, 2014b; Lappin & Kretschmer, 2005).

During initial assessments of a baby's abilities, parents may feel sadness if they perceive that their baby with CVI has "failed" one medical test after another. To mitigate feelings of sadness, assessments should take place through playful interactions as opposed to overly clinical or impersonal approaches. As a result, parents may feel more at ease because they perceive that their baby is playing rather than being tested. Similarly, the professional should complete assessment and observation forms only after a visit, never during, to avoid an atmosphere of judgement.

Referrals to other professionals and to websites with helpful information is valuable for parents at this difficult stage. Many parents feel comforted by joining support groups with other parents whose children have similar disabilities, or by being partnered with mentor parents who can share their own comparable experiences. Other parents may enjoy attending a music or movement class with their baby. Such classes can ease their sadness and depression, as well as increase their feelings

Parents who feel sad or depressed about their baby's diagnosis of CVI can benefit from sensory contact with their child. Infant massage can have a positive impact on parent/child bonding, as well as being beneficial to the baby's development.

of belonging or connecting with others, all of which can have a positive effect for both baby and parent (Metell, 2015).

Denial

A parent who is grieving may come to doubt the reality of their child's diagnosis and its implications. This denial is one way the mind can protect them from news that is otherwise too difficult to manage. Parents may now believe that the diagnosis is incorrect or that a greater power will magically fix the problem. They may even conclude that something they have done has earned them this situation. Parents in denial may sometimes act defensively when given suggestions about possible interventions. "We've already done that," or "We've tried that; it didn't work," are examples of comments from a parent in denial.

Professionals may find it difficult to communicate with parents at this stage because parents in denial are often not ready for active interventions. One way to support parents in denial is to listen attentively to their concerns about their child. In addition, making positive observations about their baby's appearance (e.g., long eyelashes or curly hair) or disposition (e.g., making "happy" sounds) can help parents feel more positive and better able to cope. An effective way to support parents during this stage is to demonstrate the activity of bathing their baby while including tactile stimulation and naming body parts. This bath activity can help parents who are in denial enjoy time with their baby. If parents' feelings of denial seem especially excessive, refer them to support groups or professionals who can help parents cope with their feelings.

Anxiety

Parents of a baby with CVI are understandably unusually anxious. Having recently experienced one unexpected revelation that upended their world, they may be anxious about receiving yet another one. They may seem excessively worried about their baby. Parents in the anxiety stage of grief may be timid, quiet, and overly preoccupied in searching for additional answers and solutions to their child's condition. They may also exhibit a strong need to control situations. Anxious parents may be so focused on the *possibility* of future problems that they are unable to focus on the *reality* of their baby's current and future needs.

When helping anxious parents, professionals should be respectful when listening to their concerns. Do not minimize their worries; do strive to provide direct, clear, and sensitive answers to any questions. Often another parent who is also experienced with parenting a child with CVI can act as a mentor and help reduce the parents' anxiety. Professionals may also suggest relaxation interventions for parents, such as chest-to-chest time with their baby. During this activity, parents can relax with their baby by using deep-breathing exercises. Parents can include their baby in their exercise routines, such as walking, stretching, or yoga. Moving together with their child can also ease parents' anxiety.

Guilt

Feelings of guilt are typical when grieving. Parents may feel that they caused their baby's disability, that it is payback for unacceptable thoughts or actions, or that they failed somehow by giving birth to a baby with difficulties. Parents with feelings of guilt may become so focused on tending to a baby with CVI that they may pay insufficient attention to their other children and to family needs in general. As with the other stages of grief, professionals can help by listening to parents' concerns, being careful not to minimize their feelings, and by referring them to support groups or to parent mentors who have experienced similar feelings. Professionals may also suggest activities that include all members

Professionals should involve a baby's siblings in interventions and activities to build the emotional bond between them. Professionals may make suggestions for ways to include all members of the family in interventions and activities. In this photo, an older sister cuddles and plays with her baby sibling.

of the family including siblings, such as participation in Sibshops (see **Appendix B**, **Resources**).

Resentment/Anger

Parents who grieve often express anger at their situation by being resentful. They may be curt or rude, blame others, leave their religious institution, experience discord with their partner, or become litigious. In this stage, it is even more vital for professionals to listen to parents with respect—and, in the author's experience, to avoid difficult discussions that can lead to further discord. In general, professionals may have difficulty presenting information and interventions to parents at this stage.

Bargaining

Another stage of grieving is bargaining. In this stage, parents might become convinced that if they do an activity unrelated to their baby's diagnosis, they will be rewarded by the baby becoming well. Bargaining can take many forms. To compensate for their situation, some parents may try to excel at any activity they undertake. They may also attempt to maximize their perceived moral standards through altruistic acts such as volunteering for charitable causes or by increasing their involvement in religious activities. Parents in the bargaining stage of grief may become obsessed with researching facts and studies related to their child's diagnosis. Again, professionals should listen to parents with respect and without judgment, and refer them to support sources, appropriate websites, or additional intervention programs as necessary. Involving parents in interventions to build visual skill ability in their child or in activities that enhance attachment to their child (e.g., baby massage) can help parents in the bargaining stage feel that they really are helping their baby. (**Appendix A** and **Chapter 6** provide such interventions.)

Acceptance

Parents in the acceptance stage of grief begin to come to terms with their baby's diagnosis. They may now appear calmer than they did in the other stages of grief. As a result, they may start to show more interest in participating in suggested interventions and demonstrate closer attachment with their baby. When parents start to feel more confident in their ability to parent a baby with CVI, they become more willing to accept a new and more realistic family concept, one which will replace their idealized vision of parenting. However, as previously stated, the stages of grief do not necessarily follow a predictable order. Again, professionals can remind parents that even though they have reached the acceptance stage, the stages of grief are not static. Stages may disappear and then reappear in reaction to a variety of events such as milestones like birthdays. When previously experienced stages of grief reappear, the same stages may now affect parents differently than they had originally. For example, a parent first experiencing the stage of anxiety might react to suggestions for interventions very cautiously, whereas a parent experiencing the stage of anxiety another time may show enthusiasm and eagerness to implement a suggestion but be anxious about an upcoming event or change. In the author's experience, when parents re-experience a stage of grief, the duration of the stage tends to be shorter.

THE NATURE OF GRIEF

In addition to understanding the stages of grief, it is helpful for family members and professionals who work with families to understand that grief, while necessary, is difficult. It can make those who grieve extremely tired, which makes it difficult to listen attentively to professionals working with their child or to implement interventions with their baby. Although it is possible to categorize its stages, it is important for professionals working with a family to understand that grief itself remains very individual. There is no "right way" to grieve, nor is there a specific chronology or duration for the process. Grief is not an illness that eventually goes away. Rather, reactions to grief may change in intensity through time. Therefore, parents will need to be prepared to recognize and cope with those feelings should they recur. Although some parents may not appear to show obvious signs of grieving when first learning of their baby's diagnosis, they usually will experience grief eventually. Teachers, professionals, and other family members help parents during this difficult time by understanding the various behaviors and feelings associated with the different aspects of grief, and listening and providing support, referrals, activities, and interventions as appropriate.

Tracy is a new parent whose baby, Jane, had just been diagnosed with CVI. During an initial meeting, Juan, her teacher of children with visual impairments, listened attentively as Tracy told her story about Jane's birth and diagnosis. Since learning of Jane's diagnosis, Tracy admitted that she cried frequently and often felt listless, tired, irritable, and nervous. She had trouble sleeping and had little appetite. Tracy confessed that she was most troubled by persistent thoughts that she could not help her baby. She also worried that feeling sad and acting listless meant that she did not love Jane.

Juan discussed the grieving process and its stages with Tracy. He assured Tracy that experiencing grief in reaction to having a baby with a disability is normal. Their discussions helped Tracy understand that her feelings and her grief were a common reaction to losing her idealized vision of her baby that she had nurtured during her pregnancy. Her reactions did not mean she did not love Jane, or that she was too weak to parent her.

Juan explained his role as their family's teacher of children with visual impairments. He would be available to offer friendly support and provide relevant information about vision and CVI. He would collaborate with the family to establish goals for Jane's development and would introduce interventions to help Jane build visual and developmental skills. Juan assured Tracy that with time, support, education, and guidance, Tracy would start to feel more confident and energized in her ability to help Jane.

SITUATIONS CAN INTENSIFY FEELINGS OF GRIEF

External situations can intensify or renew feelings of grief. For example, many parents have reported that strangers' reactions to their babies with CVI have caused their dormant feelings of grief to re-emerge. One parent reported an experience in which, just as he was starting to feel a little less distressed about his baby's diagnosis and its implications, he encountered a stranger at the store who began to weep and pray over the baby. Seeing that his baby made a total stranger react in such an extreme fashion reawakened this parent's awareness that his baby was not like other babies, causing his feelings of distress to intensify.

The following are examples of situations that may contribute to or intensify parent's feelings of grief:

- **Judgmental or unwelcome comments**—Parents are often confronted by outsiders who may pose insensitive questions or make unwelcome suggestions about their child. Even if these comments are offered by people with good intentions, their words can still arouse and intensify the parents' feelings of sadness as well as shake their confidence to properly care for their children. Years ago, I heard a woman actually ask a parent of a baby with CVI why she had not had an abortion. The comment upset the parent deeply. **Sidebar 1.2** provides suggestions for how to address judgmental or unwelcome comments about your baby with CVI.

- **Incorrect information about CVI**—Parents can feel confused about who is most knowledgeable about CVI and who is most qualified to help them and their baby. For parents of babies with CVI, this confusion can be frightening and intensify grieving. Parents must feel confident that any professional who is helping their child is up-to-date on the current and rapidly changing information about CVI. Experts should understand the different needs of babies with CVI compared to those with ocular visual impairments. They should know the specific

Managing Unwelcome Comments

Everyone carries out errands and other activities that are part of a daily routine. For parents of children who are blind or visually impaired, these activities may also involve dealing with judgmental questions, uncomfortable stares, unwelcome comments, and discourteous attitudes. These comments and actions can sometimes add to parent's already sensitive emotional state and serve to enhance their grief.

The following suggestions have been collected from both parents and professionals about how caregivers can best engage with individuals in these types of situations.

- A baby needs the experience of being in the supermarket as much as the family needs to buy food. However, on occasion it may be necessary to leave the baby at home, especially if you are in a rush, or when you need time alone.

- Remember that people ask questions simply because they do not understand. Approach the situation as a teacher and try to increase their understanding about children with disabilities. State facts simply and positively.

- Limit an uncomfortable conversation by politely ending it. For example, you may respond by saying, "I appreciate that you are interested in my child, but I am trying to concentrate on reading my book."

- Create an honest, quick, and simple story about your baby's condition. Write it down and practice it so that you can repeat it comfortably whenever a question or comment arises. You can then conclude the story with a fact about something your baby enjoys doing: for example, "Timmy has a visual condition that makes his eyes move from side to side and he doesn't see certain

needs of babies with CVI, understand the developmental differences between babies and older children with CVI, and be able to employ the most appropriate and effective interventions. Online resources provide helpful information and training for parents and less experienced teachers of children with visual impairments (see **Appendix B** for a list of these resources).

- **Discovery of additional difficulties**—Many babies with CVI have additional brain-related disabilities (Dennison, 2003). The brain event that caused CVI can also affect other areas of brain functioning such as movement development or hearing ability. If a baby with CVI receives an additional diagnosis of another disability such as cerebral palsy, different visual problems, seizure disorder, or respiratory distress, parents' feelings of grief will intensify.
- **Discord with a partner**—When both parents are experiencing the same situation with their baby, they might assume that

their experiences of grief should be identical. Do not forget, however, that reactions to grief are unique to each person. While both parents may grieve after learning that their baby is diagnosed with CVI, each parent may be at different stages in the grief process at any given time. When one partner grieves differently than the other, the other partner may conclude that this behavior is intended as a criticism of the way they are acting or feeling. Professionals can help parents understand that grieving is personal and unique to each individual, and that it is common for each partner to grieve in their own way and time. It can also be helpful to facilitate communication between both parents so each gains a better understanding of what the other partner is experiencing.

- **Unsupportive friends or family**—Family and friends of parents whose baby has been diagnosed with CVI also deal with their own personal reactions to this news. As a result, family or friends may not be ready to provide the support the parents need, which may be upsetting to the parents. In addition, regardless of a grandparent's reaction, parents may become convinced that they have disappointed the baby's grandparents because the baby has a disability. This sense of letting others down may add to their feelings of grief. Resources and websites that offer support, information, and opportunities to connect with other parents and grandparents of children with CVI can be helpful to families during this time. (Details about programs that provide support and information are found in **Appendix B**).

THE PARENT-CHILD BOND

Attachment Cues

Infant bonding and parental attachment are critically important factors in an infant's early emotional development (Chen, 2014). Babies with visual impairments often have more difficulty exhibiting familiar attachment cues to their parents than babies who are fully sighted (Chen, 2014b; Healey, 1996;

Bonding and parental attachment are critically important to a baby's development. Cuddling and play both enhance the parent-child bond.

Fraiberg, 1977). Parents' early bonding and attachment with their baby initially develops through eye contact, but babies with visual impairments are usually unable to establish eye contact early in life or to show typical signs of visual recognition of their parents' faces or expressions. The combination of a baby's inability to establish eye contact along with the parents' difficulty interpreting their baby's cues can challenge the early parent-child connection (Chen, 2014b). Parents sense that they should feel a connection to their baby yet the absence of this connection can feel like a great loss to them. Feeling unconnected may also increase parents' fears about their ability to help their baby with CVI. Parents may report feeling confused because they do not know how to communicate with a baby who does not make eye contact or show behavioral reactions or facial cues they expect (Chen, 2014b).

In addition to difficulty establishing eye contact, babies with CVI may present other challenges to parental bonding. Babies with CVI, depending on the area of brain damage, may lack the ability to recognize faces and facial expressions. They may also react slowly to a visual stimulus and show inconsistent visual responsiveness. If parents do not understand the visual characteristics of babies with CVI, they may feel rejected or ignored by their baby.

Professionals can help parents learn to build connections with their baby. Observations of parent-baby interactions can help professionals understand how a parent responds to a baby, determine how the parent-child relationship is developing, and indicate interventions that may strengthen the parent-child bond. Observing these parent-child interactions may also indicate how confident parents feel about their ability to help their child. **Figure 1.2** provides a list of behaviors that indicate whether the parent-baby bond is progressing, or whether parents can benefit from additional support and interventions. (Activities and interventions to help parents connect with their babies are provided in **Appendix A.**)

Figure 1.2
Parent-Baby Connections

Observations of parent-baby interactions can help a teacher of children with visual impairments see how parents are respond to their baby and how their attachment to their child is building. The following figure identifies actions and behaviors that are possible indicators of parents' attachment with their baby. The observations indicate how confident parents feel about their ability to help their baby. Depending how often these behaviors are carried out, it can indicate that the parent-baby bond is growing (if "Often" column is selected frequently) or that the parents can benefit from more support (if "Sometimes" column is selected frequently). Absence of many of the identified behaviors (if "Rarely" column is selected frequently) may indicate that increased attachment should be a goal for family interventions and needs to be addressed by providing support or counseling or by encouraging bonding activities.

Figure 1.2 (continued)

Action	Rarely	Sometimes	Often
Looks toward baby			
Touches baby			
Names baby in discussion			
Sits near baby			
Shows gentle touch			
Parent readily responds to baby with cues (hunger/upset/wet)			
Uses playful, loving voice			
Smiles toward baby when talking			
Displays delight about baby			
Enjoys interactions with baby			
Adjusts baby's clothes, hair, and touches baby's face lovingly			
Positions or handles baby carefully			

Additional Disabilities

Babies with CVI may also have a sensory integration disorder, a condition in which the baby cannot adequately process sensory information (Strickling & Pogrund, 2002), which may cause a baby to feel uncomfortable whenever touched. As a result of this discomfort, the baby may stiffen or move away from the parent when touched or held. Or, the baby with CVI may also have cerebral palsy, a condition that can affect typical movement reactions to stimuli.

When a condition causes a baby to react unexpectedly to their actions, parents may interpret these unfamiliar reactions as an indication that their baby dislikes them. As a result, a parent may feel disconnected from their child. These misunderstandings can hinder parent-child bonding (Fraiberg, 1977). Parents report that once they understand that these reactions are common in babies who have a visual impairment such as CVI, they are better able to cope with these bonding difficulties. For example, let's look at the science behind the baby who stiffens when picked up. This stiffening reaction, called *stilling,* is common among babies who are blind and is characterized by cessation of movement and making sounds to better attend to stimuli (Dockrell & Messer, 1999). It is important to explain to parents that stilling actually serves an important purpose—it enhances a baby's ability to smell a parent's scent, listen to a parent's voice, and focus on the parent with all of his or her attention. In short, stilling indicates that bonding between the baby and the parent is beginning. Activities such as musical interaction (Metell, 2015) or infant massage (Lappin June, & Kretschmer, 2005) that involve parents touching and holding their baby can help both the parents and the baby with CVI feel closer to one another (see **Appendix A** for suggested activities).

Supporting Bonding and Attachment

Clarify Behavioral Cues

Teachers of children with visual impairments can help parents learn to read their baby's cues. With a teacher's help, parents can begin to understand that, rather than signs of rejection, unexpected behaviors are their baby's unique adaptations to his or her visual abilities. The absence of typical responses such as a baby's ability to establish eye contact, react to smiling, and recognize parents' faces is related to the baby's vision loss, and not to the parents' behaviors.

One area of visual difficulty noted in children with CVI is the inability to recognize and attend to faces (Dutton, 2015c). This behavior can devastate parents. In the author's experience,

Babies with CVI can have difficulty attending to and recognizing faces. One way to familiarize these babies with faces is to place photos of faces, or a simple face motif like the one pictured, around the baby's environment.

providing exposure to face motifs (e.g., paper plates decorated with large eyes and a mouth in a baby's favorite color) in a baby's crib and nearby environments *significantly* increases a baby's ability to learn to respond to human faces. Parents of babies with CVI can also use sound to bond with their child. Listening to each parent's voice helps a baby learn to associate the voice with that parent, thus increasing the baby's responses of familiarity whenever they hear that parent speak.

Self-talk, a behavior in which parents actively talk about what they are doing when they perform a task, also helps a baby with CVI build language concepts and increase familiarity with a parent's voice. For example, as a parent prepares their baby's bottle, they could verbally describe their actions. Since parents of babies with CVI cannot use eye contact to bond with their child, teachers can help parents learn to use touch, holding, and speaking experiences instead.

Self-talk is a technique in which parents actively discuss and describe the actions they are performing while they complete a task, such as this mother talking to her child about the bottle she has just prepared for him. Self-talk enhances a child's language concepts and increases their familiarity with a parent's voice.

Promote a Feeling of Pride

Teachers of children with visual impairments can help parents feel pride in their baby's abilities by explaining the baby's actions and reactions to the parents and the surrounding environment, and what these actions reveal about their baby's skill development. For example, when a baby with CVI exchanges a toy from one hand to the other, this action signifies growth in the fine motor hand skills of grasp and release, resulting in the ability to transfer an object from hand to hand. Explanations of skill development helps parents better understand their baby with CVI and give parents an opportunity to feel proud of their baby's accomplishments. (See **Appendix A** for activities and techniques to promote connections between parents and their baby.)

Explain CVI and the Visual System

Parents whose baby is newly diagnosed with CVI may not fully understand this complicated diagnosis. Providing additional information about their baby's diagnosis can help parents gain confidence and encourage them to implement suggested interventions. Teachers of children with visual impairments can help inform parents about CVI and the visual system, which will help parents better understand the condition and their baby's vision. The teacher can also explain the characteristics of CVI and emphasize the possibility for improvement, or resolution, of some of these characteristics (Catteneo & Merabet, 2015; Roman-Lantzy, 2018). Babies with CVI may show some improvement in their visual abilities, but as they grow and their learning demands increase, additional visual difficulties may become more apparent. Parents must understand that although individual CVI characteristics may improve and possibly even approach typical behavior, the condition itself never fully resolves (Roman-Lantzy, 2018). For more information on this, see **Chapters 2 and 3**.

BUILDING PARTNERSHIPS

During the stages and experiences described in this chapter, a partnership is forged between the teacher of children with visual impairments and the parents. Teachers can enhance this relationship by listening to parents' concerns, acknowledging their previous experience and knowledge, respecting their customs and beliefs, and showing interest in and warm feelings toward their baby. Open communication early on is *vital* to building cooperation and understanding.

Parents' Knowledge

When a teacher of children with visual impairments first meets the parents of a baby recently diagnosed with CVI, the parents likely have already received a great deal of information about the baby's condition. They have discovered more about their child's health, abilities, likes, and dislikes. They have worried, searched for answers and information, met with many doctors, and studied their baby intensely and often. The teacher's acknowledgment of these experiences and knowledge helps to build a partnership. However, while parents may be aware of the many pieces of the puzzle that describe what is going on with their baby, they may not understand the significance of each piece or how they all fit together. They may understand that interventions are important to help build their baby's visual abilities, but they may not be able to decide which intervention is most appropriate. By observing and listening to parents' understanding of CVI, the teacher can better inform them, helping them fill in the missing pieces. Working as a team, they learn together how they can all help the baby develop his or her visual and developmental abilities.

Home Visits

When making a home visit, the teacher of children with visual impairments is not only a professional consultant but also a guest. Parents may sometimes feel threatened when teachers or therapists enter their home to observe their baby. Following each household's rules and customs, such as removing shoes when entering the home, demonstrates respect and helps parents feel more comfortable with the teacher's presence. A home visit begins by greeting the parents and taking time to informally catch up with them; this is an effective way to make the parents feel more at ease and is a useful way to transition to the real work of the session. Taking the time to help parents feel comfortable with your presence and showing nonclinical interest in their baby are important steps to building a partnership with parents. For example, if a teacher enters the home and begins to interview parents without first interacting with their baby, the parents may conclude that the teacher is not comfortable with their child. Providing an activity or intervention suggestion during the first visit will not only indicate that the teacher is comfortable with their child but is also ready to work and has the knowledge to help a baby with CVI develop.

Assessments

Early visits that initiate a partnership between the teacher and parents of a baby with CVI usually begin with asking interview questions about and observing the baby. They also include an assessment of visual and developmental abilities to determine the baby's and family's needs. However, a professional examination of a baby's abilities and needs may feel threatening to parents. An assessment may also heighten the parents' perception that both they and their baby are "failing." Seeing various evaluation forms laid out during an assessment may intimidate parents. Instead, teachers and the other team members should conduct assessments while playing with the baby and if possible complete assessment forms once a home visit has concluded. There will be time to share evaluation forms, results, and observations with the parents at a later visit.

Parents' Suggestions

Parents who already have experience raising older children with CVI are a valuable source of wisdom, inspiration, information, and support—not only for new parents, but also for teachers. These experienced parents can help teachers build the foundation of a strong and successful partnership with new parents and enable them to become more effective and perceptive teachers. Professionals who follow a standard set of procedures when working with new parents can help to establish trust, build communication, and make parents feel part of their child's team. These procedures include the following:

- Listen to the parents' descriptions of their baby's history and their own feelings
- Acknowledge the importance of parents' experience and knowledge regarding their baby with CVI
- Include parents in a discussion whenever additional professionals are present
- Respect the customs of the house and the beliefs of the family
- Plan greeting time at the start of each visit in order to check in with parents
- Interact with the baby when the baby seems interested

- Ask parents' permission before managing the baby's behavior or removing any of baby's clothing
- Make positive comments about the baby (e.g., their child has beautiful hair, silky skin, or smells wonderful)
- Give regular, positive feedback about the baby's visual skills and overall development
- Deliver new information in small doses so as not to overwhelm the parents
- Suggest activities and resources
- Summarize the visit, identify next steps, and schedule a time for the next visit

The U.S. Department of Education Office of Special Education Programs convened a national workgroup that produced several documents on key principles and best practices for early intervention services in natural environments. These documents are available on the Early Childhood Technical Assistance Center (ECTA, n.d.) website: www.ectacenter.org

CONCLUSION

A positive relationship with a teacher of children with visual impairments empowers parents of babies with CVI. This relationship gives parents the support necessary to practice and reinforce the interventions that will improve their baby's development and visual abilities. Teachers can enhance parents' willingness to work with their child by helping them understand that even though there are identifiable stages of grief, each person will respond to each stage in their own way. Teachers can also help parents understand behaviors common to babies with CVI, including actions that may lead them to mistakenly conclude that they cannot bond with their child. Improving the parent-child bond will increase a parent's willingness to work with their baby. Finally, teachers can support parents by educating them about CVI, introducing them to appropriate resources, and helping them partner with the team of professionals who will help their child achieve appropriate developmental goals and visual abilities.

CHAPTER 2

The Visual System[1]

Cerebral visual impairment (CVI) is a visual impairment that results from damage to or a disorder of the visual pathways and visual centers in the brain. However, CVI can also apply to injuries that are anatomically outside the brain's cortical region (Dutton & Lueck, 2015). To understand the effect of CVI and other similar visual impairments on early childhood development, one must first understand the ocular and the brain-based visual systems. The term *visual brain* has recently emerged as the term that refers to all areas of the brain involved in vision. The visual brain refers to "the totality of brain elements serving or supporting vision . . . that serves to map, search, give attention to, as well as recognize and interpret visual input" (Dutton & Lueck, 2015, p. 3). Simply stated, while the ocular system *manages* the light entering into the eye from the environment, the visual brain is where *seeing* actually takes place.

This chapter presents a basic overview of the visual system, including information about both cerebral and ocular visual impairments. This information is presented in order to help teachers of children with visual impairments, families, and other professionals who work with babies with CVI understand the complexities of the visual system. A fuller understanding of the visual system and of CVI benefits anyone who is involved in enhancing a baby's *visual capacity,* or the potential that the child has for visual function (Topor et al., 2004) and development. When presented to and understood by a baby's family early on, information about vision and CVI can energize the family to provide important interventions that will stimulate the visual system to increase visual capacity.

[1] Amy K. Hutchinson, MD, pediatric ophthalmologist at Emory University Eye Center, contributed substantially to the medical information provided in this chapter.

VISION TESTS

Without question, the guidance of a pediatric eye care provider is essential in caring for a child's visual health. This professional will conduct a clinical examination that will provide parents initial information about how their child uses vision. However, it is important for parents to understand that information obtained about visual ability from this examination is often based primarily on the visual acuity aspect of a child's visual abilities. Besides a medical exam, a baby's visual abilities can be evaluated using a functional vision assessment, which is described later. Parents need to understand the differences between medical exams and functional vision assessments—specifically, what each evaluation reveals about a baby's visual capacity—in order to interpret the information they receive from professionals.

Clinical Examination

Medical conclusions about a baby's vision are typically based in large part on two things: the baby's *visual acuity*, and the baby's *estimated visual potential*. *Visual acuity* is the ability to see or resolve fine detail and is measured by observing the baby's reactions to specific symbols or targets (Kran & Mayer, 2015). *Estimated visual potential* is a projection of the baby's *probable* visual ability based on the health of the components of the eye, as documented during an examination. Visual acuity is quantifiable; estimated visual potential is less definitive. Though the concrete numbers of visual acuity measurements are easier to grasp, parents (and sometimes professionals) must understand that visual acuity measures only a single aspect of vision: *the smallest symbol or object size that the visual system can effectively resolve from a specific distance.* As such, visual acuity alone does not accurately reflect a person's overall visual ability. In fact, one's comprehensive visual ability may be dramatically underestimated if visual acuity is the sole factor considered. Other factors that contribute to visual ability are discussed later in this chapter.

Clinical eye evaluations are performed using eye charts. The chart is calibrated for patients to view from a specified distance. (In the United States, that distance is usually 20 feet; but other testing distances are sometimes used.) For people with typical vision, the smallest *optotype* (letter or symbol used to test vision) that they can resolve will be on the 20/20 line of the Snellen eye chart. All lines on this chart are denoted as fractions, in which the numerator represents the specific testing distance (20 feet in this example) and the denominator indicates the farthest testing distance at which a person with typical vision can still resolve that particular size of optotype. If the person being examined were to move increasingly farther away from the chart, the optotype would need to become larger and larger in order to be resolved. However, since it is more practical to increase the size of the optotype rather than to increase the testing distance, eye charts are designed to keep the testing distance constant while increasing the size of the optotype in order to measure visual acuity. For example, when a person is said to have 20/200 vision, it means the person would need to stand 20 feet away from the eye chart in order to resolve the 20/200 size optotype. In contrast, a person with 20/20 vision can resolve that same size of optotype from 200 feet away.

Preferential Looking Tests

Preferential Looking tests are one way to measure the visual acuity of a baby who is not yet able to respond verbally to standard assessments. Preferential Looking testing techniques are based on research that finds that very young infants prefer to look at large, high-contrast patterns in which the thickness of alternating black-and-white lines (gratings) are wide enough to be seen (Kran & Mayer, 2015), rather than plain images featuring no high-contrast patterns. One version of a Preferential Looking test employs Teller Acuity Cards. Stimuli are printed on one side of these rectangular cards. A baby will typically look at the side of the card that contains the stimulus, but not at the blank side (Kran & Mayer, 2015). Grating acuity can then be estimated by noting the thickness of the lines that are too small to attract the baby's attention (Topor, 2014).

Natural environments can also be used to approximate functional visual acuity, employing targets that are both familiar and motivating to the individual child. In examinations set in natural environments, objects are placed at successively greater distances from the child. As objects move farther away, the child's response is observed and recorded. Based on the given size of an object and the greatest distance from which a child appears to see it (Topor, 2014), a child's functional visual acuity may be estimated.

Functional Vision Assessment

Additional—and often more encouraging—information about a child's vision is gathered in a nonmedical setting using a functional vision assessment (FVA). An FVA is an evaluation of a child's ability to use vision in a variety of tasks and settings (Topor, 2014), including near and distance vision use, visual fields, eye movements, and responses to environmental characteristics such as lighting and color. An FVA is usually administered only after clinical examinations have been completed. Instead of being conducted by a pediatric eye care provider or member of the medical field, the FVA is conducted by vision professionals from the educational field. These educational vision professionals are often members of a team of professionals that is similar in makeup to an early intervention team (see **Sidebar 1.1** in **Chapter 1**).

An FVA will often identify additional visual abilities than those discovered through a measure of visual acuity only. Note that the results of an FVA can vary with environmental changes, a baby's physical and emotional comfort, and a child's increasing intellectual maturity. Understanding the baby's visual abilities is essential for planning how to help the baby reach appropriate developmental goals. Additional FVAs should be conducted regularly throughout the child's life to adjust the plan as needed for their ongoing learning and development.

A family interview, in which it is determined how a baby uses vision in various activities and under specific conditions, is essential to fully understand the functional vision of a baby with CVI (Topor, 2014). An effective FVA tool to evaluate vision skills in infants is Langley's ISAVE instrument (Langley, 1998); for information about specific interview questions and history-taking forms for children with CVI, see Dutton (2015a) and Roman-Lantzy (2018). Additional information about the FVA is provided in **Chapter 4.**

Assessment Environment

Babies with CVI have unique behavioral characteristics and needs. Some of these characteristics and needs can compromise the findings of assessments if they are not taken into consideration. Babies with CVI need sufficient time prior to the assessment in which to become comfortable with both the assessor and the environment in which the evaluation is to be conducted. Babies with CVI should be assessed in an environment that has adjustable lighting to accommodate for possible light sensitivity or a tendency to light gaze. Since babies with CVI may be easily distracted, the assessment environment needs to be free of other sensory factors such as room clutter, noise, or visually distracting items such as flashy jewelry or brightly patterned clothing. Spending time to make a baby feel comfortable in the assessment environment will result in more accurate data. Since babies with CVI may have visual latency, or delayed visual reactions, they may require more time to respond visually during an interaction with the assessor.

EDUCATING PARENTS

As mentioned previously, understanding a CVI diagnosis is complicated. Parents who still have feeling of shock about their baby's diagnosis may have difficulty comprehending information provided to them about CVI. However, it is nonetheless very important that parents learn as early as possible about the diagnosis so they can both understand and evaluate information from doctors and professionals. For example, one factor that can make a CVI diagnosis especially confusing is when a baby with CVI has a coexisting *ocular visual impairment.* Unlike CVI, ocular visual impairments are caused by a disorder of the eye or optic nerve, not of the brain. If an assessment is primarily focused on a child's ocular visual impairment, CVI may go undiagnosed. If a child's CVI is not diagnosed, the CVI-related behaviors may instead be attributed to other causes (Pawletko et al., 2015). As a result, both parents and professionals may not be fully aware of the actual cause of a child's visual difficulties, which can cause the child to miss out on appropriate immediate interventions.

In both cerebral and ocular visual impairment, it is possible for children to learn to improve the use of their remaining vision. With nontreatable ocular impairments, alterations in anatomy and function are considered permanent. In contrast, a baby with CVI can experience alterations in his or her brain pathways as the brain learns to work around its limitations and rewire itself using alternative pathways. (Visual pathways are discussed later in this chapter.) In order to develop these alternative neural pathways, early interventions that stimulate the visual areas of a baby's brain must be initiated *as soon as possible.*

Parents are often confused and discouraged by a doctor's report about their baby's vision. However, their feelings may arise simply because they do not fully understand what the doctor really means. For example, when a doctor says that a baby is *legally blind*, parents may mistakenly conclude that their baby sees nothing. In this case, encouraging parents to learn basic facts about the visual system can help them better comprehend the information presented in a doctor's evaluation as well as understand their baby's true visual capacity. Appropriate early interventions can improve the baby's ability to learn and develop. The more parents understand about their baby's vision and diagnosis, the more likely they are to implement suggested interventions to help their baby.

The Initial Session

The first meeting between the parents of a baby with CVI and their teacher of children with visual impairments serves as a great opportunity for the teacher to offer support, collect information about the baby and family, begin to answer parents' questions, and help parents learn about their baby's vision. Content to cover during a first visit includes the following:

- The differences between the medical and educational models of vision
- Basic information about the visual system
- Clarification about how cerebral visual impairment affects vision
- How brain plasticity makes improvement in visual ability possible

Baby Chad was born prematurely at 29 weeks gestation—11 weeks before his due date. He weighed less than 2 pounds. He spent time in the neonatal intensive care unit to receive oxygen because his lungs were not fully developed. Chad had an interventricular hemorrhage, or a bleed of the ventricles of the brain, which resulted in damage to his brain. The bleed was determined to be moderately severe. The hospital's neuro-ophthalmologist, a doctor who specializes in brain-related visual problems, informed Chad's parents that while his eyes seemed to be healthy, because of the damage in his brain, he suspected that Chad may have CVI. As a result, Chad could be legally blind and have other developmental disabilities as well.

Chad and his parents met for an initial visit with a teacher of children with visual impairments. Jeff, the teacher, greeted the parents warmly. He tried to make them feel at ease by chatting with them and taking time to mention Chad's cute outfit and sweet face. He also presented the parents with a special handmade blanket for their baby.

As Chad's parents became more familiar with Jeff, they felt more comfortable talking about Chad's difficult birth as well as their own worries and confusion surrounding his visual abilities. They told Jeff that upon leaving the hospital, they had taken Chad to a highly recommended pediatric ophthalmologist. After he examined Chad, the doctor spoke in greater depth about Chad's vision, CVI, and possible outcomes related to Chad's vision and development. The parents admitted that the ophthalmologist's description of Chad's visual issues left them feeling both stunned and sad. They also said that they were both anxious and confused about what the doctor told them, which led them to worry about the challenges Chad might face in the future. As they talked at length about their difficult experience and tumultuous feelings, Jeff listened carefully.

Later in the visit, Jeff asked Chad's parents what they hoped to gain from their future meetings. They said that they wanted to better understand what the doctors had told them about Chad's vision and prognosis. They also said they wanted to learn more about vision and CVI, along with ways they could help Chad learn to use his vision more effectively. Jeff proceeded to tell Chad's family about the differences between the medical and educational models of vision, and that information from both models were important to fully understand Chad's visual and developmental needs. He explained that the ophthalmologist they visited had performed a clinical examination to assess Chad's visual needs and abilities. Jeff added that he and the parents would work together on a functional vision assessment, which would provide a fuller picture of how Chad was using vision and would help them identify goals for his development.

Jeff provided the parents a very simple explanation about how vision works. He also talked briefly about the differences between various types of ocular visual impairments. Jeff told them about cerebral visual impairments and how they differ from ocular visual impairments. He stressed the importance of brain plasticity. Since the brain is plastic, Jeff explained, visual problems related to CVI can often resolve themselves. Chad's parents said this information made them feel encouraged about the possibility of improving Chad's vision.

Jeff listened as Chad's parents described what they had heard from the doctors about Chad's vision, and he answered their questions. Jeff said that the information they received from both the clinical examinations and FVAs would help them set specific goals for Chad's visual development. At the conclusion of the visit, Jeff emphasized the importance of early intervention to improve Chad's vision. He gave Chad's parents a list of contacts, resources, and support groups that could provide both additional information and emotional support. He advised that they try not to be overwhelmed by the large amount of information about CVI on the internet at this early point in their journey.

VISUAL ABILITY BEYOND ACUITY

When a doctor tells parents that their baby is *legally* blind, the parents often mistakenly conclude that their child is *totally* blind. In actuality, the term *legally blind* has a specific medical meaning: The child has a visual acuity of 20/200. Legal blindness does not mean the child has absolutely no light perception or is unable to see anything. Because visual acuity is usually the first—and sometimes the only—measurement of a baby's vision that parents receive, it is often encouraging for them to learn about *visual ability,* or the entirety of how a child is using his or her vision.

The Visual Continuum

Parents are often surprised to learn that visual acuity exists on a continuum. The range of visual acuity extends from having no light perception on one end, to what is considered typical or normal vision at the opposite end. As shown in **Figure 2.1**, it is evident that having no light perception is just one form of blindness. It is not the same as legal blindness.

During an FVA or other in-depth observation, a teacher of children with visual impairments evaluates the child's visual responses. Parents can then observe their baby's specific vision-related behaviors, which may allow them to associate these behaviors with a particular point on the visual continuum. Vision simulation goggles can also help parents gain a better understanding of their baby's visual experience (see **Sidebar 2.1**).

Figure 2.1
The Visual Continuum

No light perception (NLP)	Light perception (LP)	Movement perception	Form perception	Object perception	20/200 Legally blind	20/100 Low vision	20/20 Typical or normal vision

Source: Anne McComiskey

The visual continuum line illustrates the range of visual acuities from blindness to typical sight. The line helps parents see that there is a great difference between blindness (no light perception) at one end of the continuum and legal blindness (20/200).

Vision Simulation Goggles

Parents and relatives often want to get a better understanding of what a baby with a visual impairment is experiencing visually. It is possible to create simulator goggles to represent what a person with a visual impairment might experience. It is important to emphasize that these goggles are only an approximation of what a person with a visual impairment experiences.

To create vision simulation goggles, the following materials are needed.

- Goggles: Goggles such as welding safety goggles with removable parts for the lenses and individual eye sections are the easiest to adapt. Swim goggles are another possibility, but the clear side plastic pieces will need to be blocked out.

- Scissors

- Plastic wrap, wax paper

- Black marker

- Black construction paper
- Index card
- Black tape, clear tape

Directions:

The materials listed above can be used to customize the goggles to provide a different experience depending on where a child falls on the visual continuum.

- A blind spot (scotoma) or a partial visual field loss—hemianopsia, loss of half of the visual field—can be simulated by placing dark tape in the location where the field loss has been noted.

- Total loss of vision in one eye can be represented by covering that lens of the goggles with black tape or a piece of black paper.

- Light perception can be represented by cutting the index card to fit the goggles.

- To represent no central vision, the goggles can be adapted by drawing a black circle about the size of a quarter in the center of each lens.

- Peripheral vision loss can be simulated by cutting a hole in the center of a black piece of paper and fitting the paper onto the goggles.

- Form or object perception can be simulated by cutting wax paper to fix the lens.

- Visual acuity simulation can be approximately achieved by using layers of plastic wrap:
  - 6 layers for 20/400
  - 4 layers for 20/200
  - 1 layer for 20/70

No Light Perception (NLP)

No light perception is the complete lack of light and form perception. It represents total blindness. Few babies with CVI experience no light perception or total blindness (Groenveld et al., 1990).

Photographer: Anne McComiskey

This photo shows a possible experience of no light perception (NLP), which is the complete lack of light and form perception that represents total blindness.

Light Perception (LP)

Light perception is the ability to perceive the presence or absence of light. Although a baby with light perception has severely reduced vision, he or she may still be able to perceive the difference between light and dark, or even determine the general source or direction of a light. Knowing from what source and direction a light is coming is important for travel and orientation in space. As babies mature, their ability to see light can motivate them to reach toward objects and attempt to move to other areas in their environment. Babies with CVI often respond to light; parents may notice a change in their baby's reactions when shown a light source. As observations

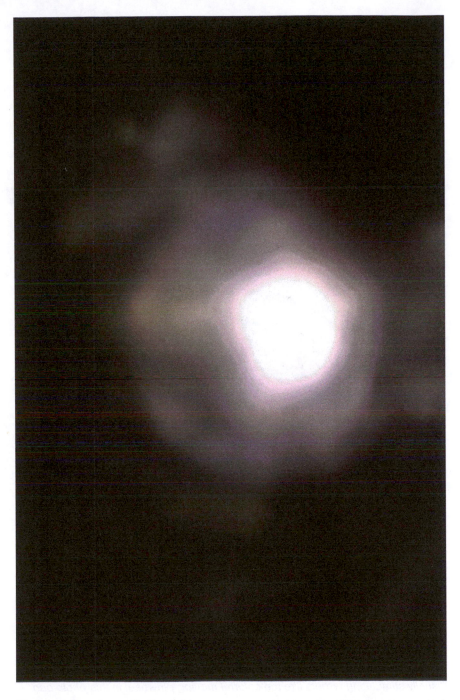

Photographer: Anne McComiskey

This photo shows a possible experience of light perception, which is the ability to perceive the presence or absence of light.

and evaluations continue over time, parents may notice changes in their child's visual responses that indicate that their baby has more visual abilities than they had initially thought.

Movement Perception

Movement perception is the ability to perceive close movement (at about 6 inches or less). Babies with CVI usually perceive moving objects better than stationary ones (Roman-Lantzy, 2018). Parents may notice a change in their baby's behavior when an object such as a spinning pinwheel or

Visually stimulating targets like the colorful moving pinwheel in this photo can help stimulate a visual reaction in a baby with CVI.

Babies with CVI

jiggled toy is placed in front of him or her, or within a preferred visual field. Parents may report that they have observed their baby "looking" at a rotating ceiling fan, with the baby responding to the movement of the fan blades.

Form Perception

Form perception is the ability to perceive a stimulus other than light or movement. Babies with CVI may be able to perceive movement, they may also notice particular colors more readily than others. Depending on the characteristics of an object and the nature of the environment in which an object is encountered, movement and color can enhance a baby's ability to glean the presence of a form near him or her.

Photographer: Anne McComiskey

This photo shows a possible experience of form perception, which is the ability to perceive something other than light or movement.

Object Perception

Object perception is the ability to perceive an object—such as a pacifier or favorite colored or patterned toy—up close. When a baby perceives an object in close proximity, his or her face may become more animated. The baby may even move his or her body in a way that suggests that he or she is trying to reach this target. This visual behavior indicates that the baby is able to perceive some details of familiar objects, at least some of the time and in some conditions.

20/200: Legal Blindness

As previously discussed, legal blindness is the visual acuity of a person who can only see an object from 20 feet away that a person with typical vision can see from 200 feet away. The term *legally blind* is important because it is the designation used in North America and most of Europe to determine whether a person is entitled

Photographer: Anne McComiskey

This photo shows a possible experience of legal blindness (20/200), which is the visual acuity of a person who can see at 20 feet what a person with typical vision sees at 200 feet.

to a range of services, benefits, and rights based upon their vision. As the photo below demonstrates, a person who is legally blind still has *some* vision. Again, it is important to stress to parents that legal blindness does not mean their baby lacks all visual ability.

20/100: Low Vision

A person whose visual acuity is measured at 20/100 can only see an object from 20 feet away that a person with typical vision can see from 100 feet away. The measurement 20/100 designates *low vision.* Low vision is an uncorrectable vision loss that is severe enough to interfere with a person's ability to learn or to perform daily activities. Some eye care professionals use the term *low vision* to indicate any instance of permanently reduced vision between 20/70 and 20/100 that cannot be fully corrected with regular glasses, contact lenses, medicine, or surgery (American Optometric Association, 2018).

20/20: Typical Vision

The typical vision of people with unimpaired vision establishes the norm for visual acuity. It is measured at a distance of 20 feet. A person with 20/20 vision can see an object or symbol on the 20 line of a vision chart clearly from 20 feet away. However, having 20/20 vision does not mean a person has *perfect* vision. For example, people who have *hyperopia* (farsightedness) can clearly see objects at a distance but are unable to bring closer objects into focus. In contrast, people who are *myopic* (nearsighted) can see items that are close to them, but cannot clearly see those that are farther away (American Optometric Association, 2018). In most cases, glasses, contact lenses, or vision therapy can help improve vision for people who are farsighted or nearsighted.

THE VISUAL SYSTEM

Vision is the complex process by which light from the environment moves through or stimulates the various components of the visual system. Light travels through the eye to the retina, where it is converted to electrical signals that are transmitted through both the brain's visual structures and the optic nerve to the occipital lobes. The occipital lobes at the back of the brain contain millions of cells that process and use these electrical signals to reconstruct and produce a visual scene that is a replica of the one in the environment (Roman-Lantzy, 2018).

From the occipital lobes, the visual information is next divided into two systems, or pathways, of visual processing that create a complete picture based on the visual information. The *dorsal stream,* or the "where" system, is involved to guide actions and recognize where objects are located in space; it processes attention to movement and the perception of form and light (Roman-Lantzy, 2018). This stream stretches into the brain's posterior parietal lobe. The *ventral stream,* or the "what" system, is involved to recognize and identify objects visually. It also plays a role in the development of the vision required to perceive details, including targets in complex arrays and at distances (Roman-Lantzy, 2018). The ventral stream extends into the brain's temporal lobe. The dorsal and ventral streams are general concepts and do not refer to actual anatomical pathways; however, they are helpful to understand the clinical manifestations of CVI, allowing them to

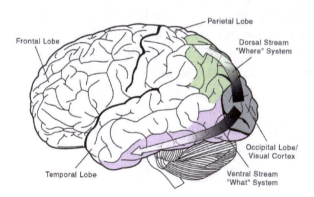

Source: Adapted from Selket, made from File:Gray728.svg, CC BY- SA 3.0. Retrieved from https://commons.wikimedia.org/w/index.php?curid=1679336

Visual information from the occipital lobes is divided into two systems or pathways of visual processing, the dorsal and the ventral streams, to create a complete picture of the visual information.

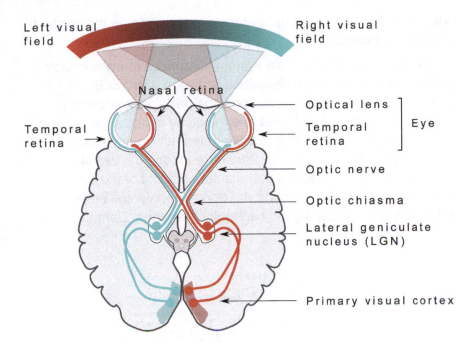

Left visual field

Right visual field

Nasal retina

Temporal retina

Optical lens

Temporal retina

Eye

Optic nerve

Optic chiasma

Lateral geniculate nucleus (LGN)

Primary visual cortex

Source: By Miquel Perello Nieto - Own work, CC BY-SA 4.0, https://commons .wikimedia.org/w/index.php?curid=37868501

The visual system is made up of the ocular (eye and optic nerve) and perceptual (brain areas that detect and recognize what is seen) parts of vision.

be related to anatomical abnormalities found on the MRI scans of children with CVI.

In order for vision to function correctly, all structures and components of the visual system must operate precisely and efficiently. In addition to the health and condition of the visual system itself, visual ability is influenced by environmental conditions as well as a person's health and emotional state. As a result, each person's visual experience is unique.

The visual system is made up of ocular (eye and optic nerve) and perceptual (brain areas that detect and recognize what is seen) components. *Cognition* is an extension of visual perception. It involves a person's capacity to process what is seen, consider its significance, and then use and manipulate both the incoming image data and stored imagery in the context of creative thought.

Each section of the visual system comprises many complex parts. The Tree of Vision described in *Vision and the Brain* (Lueck & Dutton, 2015b depicts how the principal processing areas are connected and what role they play in visual perception and cognition. The tree diagram illustrates how image data received from the eyes is then transferred along the visual pathways of the trunk to the occipital lobes. Most of the visual information is transferred along the dorsal and ventral streams, which are represented by the two major branches. Damage at any

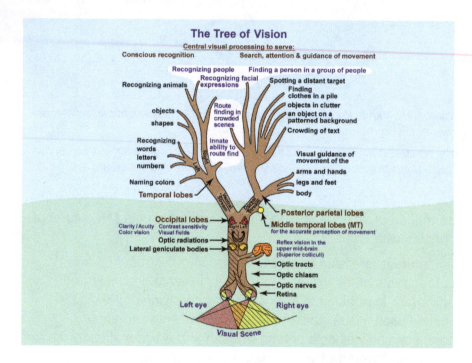

Source: Reproduced with permission from Dutton, G. N., Bowman, R., & Fazzi, E. (2014). Visual function. In B. Dan, M. Mayston, N. Paneth, & L. Rosenbloom (Eds.), Cerebral palsy: Science and clinical practice. *London: Mac Keith Press*

The Tree of Vision (Lueck & Dutton, 2015b) depicts how the principal processing areas are connected and what role they play in visual perception and cognition.

location in this system leads to impairment of the functions that exist above that level (Dutton, 2015b).

The many branches radiating from the ventral and dorsal stream trunks symbolize the clusters of visual difficulties that are commonly observed in children who have a cerebral visual impairment (Dutton, 2015c). For example, visual difficulties shown branching off of the left trunk, which symbolizes the *ventral* or "what" stream, include issues recognizing objects, symbols, faces, and facial expressions. Visual difficulties shown branching off the right trunk, which symbolizes the *dorsal* or "where" stream, include problems with visual complexity and clutter, visual motor planning, and visual field inattentiveness.

An abnormality in or disruption of any component of the visual system can result in visual difficulties or disabilities. Some medical syndromes and congenital issues can interrupt the formation of parts of the eye and the optic nerve. Many of the disruptions that occur specifically within the ocular portion of vision are correctable with eyeglasses, contact lenses, or surgery.

As mentioned earlier, babies with brain-related visual impairments—and especially those with CVI—may have coexisting disabilities along with ocular abnormalities. The Model Registry of Early Childhood Visual Impairment showed that only 21% of children with CVI had no other coexisting conditions in addition to the visual impairment (Hatton, 2001). A retrospective study of 100 children with CVI, by Brodsky et al. (2002), showed that 82% had coexisting strabismus, a misalignment of the eyes. The CVI lecture series (Hyvärinen, 2004) identified the following coexisting conditions with CVI: cerebral palsy (53%), seizure disorder (50%), neurological disability (75%), and hearing impairment.

The very existence of other ocular abnormalities may mask coexisting CVI in a baby, and a diagnosis of a CVI may overshadow a coexisting ocular impairment (Roman-Lantzy, 2018). During a baby's FVA, teachers of children with visual impairments often identify characteristic behaviors associated with CVI, even when other known ocular abnormalities are present. Teachers can recommend appropriate interventions to address the issues related to both ocular visual impairments and CVI. However, while teachers of children with visual impairments assess functional vision, they do not diagnose visual impairments or other conditions. **Table 2.1** describes how a disorder in each part of the eye affects overall vision. (An in-depth discussion of ocular impairments that frequently accompany CVI is outside the scope of this book; for additional information, readers can refer to Erin et al., 2002; Topor et al., 2004; and others).

Ocular Part of Vision

The Eye

Light enters the visual system through the eyes (see **Figure 2.2**). Both eyes contain intricate systems that receive, filter, and bend light so that it focuses on the retina, where a photochemical reaction occurs. This reaction stimulates transmission of electrical signals to the brain. The slightly different vantage points of each eye result in the perception of depth through a process known as *stereopsis*. Disruption of vision in one eye will impair binocularity (coordinated use of both eyes) and compromise a person's ability to perceive depth. However, as children with visual impairments continue to use their vision, they can learn to interpret depth through environmental cues even if stereopsis is not present. However, the lack of binocularity can affect development of sitting and standing balance in small children and delay achievement of these milestones.

The Optic Nerve

The optic nerve consists of hundreds of thousands of nerve fibers that arise from the ganglion cells located near the inner surface of the retina. It behaves much like a fiber optic cable, relaying electrical impulses from the retina to the brain. About half of the optic nerve fibers from each eye cross over to the other side of the brain at the *optic chiasm*, which allows the visual cortex to receive visual information from both eyes. If the optic nerve is underdeveloped, the visual information transmitted to

Table 2.1
Ocular Abnormalities in Babies With CVI

Ocular Abnormality	Description	Effect on Vision
Ptosis and other eyelid malformations	Drooping or other malformations of the eyelids	Can completely block vision or produce distortion in the visual image sent to brain
Microphthalmia with or without coloboma	Small and sometimes incompletely formed eyes	Can span from near normal to complete loss of vision
Corneal opacities or cataract	Opacity or cloudiness in the cornea or lens	Can completely block vision or produce distortion in visual image sent to the brain; images may be blurry or fuzzy and colors may seem faded
Iris abnormalities including aniridia, coloboma, albinism	Partial or complete absence of the iris (aniridia); cleft or gap in part of the eye, such as the iris, lens, or retina (coloboma); or lack of pigmentation in eyes, skin, or hair (albinism)	Impaired vision; sensitivity to light and glare; may cause distortion of image
Strabismus	Misalignment of the eyes	Can suppress the image coming from one eye; can lead to amblyopia, impaired depth perception, or both
Nystagmus	Involuntary, rapid, or repetitive eye movements	Can span from near normal to severe visual impairment; often associated with some other underlying eye or brain condition

(continued)

Table 2.1 (continued)

Ocular Abnormality	Description	Effect on Vision
Amblyopia	Vision does not develop properly because the eye and the brain are not working together correctly; commonly known as "lazy eye"	Blurred vision in affected eye; if left untreated, may lead to permanent vision problems
Glaucoma	Pressure of fluid inside the eye is too high, resulting in loss of peripheral vision; if not treated, the increased pressure can damage the optic nerve	Loss of peripheral vision; if left untreated, may eventually lead to blindness
Refractive errors such as hyperopia, myopia, and astigmatism	Farsightedness (hyperopia); nearsightedness (myopia); irregularly curved cornea or lens (astigmatism)	Difficulty focusing on near and distant objects; blurred vision, eyestrain, headaches
Retinopathy of prematurity	Abnormal development of retinal blood vessels due to prematurity; sometimes progressing to retinal detachment	Can lead to reduced vision or blindness
Optic nerve hypoplasia or atrophy	Underdeveloped or degeneration of the optic nerve; cannot adequately transmit visual information from eye to brain	Little or no visual impairment to near-total blindness; dimmed or blurred vision, reduced field of vision, difficulty seeing contrast and fine detail

Note. This table describes how a disorder in each part of the eye affects overall vision.

Figure 2.2
Components of the Eye

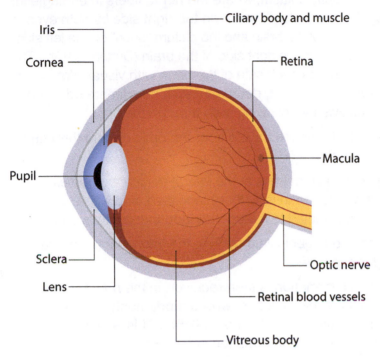

Note. Components of the eyes receive, filter, and bend light so that it will focus on the retina, where a photochemical reaction occurs to begin transmission of electrical signals to the brain.

the brain is limited, even if the eye is completely normal. Many babies with CVI also have damaged optic nerves because both conditions result from similar causal factors.

Perceptual Part of Vision

The perceptual system of the brain affects how one understands the visual information received from their eyes. The perceptual system is analogous to a computer within the visual system. The eye is the camera, connected to this computer via a cord (the optic nerve). The brain's perceptual system receives visual information from the retina, transmitted through the optic nerves. The optic nerves intersect at the optic chiasm, where the nerve fibers intermingle in such a way that the picture "seen" on the right side by both eyes is sent to the left side of the brain and the picture "seen" on the left side by both eyes is sent to the right side of the brain (Dutton, 2015b). The optic chiasm provides each side of the brain with visual information from both eyes. As a result, depth perception is generated. Vision information follows the following path through the brain:

- The visual information travels from the optic chiasm through the *optic tracts*.

- The optic tracts terminate at the *lateral geniculate bodies,* where the information is further processed, and where some information is routed to a feedback loop that controls pupil size.

- From the lateral geniculate bodies, the information next travels through *optic radiations*.

- The visual information is then received in the *primary visual cortex* of the occipital lobes, where fundamental image processing takes place (Dutton, 2015b). This is where the most detailed visual information is first broken down into its component parts, and then converted into symbolic patterns representing data such as color, detail, and movement. It takes about one-tenth of a second for the visual information to reach the occipital lobes from the eye's retina (Dutton, 2015b).

- From the occipital lobes, the information travels along the dorsal and ventral visual streams (or pathways) to the parietal and temporal lobes. As mentioned earlier, these two lobes are the principal areas of the brain that serve the higher functions of vision, including visual search, visual attention, visual guidance of movement, and image recognition (Dutton, 2015b).

The dorsal stream runs from the occipital lobe to the posterior parietal lobes of the brain, functioning at a subconscious level (Dutton, 2015b). The dorsal stream is referred to as the "where" stream because it supports visual guidance of movement. The ventral stream runs from the occipital lobes to the *temporal lobes* of the brain. It is often referred to as the "what" system because it supports visual recognition, or determining what things are. Unlike dorsal stream vision, ventral stream vision functions at a conscious level (Dutton, 2015b).

Damage in the Perceptual Part of Vision

The term *ocular visual impairment* typically refers to damage to the regions of the body involving the eye, optic nerve, and optic chiasm. In contrast, *cerebral visual impairment* involves damage specifically to those visual areas located behind the optic chiasm (Kran & Mayer, 2015), where the perceptual part of vision is located. Babies with CVI often experience damage somewhere within the perceptual areas of the visual system; although, as mentioned earlier, it is not uncommon for them to experience damage in ocular areas as well (Kran & Mayer, 2015). Each area of the visual perceptual system is critical to the brain's ability to interpret what is seen accurately. Damage in the visual brain impedes the brain's ability to receive and process visual information properly. The specific location of damage within the visual brain will affect how the visual image is impaired.

Damage in the posterior parietal lobe of the brain results in fewer brain cells and nerve fibers being available to process incoming information; as such, a person with damage in this region of the brain would find it difficult to conceptualize a mental map of their surroundings. Movement through visual space would be less accurate because of impaired visual guidance, or *optic ataxia*. Children with optic ataxia tend to bump into things and may not be able to detect items within their visual space. Children with a disorder of the dorsal stream usually have complete or partial lower visual field loss, which can affect a child's ability to see their own feet, notice obstacles on the floor, or detect drop-offs or changes in level. Children with dorsal stream dysfunction can also have impaired visual guidance of the lower (and less often, upper) limbs (Dutton, 2015c), as well as difficulty using vision while simultaneously doing something else, such as walking and talking at the same time (Topor, 2014).

Table 2.2
Visual Features of CVI to Consider Looking for in Relation to Damage in Specific Brain Locations Reported on a Brain MRI Scan

Area of Damage Seen on MRI Scan	Visual Features to Look For
Occipital Lobes	
Left occipital lobe	• Lack of visual field on the right side for both eyes
Right occipital lobe	• Lack of visual field on the left side for both eyes
Both occipital lobes	• Impaired central visual functions of acuity, contrast, and color
	• Lack of visual field on both sides (often manifesting as visual field constriction)
	• Severe damage causes profound visual impairment
Posterior Parietal Lobes	
Left posterior parietal lobe	• Intermittent lack of attention on the right side
	• A tendency to miss people and events on the right side
	• A tendency to bump into people and objects on the right side, especially when upset or tired
	• Reduced accuracy of visual guidance of movement of the right side of the body
	• A tendency to be left-handed (because this becomes the dominant hand)
	• Weakness of the right side of the body (as a result of damage further forward in the brain)
	• Difficulties with spoken or written language (because the left parietal lobe serves language)
	• When drawing, the right side of the picture can be distorted

Table 2.2 (continued)

Area of Damage Seen on MRI Scan	Visual Features to Look For
Right posterior parietal lobe	• Significant lack of attention on the left side and intermittent lack of attention on the right side (Ting et al., 2011) • People and events on the left side are frequently missed • People and objects on the left side are frequently bumped in to • A tendency to be right-handed • Weakness of the left side of the body
Both posterior parietal lobes *Severe damage affecting the cortex, white matter, or both*	• Inability to see more than one or two items in a visual scene at once (simultanagnosia), despite the requisite visual field • Inability to use vision to guide movement, accurately despite sometimes having clear three-dimensional vision (stereopsis), in rare cases, resulting in colliding with walls and obstacles, bumping into people and objects, and not being aware of drop-offs • Inability to give attention to more than one or two things at once • Noise or conversation can make the child lose visual attention • Inability to move the eyes from one target to another at will, despite ability to move the eyes • Profound lack of ability to see moving targets is common • Lack of lower visual field below the horizontal midline • Impaired movement of all four limbs as a result of quadriplegic cerebral palsy is common

(continued)

Table 2.2 (continued)

Area of Damage Seen on MRI Scan	Visual Features to Look For
Limited damage to parietal white matter	• Behavioral patterns of dorsal stream dysfunction • Lack of ability to see moving targets is occasionally observed • Lack of the peripheral lower visual field means that the feet cannot be seen while walking • Impaired ability to move feet over floor boundaries, or walking around patterns despite looking at them, suggests optic ataxia of the lower limbs • Reaching for patterns on plates as if they are three-dimensional is observed in some young children

Temporal Lobes
(The patterns described for damage to one side apply to acquired damage, but can be variable. Damage from birth tends to affect all forms of recognition.)

Left temporal lobe	• Impaired object recognition (object agnosia); color recognition may be used to compensate • Impaired shape recognition (shape agnosia) • Difficulty learning the shapes of letters (alexia)
Right temporal lobe	• Impaired face recognition (prosopagnosia) • Impaired ability to see meaning in facial expressions • Difficulty being orientated (may be profound) and navigating known environments (topographic agnosia)
Both temporal lobes	• Combination of the impaired abilities described for the left and right temporal lobes (integrative agnosia) • Difficulty knowing the length and orientation of lines, or size of objects • Impaired visual memory (often with reliance on auditory memory and language ability)

Damage in the temporal lobe of the brain results in fewer brain cells and nerve fibers being available to process incoming information. Ventral stream dysfunction can result in *prosopagnosia* (difficulties recognizing faces), as well as difficulty interpreting facial expressions; recognizing animals, shapes, objects, colors, and words; forming visual memories; and finding routes for travel (Dutton, 2015c; Topor, 2014). **Table 2.2** outlines the visual features of CVI in relation to damage in specific brain areas.

CONCLUSION

Babies with CVI frequently have additional eye-related visual impairments. In order to employ the most effective interventions, it is necessary for both professionals and parents to understand the differences between *ocular* and *perceptual* visual impairments. Providing parents with information also serves another important role: Once parents gain a deeper understanding of the visual system and learn more about their baby's particular visual abilities and disabilities, they feel less confused about the diagnosis of CVI and begin to feel empowered to address their baby's early visual diagnosis. Besides simply providing parents with interesting facts, teaching parents about their baby's visual experiences through simulation serves an even greater goal: fostering an emotional connection with their baby.

CHAPTER 3

Cerebral Visual Impairment[1]

The assertion that "the most difficult aspect of CVI is to understand its nature" appeared in a handbook about cortical visual impairment in children published in 1989 (Steendam, 1989, p. 1). It still holds true today. Confusion about CVI extends from keeping track of its changing names to understanding its impact on babies' behavior and development. **Chapter 2** introduced the visual system, including the component parts of the eye along with the brain's role in the vision process to manage perceptual visual functioning. This chapter explores the nature of CVI, which has been referred to as a "complex and multifaceted condition" (Dutton & Lueck, 2015, p. 3).

This chapter provides even more information for professionals to share with families. As a parent's knowledge about CVI grows more sophisticated, their ability to understand, connect with, and parent a baby with CVI increases. However, bringing a parent's grasp of CVI to the next level can be difficult. In other words, since even professionals sometimes find all of the nuances of CVI difficult to understand, one must not forget the confusion parents of a baby newly diagnosed with CVI may feel. **Sidebar 3.1** addresses some of the questions that parents may rely on a professional to answer.

CEREBRAL VISUAL IMPAIRMENT

When first discussing CVI with parents, start with the basics. A good approach is to consider the questions most parents have about CVI. It can be useful for teachers of children with visual impairments to frame the discussion by considering the following frequently asked questions. Suggested replies to parents'

[1] Amy K. Hutchinson, MD, pediatric ophthalmologist at Emory University Eye Center, contributed substantially to the medical information provided in this chapter.

Frequently Asked Questions About CVI

Teachers of children with visual impairments report that most parents of babies with CVI have similar questions about the diagnosis. Some of these include the following:

1. What is a cerebral visual impairment (CVI)?

2. Is CVI a visual impairment or a learning disability?

3. Why do professionals use different names for this diagnosis?

4. Does CVI occur often?

5. What causes CVI?

6. How do professionals diagnose a baby with CVI?

7. What tests are used to diagnose CVI?

8. Why did the doctor say that my baby's eyes are fine if my baby is blind?

9. Will eyeglasses fix CVI?

10. Can my baby have other eye problems in addition to CVI?

11. Can babies with CVI also have additional disabilities?

12. What is my baby's visual experience like?

13. Why does my baby sometimes seem blind and other times appear to use vision?

14. Will my baby outgrow this problem and develop normal vision?

15. How can vision loss and CVI affect development?

16. What can I do to maximize my baby's vision and learning potential?

questions consistently emphasize the importance of timely intervention.

What Is CVI?

CVI is an abbreviation referring to two definitions of brain related visual impairment. CVI is a visual impairment that results from damage to or disorder of the cortical area in the brain. In some cases, however, doctors and other professionals may use the term CVI in a more inclusive sense, applying the term to a broader range of vision impairments. CVI can also apply to a visual impairment that results from disorders of the visual pathways and visual centers of the brain (Dutton & Lueck, 2015).

Helping parents understand the various aspects and terminology of CVI is a challenge for both medical and educational professionals. In this photo, a mother holds her baby as she discusses the diagnosis with a medical professional.

Names for CVI

Why Do Professionals Use Different Names for This Diagnosis?

As understanding of the role the brain plays in vision has increased, so have the names professionals have used to identify what is now called CVI. Scientists have been aware that the brain plays a role in vision as early as the 1700s (Hoyt, 2003). However, understanding of the brain's role deepened in the 1900s as scientists studied how shrapnel injuries to the brains of injured soldiers affected their vision (Dutton & Lueck, 2015). As scientists' understanding of the vision processing centers of the brain grew more sophisticated, the terminology used to discuss the range of visual processing disorders included in CVI has evolved to more accurately reflect CVI's impact on visual processing. It is almost certain that medical, visual impairment, and blindness professionals will continue to debate what the condition we now call CVI should most appropriately be called in the future. As the terminology evolves, professionals and parents alike may find themselves confused at times.

Neurological visual impairment is a term that refers broadly to visual impairment caused by the brain. Other diagnostic terms are more specific. For example, *cortical* visual impairment (referred to as CVI) is a type of brain-based visual problem to which specific physical and behavioral criteria can be applied (Roman-Lantzy, 2018). In neurological terms, cortical visual impairment is impaired vision resulting from bilateral dysfunction of the optic radiations, visual cortex (occipital lobe), or both (Roman et al., 2010). In contrast, the similar-sounding *cerebral* visual impairment (also referred to as CVI) is a broader term than cortical visual impairment and describes disorders of the visual pathways and visual centers in the brain (Dutton & Lueck, 2015). Cerebral visual impairment is generally considered to be a name that is wider in scope and includes cortical visual impairment within it.

After World War II, many veterans returned home with damage to the occipital cortex (visual center) of their brains. At that time, what we now call CVI was usually called *cortical blindness,* since many soldiers' brain injuries did, in fact, result in blindness. However, cortical blindness is no longer the most accurate term used to describe all CVI. As previously discussed, most babies with CVI can see something and it is possible for their vision to improve (Cattaneo & Merabet, 2015; Roman-Lantzy, 2018), whereas a person with cortical blindness cannot see and their vision is not expected to improve.

Another term that professionals sometimes use for brain-related visual disability is *delayed visual maturation* (DVM). DVM is a delayed myelination of cortical areas of the brain. The visual abilities of children with DVM improve naturally and continue to develop normally (Russell-Eggitt et al., 2008). Although babies with DVM will start to develop typical vision within their first year (Russell-Eggitt et al., 2008), they can still benefit from early interventions intended to compensate for any early visual learning they have missed (Erin et all, 2002, p. 86). In the author's experience, doctors may diagnose DVM when a baby's visual milestones are delayed; but CVI is not immediately apparent from brain imaging. Children diagnosed with DVM by one doctor are sometimes diagnosed with CVI at a later date by a different doctor. In fact, the diagnosis of DVM should only be made in retrospect, once vision has developed normally because, as already mentioned, infants with DVM characteristically outgrow their visual problems (Topor I., 1999).

Since parents and professionals expect the vision of babies with DVM to improve without treatment, they unfortunately may postpone critical early interventions for children initially diagnosed with DVM. If parents and professionals are unsure whether a child has DVM or CVI, it is essential to try to verify a diagnosis as soon as possible. Babies with DVM will experience improved vision naturally, but babies with CVI need interventions as soon as possible to improve their visual abilities to the maximal potential. A mistaken diagnosis could mean that a baby misses out on important early interventions during the critical period of development (A.K. Hutchinson, personal communication, December 15, 2017). Characteristic behaviors of CVI discussed later in this chapter will help identify this diagnosis.

Incidence of CVI

Does CVI Occur Often?

CVI has become the primary cause of visual impairment in children in developed countries (Lueck & Dutton, 2015a). The American Foundation for the Blind's statement on cortical visual impairment reports that 30–40% of children who are visually impaired have a cortical visual impairment (Roman-Lantzy, 2018). A key factor in the increase of children with CVI is the improvement in infant mortality rates. Advances in medical science to treat babies born prematurely (less than 37 weeks of gestation) mean that children are now able to survive increasingly shorter gestational ages. Babies born with shorter gestational durations are at high risk of brain injuries, including those that cause CVI. As a result, the population of prematurely born children with CVI is rising (Lueck & Dutton, 2015a).

What Causes CVI?

Brain damage can occur at any stage—in utero, during the birthing process, or after birth—as a result of an anatomical disorder, accident, or illness. The brain needs both oxygen (for growth and healing) and glucose/sugar (fuel for energy within the brain) to remain nourished and healthy and can become damaged without this oxygen and glucose supply. Any event that reduces or stops the delivery of oxygen and glucose to the brain either before or after birth can cause brain damage (Roman-Lantzy, 2018). The longer the brain is deprived of oxygen or glucose, the greater the damage (Dutton, 2015c). Because the brain of the fetus is in the beginning phase of development, deprivation of oxygen or glucose causes more significant damage than an older baby might experience.

While depriving any area of the brain of oxygen and glucose may damage it, CVI results specifically when there is "damage or malfunction of visual pathways and visual centers in the brain . . . including the optic radiations, the occipital cortex, and the visual associative areas" (Boot, 2010; Fazzi, 2009; Ortibus, 2011; as cited in Dutton, 2015).

Damage to these perceptual areas in the brain can create a situation analogous to a traffic disruption on a major roadway. Damage within the visual areas of the brain disrupts or stops the flow of electrical impulses and impedes their travel through the areas of the brain responsible for sight. This disruption of the normal flow of electrical impulses negatively affects how visual information is received and processed.

The most common causes of CVI include malformations of the brain or other anatomical abnormalities. These may include microcephaly, hydrocephalus, tumors, viruses such as meningitis and encephalitis, bacteria, parasites such as toxoplasmosis, complications in utero (difficulties with the umbilical cord or placenta, or fetal stroke), brain damage related to prematurity (intraventricular hemorrhage or periventricular leukomalacia), complications during delivery such as asphyxia at birth, rubella and other infections, cytomegalic inclusion disease, seizures, head injury from trauma, or shaken baby syndrome (Dutton, 2015c; Roman-Lantzy, 2018; see **Table 3.1**).

Diagnosing CVI

How Do Professionals Diagnose a Baby With CVI?

As stated earlier, a CVI diagnosis may be confusing. There is currently no single established procedure for diagnosing CVI (Roman-Lantzy, 2018). The fields of special education and medicine continue to dialogue about definitions of CVI, appropriate terminology, diagnostic criteria, directions for research, evidence-based interventions, and educational practices (Roman-Lantzy, 2007). Even in cases in which an ophthalmological exam shows that both the eye structures and the optic nerve are healthy, a child's behaviors can still indicate that vision is not being correctly processed. This is especially true if there is a history of brain damage or medical imaging that suggests it. Both medical and nonmedical assessments can indicate the probable presence of CVI, but a formal diagnosis is made by a medical professional. A teacher of children with visual impairments can initiate appropriate interventions if CVI is suspected since in the early years of development these strategies are appropriate for babies with both ocular and neurological visual impairments.

What Tests Are Used to Diagnose CVI?

CVI is diagnosed through medical assessments and observed behaviors. Major brain damage can often be identified by

Table 3.1
Causes of Damage to the Visual Brain*

Cause	Comment
Anatomical disorders of the visual brain	For example, *occipital encephalocele* (protrusion of brain tissue through the skull in the occipital region).
Brain malformations	A wide range of abnormalities of brain structure can impair vision.
Blocked shunts in hydrocephalus*	If the plastic tube used to treat hydrocephalus gets blocked, vision can be severely affected.
Chromosomal and other genetic disorders	Disorders of both brain structure and function can impair vision.
Closed head injury*	Bleeding, blunt injury, and high pressure in the head all contribute to a range of patterns of visual impairment.
Focal damage to specific brain locations	Disorders of visual function depend on the brain structures damaged.
Hemorrhage*	A broken blood vessel leaks blood into a part of the brain.
Tumors*	A wide range of tumors can cause damage in specific locations.
Cortical dysplasia	A part of the cortex of the brain does not develop properly. Vision can be affected if the visual brain is involved.
Hydrocephalus*	Water (cerebrospinal fluid) is unable to escape normally from the spaces where it is made. The water spaces expand under pressure, causing damage to white matter.

(continued)

Table 3.1 (continued)

Cause	Comment
Hypoxic ischemic encephalopathy at term	A blocked blood vessel in the brain, or poor blood and oxygen delivery to the brain, causes damage in a single location or in many locations in the brain.
Infantile spasms, and epilepsy*	The electrical discharge in the brain resulting from seizures can impair vision. This may be the first sign of the disorder.
Injury to the periventricular white matter	Damage to the white matter nerve fibers (or *cabling*) surrounding the water spaces, or ventricles in the brain, has many patterns, and is mainly due to poor oxygen or blood supply during early development. Vision is commonly impaired. Premature birth and *spastic diplegia* (a form of cerebral palsy) are common, but not universal, associations.
Metabolic disorders*	A wide range of rare disorders of how brain cells function can impair visual functioning. Some of these conditions can be progressive in nature.
Meningitis and encephalitis*	Viruses, bacteria, and the parasite toxoplasma can all cause damage.
Neonatal hypoglycemia (low blood sugar)	Low blood sugar shortly after birth causes damage.

*All causes listed can occur early in life. Asterisks denote conditions in which damage to the visual system can also develop in later childhood.

magnetic resonance imaging (MRI), a medical procedure that uses magnetic fields and radio waves to produce anatomical images of a brain in great detail (Fazzi et al., 2015). Since an MRI takes anywhere between 30 and 60 minutes to complete, sedation is often required if a baby cannot remain still enough for the duration of the exam.

The images produced through an MRI then require in-depth analysis by a radiologist and an ophthalmologist to pinpoint the exact location and extent of damage within the brain. While an MRI is the most useful method to support a diagnosis of CVI in a baby, it is not sufficient by itself. To diagnose CVI, the results of an MRI must be correlated with clinical findings of an ophthalmologist (Hutchinson personal communication, 2018). New investigative tools, such as functional magnetic resonance imaging (fMRI) that examines changes in blood oxygenation and flow within the brain, permit observation of the brain in action when performing a particular task. Although an fMRI may provide more detailed information (Fazzi et al., 2015), it may not be an appropriate test for an infant because it requires the baby to complete a task. The presence of specific visual inabilities such as lack of a visual field or impaired object perception will help a radiologist and doctor identify which areas of the brain are damaged (Dutton, 2015c). **Table 3.2** presents visual behaviors that arise from damage within different areas of the brain.

Roman-Lantzy (2018) presents three criteria that together can indicate the presence of CVI: medical, neurological, and behavioral. The medical criterion is based on data obtained through a medical eye exam. This exam focuses only on damage to the eye and optic nerve, but does not formally take into account a child's visual behavior. The neurological criterion is obtained through the child's history of any major neurologic events. This information is typically gathered from a child's parents, who are asked about this history during a doctor's visit or an educational assessment. The behavioral criterion is when a baby demonstrates visual and behavioral characteristics typical of children with CVI (Roman-Lantzy, 2018;

Table 3.2
Common Clues to the Possibility of CVI and Its Potential Features

Possible Indications of the Presence of CVI	Visual Features to Look For
Medical Features	
Premature birth (if damage is subtle, MRI may be normal)	• Low visual acuities with no optical or eye disorder • Inability to find someone in a group, or objects in a pile • Lower visual field impairment (very peripheral in mild cases) • Inaccurate visual guidance of limb movement • Difficulty reading crowded text
Hydrocephalus (can have periventricular white matter injury)	• Many have visual acuity or visual field impairment • Over 50 percent have perceptual impairments that can affect both dorsal and ventral streams
History of seizure	• *West syndrome (infantile spasms or early-onset epilepsy):* low vision (low vision may lead to the diagnosis) • *Grand mal seizures:* CVI symptoms and reduced vision lasting for hours or days after a seizure • *Continuous epilepsy with variable vision* that can be controlled with anti-epileptic drugs • *Occipital seizures:* unformed images that are not actually there (hallucinations), resulting from electrical activity in the visual brain
Low blood sugar or respiratory arrest in early weeks after birth (leads to damage to visual brain if sugar or oxygen does not reach the brain cells)	• Occipital or posterior parietal lobe damage, or both; severity of damage and outcome varies • Low visual acuities with visual field reduction unexplained by eye or refractive disorders • Features of dorsal stream dysfunction common • Possible Balint's syndrome • Ventral stream dysfunction can predominate in some cases

Table 3.2 (continued)

Possible Indications of the Presence of CVI	Visual Features to Look For
Meningitis (infection around lining of brain) or encephalitis (infection of brain) (can lead to multiple foci of damage with outcome ranging from mild to severe visual dysfunction)	• Photophobia • Visual acuity impaired (worse when tired) • Vision can fluctuate during recovery • Visual field constriction • Visual perceptual disorders (impaired color naming, inability to recognize shapes, letters, or words) • Faces can look distorted or are not recognized • Getting lost • (Note: Progressive recovery needs to be sought and the approach to the child modified accordingly)
Hyoscine patches to control salivation	• Large pupils, causing photophobia • Poor or absent accommodation (ability to focus) causing reduced vision in the long farsighted (long sited), and minimal near vision
History of major head injury	• Any type of CVI can result
Appearance	
Microcephaly (small head), with flattening at the back, more so on one side	• Low visual acuities • Lack of vision/visual field on side opposite to the greatest degree of flattening
Spastic diplegia	• Lower visual field impairment • Impaired visual search • Difficulty reading crowded text
Hemiplegic cerebral palsy or Consistent repeated bruising on one leg	• Lack of vision (often relatively asymptomatic) or impaired visual attention on the weak or bruised side

(continued)

Table 3.2 (continued)

Possible Indications of the Presence of CVI	Visual Features to Look For
Spastic quadriplegia	• Any aspect of visual functioning can be impaired
Dyskinetic cerebral palsy	• Impaired focusing (accommodation)
Horizontal nystagmus (some children have undiagnosed periventricular white matter disease [PVWMD])	• The same features as for premature birth need to be looked for (only a small proportion of cases affected)
Visual Behaviors	
Visual search difficulties (any of these features should trigger a search for the others)	• Inability to find a distant target being pointed out • Inability to find a person in a group • Inability to find a clothing item in a pile of clothes • Inability to find a toy in a toy box • Inability to read crowded text
Running out in front of traffic	• Low visual acuities • Visual field impairment • Impaired visual attention • Impaired perception of movement • Visual inattention
Not looking at someone who is talking to him or her	• Low visual acuity precluding interpretation of facial appearance and expressions • Evidence of dorsal stream dysfunction with impaired splitting of attention between sight and sound • Impaired perception of movement precluding fast-moving facial expressions from being seen

Table 3.2 (continued)

Possible Indications of the Presence of CVI	Visual Features to Look For
	• Inability to recognize faces • Inability to interpret the language of facial expression
Refusing to run down a hill	• Lower visual field impairment, often very peripheral, precluding the extended foot from being seen
Drawings poor on one side of the page	• Evidence of visual inattention on the side of the poor drawing
Reading difficulties, starting around age 8 (resulting from smaller print size and increased crowding)	• Lack of focusing (accommodation) • Difficulties with visual crowding
Reactive Behaviors	
Not looking at what is being reached for	• Lack of central vision • Features of ventral or dorsal stream dysfunction
Striking an adjacent restless child, while continuing to work	• Limited visual attention, leading to a need not to be distracted when completing a task
Displaying anger when furniture is moved	• Lower visual field impairment • Features of dorsal stream dysfunction
Exhibiting fear in straight symmetrical corridors	• Lack of visual attention on one side can render symmetrical environments frightening, perhaps because one side becomes less evident
Exhibiting distress in crowded places	• Features of dorsal stream dysfunction

(continued)

Table 3.2 (continued)

Possible Indications of the Presence of CVI	Visual Features to Look For
Compensatory Behaviors	
Sitting very close to the TV	• Low visual acuity • Features of dorsal stream dysfunction
Watching the TV upside down, lying on back with head back	• Lower visual field impairment (using the intact upper field to watch the TV)
Feeling the ground ahead at floor boundaries	• Low vision • Lower visual field impairment • Other features of dorsal stream dysfunction
Organizing possessions in fixed locations	• Other features of dorsal stream dysfunction

see **Sidebar 3.2**). The child's parents and teacher of children with visual impairments can formally identify characteristic behaviors through observation during a functional vision assessment (discussed in **Chapter 4**).

Is My Child Blind?

Understandably, parents may be confused when presented with a seeming contradiction: If a doctor determines that their baby's eyes and optic nerves are free from damage, why is their child visually impaired? The answer is that the problem lies in the *brain,* not in the eyes. Even when a baby's eyes and optic nerves are structurally sound, if the brain itself is unable to process the visual data it receives, the child will still have a visual impairment. The visual difficulties associated with CVI vary depending on where the injury to the brain is located. It is worth reminding

Visual Behaviors Characteristic of CVI

Children may exhibit characteristic visual behaviors that, when observed, help confirm the presence of CVI. Children are unique, and so are the causes, severity, and locations of their visual dysfunction. Depending on the severity of the condition, the amount and level of related behaviors will vary, as will their effect on visual functioning (Roman-Lantzy, 2018).

Visual responses may fluctuate depending on many factors, both environmental and personal. A child will not attend well to visual targets if the child is uncomfortable, distracted, upset, ill, or feels threatened. Environmental conditions affect vision use, such as too much or too little light, loud or distracting noises, too small a target or one placed too far away, an uninteresting target, or a target set against a crowded background. Babies with CVI may also exhibit hypersensitivity to tactile, auditory, or visual inputs. They may cry or cover their ears in response to certain noises. The child may not see objects in certain visual fields, leading observers to conclude that the child with CVI sometimes has vision while at other times does not. These visual fluctuations are characteristic of CVI and can be misunderstood by both professionals and parents who might incorrectly assume that the child sees well and is therefore choosing to be unresponsive. Visual responses are involuntary, so it is not possible for a small child with CVI to voluntarily choose to use vision more effectively.

- Color preference: Some colors are more visually engaging than others, which may help a baby maintain visual attention to a target. Highly saturated and vibrant colors such as red and yellow are especially preferred by many children with CVI.

- Need for movement: It is possible to increase a baby's ability to view an object and maintain visual attention to

(continued)

it by either moving the object itself, or by continuing to move the child in relationship to the object. Motion can increase the child's ability to view the object and maintain visual attention to it. For example, a shaking toy can be more visually stimulating than a stationary one.

- Visual latency: Visual latency is a delay in reacting to a visual target. When an appropriate target is presented within a child's optimal area for viewing, there may be a delay before the child gazes at or regards the target.

- Visual field preferences: Visual field preferences is the preference or ability to see target objects within some visual fields but not others.

- Difficulty with visual complexity: This difficulty manifests as an inability to discriminate details. For example, a target object grouped with other objects, such as in a toy box, may be more difficult to find. In contrast, a target object grouped with just a few others, such as on a toy shelf, may be visually easier to find. An item presented against a cluttered or patterned background may be difficult for a baby to locate visually.

- Discriminating faces or recognizing unfamiliar faces may also be difficult for a baby with CVI.

- Need for light: Children with CVI may light-gaze at bright lights, becoming attracted to sources of light and to reflective materials. For example, a ceiling light may capture a child's visual attention to the exclusion of other targets. A child with CVI may also be hypersensitive to lights (photophobia), especially those that produce a glare. While a baby with CVI may sometimes seem to gaze at nothing or into empty space, this behavior is actually a purposeful response. For example, looking off into space may calm the child, help to filter out distracting stimuli, reduce visual confusion, or provide relief from eye fatigue.

- Difficulty with distance viewing: Targets that are near the child are easier to see and isolate than those in the distance. A child may behave as if nearsighted.

- Atypical visual reflexes: A child may have an absent or impaired blink response in response to an approaching target, such as when tapped on the bridge of the nose. There also may be a slow or absent pupillary response to change in light if there is a coexisting retinal problem or optic atrophy. Pupils are often normal in babies who have CVI with no other visual disabilities (A. K. Hutchinson, personal communication, October 15, 2017).

- Difficulty with visual novelty: A child is more likely to respond visually to a familiar and favorite target than a novel one.

- Absence of visually guided reach: The acts of looking at an object and reaching for it are typically performed separately. A baby with CVI will look at the target, look away, and then reach toward the target.

parents that babies with CVI are rarely completely blind. With appropriate interventions, it is possible for them to improve their visual abilities. These visual abilities, such as visual alerting, visual engagement, and visual integration, are discussed in **Chapter 6.**

Can Eyeglasses or Contacts Fix CVI?

Corrective lenses such as eyeglasses or contact lenses are used to compensate for irregularities of the eye's cornea and lens. As explained in **Chapter 2,** these structures bend light from the environment to focus accurately on the retina of the eye. If these structures are irregular, they will not bend light received from the environment accurately. Since this light cannot focus accurately on the retina, a refractive error will occur. A refractive error causes a focused image to be projected either in front of or behind the retina, which results in a baby perceiving a blurry or diminished image. Corrective lenses work by readjusting the focus of the light as it enters the eye, enabling it to reach the retina accurately. Concave or minus lenses are employed when the eye causes light to project in front of the retina (myopia); convex or plus lenses are used when the eye causes light to project behind the retina (hyperopia). By making sure that visual information accurately reaches the retina, corrective lenses make visual images clearer. Children with CVI are susceptible to coexisting ocular impairments, such as refractive errors, that might benefit from correction (Saunders, 2015). While corrective lenses cannot "cure" CVI, ensuring that a baby with CVI's ocular visual ability is optimized can enhance his or her ability to learn to use vision (Orel-Bixler, 2014).

Occasionally, even in cases in which a child's visual focus will improve through the use of corrective lenses, a doctor may decide that a child can be spared the additional discomfort of learning to wear lenses and will postpone encouraging the uses of eyeglasses. Parents and professionals should work together to decide the importance, appropriateness, and timing of introducing eyeglasses.

Anecdotal information suggests that some children with CVI whose eye examinations do not indicate refractive errors may still be able to increase their visual alerting with lenses with plus accommodation such as used in reading glasses. In such cases, corrective lenses may compensate for weak accommodation that a medical exam was unable to detect. In children with CVI who also have accompanying conditions that cause hypotonia (low muscle tone)—for example, cerebral palsy or Down syndrome—hypotonia may affect muscles inside the eye, resulting in accommodation that is weak or nonexistent. It is recommended that a child who seems to become more visually alert when wearing plus-4 lens or higher eyeglasses should be thoroughly reassessed by a teacher of the visually impaired.

CVI and Other Disabilities

Can My Baby Have Other Eye Problems in Addition to CVI?

As explained in **Chapter 2,** a child may have other ocular impairments along with CVI. The most common include strabismus, nystagmus, myopia, hyperopia, optic nerve hypoplasia or septo-optic dysplasia, optic atrophy, corneal opacities or cataracts, glaucoma, and retinopathy of prematurity (for more information see **Table 2.1** in **Chapter 2**). If a child with CVI has an ocular abnormality that can be treated with corrective lenses, then he or she will certainly benefit from using eyeglasses to maximize visual ability (L. Hyvärinen, personal communication, January 2, 2018).

Can Babies With CVI Also Have Additional Nonvisual Disabilities?

A neurological event that damages visual areas of the brain in a baby with CVI can also damage other nonvisual areas. Cerebral palsy, seizure disorders, sensory integration disorder, hydrocephalus, cognitive impairment, microcephaly (abnormally small head), meningomyelocele (spina bifida), hearing loss, and memory dysfunction are some of the disabilities that can coexist with CVI (Dennison, 2003; Dutton, 2015c; Roman-Lantzy, 2018; Steendam, 1989).

THE BABY'S VISUAL EXPERIENCE

It can be hard to understand the visual experience of a baby with CVI simply because a baby is unable to describe their vision verbally. We know what it is like for an adult to have CVI since adults with an acquired brain injury that results in CVI can usually describe their visual experience. However, it is likely that the visual experience of a baby with brain damage is probably very different than that of an adult because of a baby's lack of both life experiences and visual memory.

What Is My Baby's Visual Experience Like?

Even though a baby is unable to describe his or her actual visual experience, it can be determined through brain imaging which parts of the brain are injured. Once the damage is located, it is possible to draw general conclusions about what a baby's visual experience probably is like. We would expect that the visual experience of a baby with CVI is likely changing and confusing. What follows is a hypothetical impression of what a baby's visual experience might be like, based on known characteristic visual behaviors of older children with CVI. It can be useful to share the following description with concerned parents.

A Hypothetical Experience

Imagine a world where nothing seems to remain visually consistent, where changes to what you see seem to be entirely random. For example, the background might appear foggy, with varying levels of brightness coming from different locations. Then unexpectedly, something of visual interest may suddenly appear in your visual field. This form may appear blurry. What is it? Is it a toy or a face? An overhead light? The bright color of a mother's blouse? Is it something that is in motion, such as a ceiling fan, that attracts the baby's visual attention? Or perhaps it is a bright red object, a shiny mirror, or a lighted toy that has moved into a baby's visual field and then moved away again. When a baby with CVI's vision is engaged by something, he or she may remain attentive for a while but then become confused or bored because the item has no understood significance or meaning. At this stage, the baby may respond by staring off into space or by closing his or her eyelids.

Now suppose that a parent has picked up the baby. The baby now hears the familiar sound of a parent's voice warmly talking about eating, along with the sound of the parent's fingers tapping a plastic bottle. Since these sounds frequently occur together, the child has come to

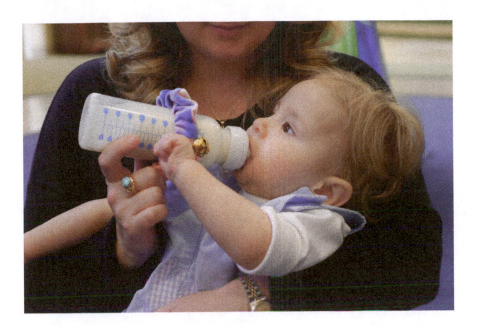

A baby's bottle decorated with colorful and highly visually motivating items can motivate visual alerting and attention. In this photo, the baby plays with a colorful hair scrunchy on the bottle. Hopefully, he will then look at the bottle between sips as his parent moves it to different places in his visual field.

associate these sounds with concepts such as "caring person," "drinking something pleasing," and "bottle." If a parent attaches something visually exciting to the bottle, such as shiny paper or red and yellow stripes, it increases the chances that the baby will be stimulated to first look at the decorations, but eventually, the bottle itself. The baby can now associate the decorated bottle with the love of a parent and the experience of eating. As a result, the baby's visual experience in this situation is no longer confusing. Their visual experience is now connected to concepts that are both meaningful and positive. So perhaps the baby will start to be motivated to use vision while drinking a bottle. Perhaps the baby will eventually try to look toward the bottle as the parent carries it slowly closer.

Fluctuating Visual Ability

Why Does My Baby Sometimes Seem Blind, Yet at Other Times Appears to Use Vision?

CVI often creates a kind of short circuit within the visual system. As a result, visual ability may fluctuate under the influence of several factors. The "vision switch" may appear to be turned off in some environments or situations, yet it is engaged in others.

Babies do not easily tolerate confusion or stress, so they tend to ignore a stimulus that causes either feeling. For example, when placed within a confusing or stressful situation, the baby may appear not to see. Also, additional activity within an environment along with the characteristics of visual targets will affect how a baby with CVI can perceive targets (Roman-Lantzy, 2018). What a baby hears or touches, as well as how he or she feels physically or emotionally, can affect a baby's ability to attend visually. If a baby is interested in or is already familiar with a visual target, if there is sufficient light without glare, if a target has certain familiar characteristics, if the target is not located in a crowded area, and if a baby is given sufficient time to respond to the target, the baby may visually respond to the target. In situations when a child feels comfortable and safe, and when the target and background are carefully chosen, the baby may be able to use vision and not appear to have a visual impairment. **Sidebar 3.3** discusses which visual targets might be most stimulating to a baby with CVI, and **Sidebar 3.4** discusses situations that may interfere with a baby's visual behavior.

INCREASING EARLY VISION

Brain Plasticity

Will My Baby Outgrow This Problem and Develop Normal Vision?

Early exposure to visual activities is extremely important for visual development. An important factor to consider when discussing young children and visual impairment due to damage

Visually Motivating Targets

Children who have CVI often respond visually to highly motivating objects when these are moving or lighted, or if these objects appear in the children's preferred colors. (Roman-Lantzy, 2018). Objects with more than one engaging characteristic help attract a baby's visual attention. For example, a happy face toy that also plays music, or a shiny pinwheel that moves and has projectiles, are often favorite visually motivating targets. Light boxes can also help a baby with CVI focus visual attention. Objects that may attract visual attention in babies with CVI include the following:

- lights
- black-and-white patterns
- specific bright colors, especially red or yellow and neon
- shiny surfaces
- movement
- stripes
- geometric designs
- projectiles-items with extensions such as a pinwheel
- highly contrasting colors
- strong contours such as a toy with several different and distinct color sections
- familiar objects

Although human faces or pictures of faces such as a happy face motif may also alert vision in babies with CVI, babies with ventral stream dysfunction may have difficulty recognizing faces (Dutton, 2015b). In the author's experience, babies who have been consistently exposed to face motifs from early ages seem to begin to respond to face patterns and start to recognize familiar faces. Decorating a baby's crib with paper plates decorated with smiling faces is an effective, easy-to-implement intervention to help a baby regard and recognize faces.

Situations That Can Interfere With Visual Behavior

Babies and toddlers with CVI often cannot attend to more than one thing at a time (Roman-Lantzy, 2018). Situations that compete for attention can interfere with a baby's ability to attend visually.

- **Physical well-being:** A child who is ill, hungry, wet or soiled, uncomfortable, in pain, very tired, having seizures, or very medicated is less able to attend to visual targets. For example, a child who is hungry may attend to the sensation of hunger and not visually attend as well as when they feel full.

- **Emotional well-being:** A basic human need is to feel safe (McLeod, 2017). A child who is upset, sad, afraid, or confused is less able to attend to visual targets than a child who feels safe. Some children will attend and show interest with one professional but will not open their eyes in the presence of another. The child may feel less safe with one professional than with the other.

- **Physical support:** A child who is not well supported physically will have more difficulty attending to visual targets than a child who is well supported with the head, neck, body, and legs appropriately positioned. A child who is lying down and in a comfortable position with the head in line with the trunk and well supported can better attend visually than a child who is slumped in a chair or precariously balanced on an adult's knees.

- **Distractions:** A child who is distracted by noise, sudden movements, or the presence of another interesting activity may have difficulty visually attending to a target activity. For example, a baby engaged in an activity using vision may shift attention when a parent arrives home. Children in a group setting might be more interested in the sound and activity from another group and be distracted from their target activity.

- **Motivation and function:** A child who is not motivated or interested in an activity that requires visual attention is less likely to participate visually than a child who is presented with an activity in which they have interest and motivation. Finding what motivates a child may a challenge for the professional, but it is an important step for successful interventions. For example, in one case a professional sang a song whenever the child gazed toward a presented target. Soon the child stopped gazing at the target as soon as the tune started. In contrast, the child's parent practiced the same activity, but remained quiet whenever the child gazed at the target. The child repeatedly established a prolonged gaze at the target. The parent and teacher decided that the child was either distracted or simply did not like the song being sung, and was more motivated to look at the target when the environment was quiet.

- **Target characteristic:** A child is more likely to gaze toward visually motivating targets (see **Sidebar 3.3**) than at targets that are visually bland or uninteresting. For example, one particular parent always puts a baby's favorite pacifier directly into the child's mouth. The teacher of children with visual impairments concluded that the pacifier would be a very motivating target for the baby to look toward. The teacher suggested adding silver bells to the handle of the pacifier and showing the baby these moving, shiny bells before giving the baby the pacifier. The parent then placed the pacifier into the baby's mouth as soon as the baby approximated a gaze. The baby soon looked toward the pacifier when it was held for their gaze.

(continued)

- **Target placement:** Children with CVI often have a visual field loss that is related to the location of damage in the brain. Some children may have blind spots in their vision called scotomas. Targets that are placed within these areas cannot be seen. During an FVA, the teacher will try to determine whether there is a field loss and, if so, locate areas where the child has more difficulty establishing a gaze. Once the extent of a child's visual field loss is determined, targets should be presented in the child's best visual field.

- **Pace:** Children with CVI often show a delay between the time an appropriate target is presented and when they actually gaze toward it. These children simply need extra time to process visual targets before reacting to them. For example, once a child is well supported and an appropriate target and environment is selected, only then should the target be presented to the child. After sufficient processing time, which may last as long as several seconds, the child will start to gaze or reach toward the target. Patience is essential when waiting for a baby with CVI to process a visual target.

of the brain is the ability of the brain to "continuously reorganize itself as it develops" (Catteneo & Merabet, 2015, p. 105), especially following a brain injury. The brain's ability to reorganize continuously is called *brain plasticity* or *neuroplasticity*. Because of brain plasticity, children with CVI can gain or improve some visual capacity through specific interventions.

Even though brain plasticity exists throughout an individual's lifetime, the most critical or sensitive period of visual brain plasticity takes place during infancy and early childhood (Catteneo & Merabet, 2015). During this critical period, other areas of the brain responsible for visual functioning can more readily reorganize and rewire to take over neural processing from damaged areas of the visual pathways and the primary visual cortex (Catteneo & Merabet, 2015; Tychsen, 2001).

Appropriate Interventions

Consistent and strategic visual activities can often help the brain increase neural pathways (Roman-Lantzy, 2018). With appropriate interventions, visual abilities of babies with CVI can improve, although never to the extent of a child with typical or normal vision (Roman-Lantzy, 2018). In the author's experience, improvements in visual ability and the resolution of problematic visual behaviors depend on many factors, including the timing, duration, and area of damage, as well as the family and support team's ability to implement appropriate interventions consistently. In order for a baby with CVI's vision to improve, it will take a trained team that follows a systematic approach.

Among early visual skills, there are three that, in the author's experience, serve as the main gateway to increased early visual development in a baby with CVI: visual alerting, visual engagement, and visual integration with other developmental skills. (These skills are discussed in more detail in **Chapter 6**.)

VISUAL IMPAIRMENT AND EARLY DEVELOPMENT

Parents frequently ask how vision loss affects their baby's behavior and development (see **Sidebar 3.5**). This section offers some general information about how both ocular and cerebral visual impairment influence development. The reference section of this book includes additional sources that provide a more in-depth examination of this subject.

Each baby's learning experience is unique, and progress in development is individual. It is not helpful to compare the development of a baby with CVI to that of a fully sighted baby because their learning approaches are different. As previously

Frequently Asked Questions About Development and Behavior

Parents' early questions to their child's teacher of children with visual impairments are frequently about how vision loss and CVI affects their baby's behavior. The following questions and sample answers are drawn from teachers' experiences.

1. Why does my baby keep his or her head down all the time?

    Parents may wonder why their baby keeps his or her head down on the chest instead of holding it up. This posture does not always indicate that a baby is withdrawn or sleepy. It may, instead, be related to muscle weakness related to other disabilities such as cerebral palsy; or it may result from the baby not looking around or moving the head enough to build muscle strength in the neck.

2. Why doesn't my baby sit without support, or stand independently?

    Sitting and standing are skills that require muscle strength as well as balance. The development of these skills frequently takes longer for a baby who has a visual impairment because the baby needs to learn the motor skills of sitting and standing through experience, without the benefit of incidental learning by watching others. Many babies with CVI have strabismus, a condition in which both eyes do not work in a coordinated manner, which can affect the baby's depth perception and balance. Babies with CVI may have additional disabilities such as cerebral palsy that affect muscle strength and motor ability. Additionally, babies with visual impairments develop motor skills differently than fully sighted infants.

Comparisons between the two groups may lead to an unfair evaluation of the abilities of the child with vision loss (Fazzi et al., 2015).

3. Why doesn't my baby respond to me or seem to know me?

A baby with vision loss may not recognize a parent until the baby can experience a familiar touch, scent, or sound. Babies with CVI have difficulty with facial recognition and may not be able to recognize a parent until the introduction of one of these other nonvisual cues.

4. Why doesn't my baby look at me or smile when I am playing with him or her?

A baby with a visual impairment does not observe the smiles of others. Therefore, they do not smile reciprocally to parents, or in pleasure until much later than sighted babies (Fraiberg, 1977). Additionally, a baby with a visual impairment or CVI may not be able to see a parent's facial expressions. However, the baby may use different cues to show positive responses to a parent, such as becoming very still and quiet. As mentioned previously, a baby with CVI has difficulty recognizing faces and expressions and typically will not smile reciprocally until more visual ability has developed.

5. Why does my baby say "hi" all of the time?

Sometimes babies with a visual impairment use word repetition to initiate a verbal response from people around them. This behavior becomes more like an echo than a greeting. Since a baby who is unable see in the distance may still be curious about who is around, the baby might use this echo to locate people in the surrounding environment. Sometimes

(continued)

this behavior may seem strange to others and make them feel uncomfortable with the child. Interventions such as modeling other verbal communicators and parental guidance (perhaps parents could teach the baby to limit the number of times a word is repeated) will help babies learn early social communication and language.

6. Why isn't my baby talking like other babies?

   Babies who are blind or visually impaired have longer stages of preverbal exchanges and language play because of the absence of visual cues and inability to watch facial expressions. Babies with vision loss and those with CVI remain in a preverbal phase of language development longer than typically sighted babies (Fazzi & Klein, 2002).

7. Why does my baby press his fingers in his eyes and move his head back and forth? Will these behaviors hurt him?

   Babies who are blind or visually impaired frequently demonstrate repetitive behaviors such as eye poking, eye pressing, finger waving, and head movements. These behaviors, sometimes called mannerisms, may indicate a need for sensory stimulation or a need to escape from uncomfortable situations. Understanding the child's motivation for these behaviors and finding a replacement for these mannerisms is important for several reasons. Some mannerisms, such as eye poking, can disturb the eye structure over time. Mannerisms can also be uncomfortable to watch (Pruett, 2002) and may possibly interfere with the baby's socialization opportunities.

stated, babies who are blind or visually impaired because of ocular or perceptual disabilities require specific early intervention strategies and guidance to maximize their developmental potential (Chen, 2014a). Strategies are discussed further in **Chapter 5.**

Learning Challenges

How Can Vision Loss and CVI Affect Development?

A significant visual impairment alters a baby's early learning (Fazzi & Klein, 2002) because babies acquire their earliest information through their senses (Barraga & Erin, 1992). Since 80% of all early learning is believed to be visual a child who is blind or visually impaired is understandably at risk for developmental delays. For example, without the ability to use distance vision to look at the environment beyond his or her own body, a baby's stimulation and early learning opportunities are limited to the body and whatever it may touch. As already noted, babies with CVI have unique behavioral characteristics, and may possibly possess coexisting disabilities that can further challenge typical development. Vision loss in general, and CVI in particular, can affect developmental areas such as sleep-awake patterns, gross motor functions, spatial concepts, cognitive abilities, attention and memory, communication skills, learning processes, behavior, bonding, social responsiveness, and communication (Fazzi et al., 2015; Lueck et al., 2008).

As evidenced by developmental inventories such as the Denver Developmental Scales and the Oregon Project Skills Inventory, early interventions initially focus on the developmental areas of gross and fine motor skills, concept development and cognition, self-image, social connectedness and bonding, and early communication.

Gross Motor Development

Gross motor *skills* involve large muscle movements, such as movements of the arms and legs. In contrast, gross motor *development* encompasses both static body postures, such as sitting and standing, as well as any movement skills, such as reaching out to touch a desired object (Anthony et al., 2002). Much of early gross motor development is stimulated by vision (Barraga & Erin, 1992). Babies with vision loss typically learn to develop gross motor skills differently than fully sighted babies, mainly gaining skills through trial and error. Developmental milestones usually develop later in babies with CVI than in babies with typical sight (Strickling & Pogrund, 2002) who are able to learn by watching.

Babies with higher levels of visual ability show less delay in gross motor development (Fazzi et al., 2015). Babies with typical vision are able to scan visually and attend to what attracts their interest in the environment. They are also able to learn about movement by watching the people around them, which can inspire a baby to attempt to move their body toward a specific object or person. Also, in order to look around an environment, a baby's head must be able to move independent of the body (Strickling & Pogrund, 2002). As the baby continues to move his or her head, the neck muscles strengthen. As neck muscles strengthen, the baby can then start to start to perform movements that will further develop other muscles in the body, which will expand gross motor skills and coordination. It follows that babies who are not able to see also cannot look around, meaning that they will have weaker neck and trunk muscles, which will affect their overall gross motor development.

Without vision as a stimulus, babies with CVI will benefit from alternative movement experiences and early activities that build head, neck, and body strength along with motor skills. For example, parents can help a baby strengthen neck and core muscles by holding him or her facing outward instead of snuggled face down into a parent's shoulder. When understood, concepts such as object permanence (awareness that an object continues to exist even when not perceived), spatial awareness, and formation of mental images are important milestones that contribute to gross motor development (Fazzi et al., 2015). When a baby is interested in an object, he or she is more likely to try to reach, touch, or manipulate it. One indication that a baby with CVI is beginning to grasp the concept of object permanence is

Moving the head and neck to look around helps build head, neck, body strength and motor skills. In this photo, the adult holds the baby facing out and holds a visually interesting object to touch and hopefully regard.

when they try to reach out towards a sound source. Once a baby understands that an object still exists even when they are not touching it, it will motivate experimentation with additional motor movements to reach an object.

Babies with CVI have varying degrees of dysfunction in the perceptual areas of the brain that can further impede normal gross motor development. When a baby cannot form images of or recognize objects, it can limit a baby's curiosity and motivation to move. Other issues babies with CVI may have include spatial awareness difficulty or lower visual field loss, which can also affect a baby's interest in practicing movement skills. For example, if a baby cannot correctly gauge spatial distance or does not see an obstacle because of a visual field loss, the baby may accidentally bump into objects, which will discourage him or her to repeat movement efforts.

Gross motor development in a baby will benefit from time spent in a well-supported position on the stomach and engaged in play. In this photo, the baby is on a floor blanket with a wedge to help elevate the head and reaches and looks toward a fun toy.

As stated, babies with CVI may also have coexisting disabilities, such as cerebral palsy and neurological disabilities, which because of the muscular problems or sensory sensitivity can further compound the difficulty of building gross motor skills. While a child with typical sight generally develops gross motor skills without being specifically taught them, the gross motor development of babies with CVI will benefit from teaching interventions that stimulate small segments of gross motor action at a time that are conducted in a familiar and safe area, such as laying on a favorite blanket, or within a play area with interesting toys or objects nearby.

Fine Motor Skills

Fine motor skills include the small, precise movements performed by smaller muscles in the body, such as those in the hands and fingers, that can be used to grasp objects. Reaching out to touch or engage with a viewed object in the environment stimulates a baby's interest, curiosity, and efforts to use the hands. Without early guidance, babies who are unable to see their own hands or the hand movements of others, or who are unable to perceive nearby objects that might pique curiosity, subsequently develop fine motor skills at a later age than typically sighted babies (Bishop, 2000). Since babies with CVI cannot readily look around their environment and then attempt to find, touch, and handle the objects they see, they have less opportunity to practice hand skills and to increase their interest in objects in their environment in comparison with babies with typical sight. Without awareness or interest in objects, babies who are blind, visually impaired, or have CVI may instead become focused on activities geared towards self-stimulation (Strickling, C., 1998) such as eye pressing, hand flapping, or rocking.

Interest in objects can be fostered by mutual hand guidance. In this photo, the adults and baby are physically close and playing together with a visually interesting and fun toy.

Babies with CVI

Babies interact with items that are consistently around them. Object awareness and interest in objects can be fostered in babies with CVI by planned interventions that include mutual hand guidance to reach toward and interact with objects, as well as extended opportunities to practice reaching and touching (Bishop, 2004). Time spent with objects near enough that the baby can incidentally touch them can promote object interest, play, and fine motor skills. Once babies with visual impairments have developed sufficient gross motor strength and coordination to maintain a prone (lying face down) position and manage upper-body weight bearing, they will then have more opportunities to interact with objects in the environment and begin to develop fine motor skills (Strickling & Pogrund, 2002).

Babies with CVI may have additional difficulties that can impede the development of fine motor skills. For example, brain damage can create issues with object recognition, field loss, and managing visual clutter, which can result in difficulty locating or recognizing objects in an environment and deter from object exploration. Additionally, babies with CVI can sometimes have a sensory perception difficulty that affects how they experience touch. In this case, an unpleasant touch sensation can discourage a baby from engaging with and building interest in interacting with items in his or her environment. In general, babies with CVI may not attend to novel objects or remember previously experienced objects. They may also be distracted by sounds or actions in the environment, such as a sibling at play, because of difficulty with attention. A properly staged environment, relatively free of distracting noise and visual clutter, that includes interesting objects close to or on the baby's body can enhance incidental interactions with objects. Opportunity to spend time in a controlled and staged area is an important strategy that will encourage a baby with CVI to develop fine motor skills, increase object interest, and expand awareness of the larger environment. Information about controlled learning environments is explained in **Chapter 5.**

Early Concept Development

A baby's early concept development includes building object permanence, self-image, social connectedness, and concepts about immediate surroundings. A severe visual impairment can reduce a baby's opportunities to build these concepts and to learn about the environment (Fazzi & Klein, 2002). The lack of distance vision and the delay of motor skills together reduce opportunities for learning about objects farther away in the environment and limit the ability of a baby with CVI to learn about interactions through observing. In order to help build concepts, it is extremely important that teachers of children with visual impairments teach parents to make a baby's near environment and personal interactions as interesting and dynamic as possible in order to foster object awareness. *Near learning environments* (discussed in **Chapter 5**) foster the crucial concept of object permanence— the awareness that an object exists even when a baby with CVI is not touching it—and will encourage the act of reaching toward the sound of an object. Object permanence is thought to be the gateway to other developmental skills (Catteneo & Merabet, 2015

Strategies, activities, and interventions that build and enhance early concept development should address several areas of development simultaneously. Interventions to support object permanence can also encourage concept awareness, language development, and the understanding of cause and effect. For example, a toy such as a wrist rattle helps a baby understand that the object exists even when it is not being touched (object permanence), while also encouraging the use of both hands when one hand explores the wrist rattle on the other hand (bilaterality). Toys such as a wrist rattle that make sounds when activated, reinforce the concept of cause and effect—the idea that "I do something, and this happens."

A baby with CVI can practice and reinforce cause and effect if the toy is consistently available. In addition to sounds, bright colors can also attract the attention of a baby with CVI. The added benefit of a brightly colored toy, such as a red apple that makes a chiming sound, helps attract the visual attention of babies with low vision and those with CVI, encouraging them to reach toward the toy (reach on sound and visual cue). Massage activities help increase a baby's concepts about his or her body in addition to fostering a connection to the parent providing the massage. Concept development is further enhanced when parents actively talk about and describe the actions or events that they or the baby are experiencing. For example, if the baby is wiggling her foot, a parent might say, "Your foot; you're moving your foot." Touching the baby's foot while providing this explanation can also draw the his or her attention to the body part itself, which will reinforce his or her understanding of the word *foot*. Other opportunities to describe an activity verbally to a baby include diapering, bathing, or drying after a bath. All offer a chance to help a baby build language concepts.

Self-Image

A baby's positive self-image is developed by seeing his or her image, by feeling cared for, and by how capable he or she feels (Bishop, 2004). Mirrors can help a baby with CVI, despite visual issues, perceive an image of self. As discussed previously, certain characteristics of objects stimulate visual interest in babies with CVI. Mirrors happen to have a few of these characteristics: They are shiny, reflect light, and reflect movement. Often a safety mirror, such as a crib mirror, that is placed very close to a baby can attract a baby's visual interest. Ultimately a baby with CVI might increase visual attention to the mirror enough to distinguish his or her image, enhancing an awareness of self.

A baby may feel comfortably attended to by parents through touch and attention. A body massage or being held in a body carrier are two examples of interventions that promote closeness and help build a baby's positive self-image. A baby's positive self-concept is enhanced as they continue to acquire the skills that will enable him or her to perform tasks independently such as holding a bottle, using a spoon, or reaching for and grasping a desired object. Teachers of children with visual impairments can help parents by providing them strategies to teach babies with CVI the skills that will both increase their independence and promote a positive self-image. Unfortunately, a child with vision loss often depends on others to provide everyday needs and wants for a longer period of time in early life than do babies who have full sight. This inability to perceive visual cues can make a baby with CVI reliant on others to interpret or assist in interactions within the social environment (Sacks & Page, 2017). This reliance can negatively impact the development of positive self-image.

Achieving the self-sufficiency that encourages positive self-esteem might also be delayed as a result of "learned helplessness," a perception of the lack of personal control and ability (Pogrund, 2002a; Sacks & Page, 2017). Sometimes, a parent may consistently do things for their baby without encouraging the child to try to learn new skills that would increase independence (Fazzi et al., 2015). This overprotectiveness can also adversely affect the development of positive self-esteem. A teacher of children with visual impairments can coach parents about helping their child increase independence and build a positive sense of self-esteem.

Social Connections

Social connectedness is important for everyone. A baby's first connections occur with parents, so early parent-child interactions are critical to a baby's development. Babies with CVI can have difficulty achieving this important social connectedness because they do not use vision well enough to establish eye contact and see facial details. This can detract from their ability to attract their parents' attention, seek comfort (Lueck et al., 2008), and respond to a parent's overtures, which can interrupt or postpone early parent-child bonding. Actually, a baby with reduced vision may be responding to his or her parents or to other people but may exhibit different cues and responses than do sighted babies (Fazzi et al., 2015) who may look towards a parent, wriggle, and show animation. Nonstandard reactions from a baby with CVI could lead parents to misinterpret their baby's intentions. For example, instead of moving, smiling, and showing anticipation, a baby with CVI may instead become still, showing little apparent affect. However, a baby with CVI may react in this way specifically to better listen to a parent. Judging these nonstandard reactions negatively, parents may mistakenly conclude that their baby feels no connection to them. In other cases, parents may interpret this seemingly passive listening behavior to indicate that their baby would prefer to remain in the crib instead of participating in the activities, interactions, and interests of active life. A teacher of children with visual impairments can help parents build social connectedness with their baby by interpreting these unexpected behaviors and cues for them. The teacher can also emphasize the importance of including the baby in family activities. This involvement will benefit babies with CVI by increasing tactile, auditory, and movement learning opportunities, as well as interactions with others.

Joint attention, in which the baby and parent both regard and react to the same event or object, is another activity that is crucial in supporting the development of attachment and bonding. Diminished visual ability in a baby with CVI unfortunately reduces opportunities for joint attention (Fazzi et al., 2015). One way to help foster attention and attachment in babies with CVI is through mutual play activities guided by the baby's interests. For example, when a parent and their baby play with and explore a favorite toy or item, the parent's and child's hands work together while the object is shared. In addition, the parent can talk to the child about the toy or object, perhaps by naming parts or describing textures. Parents can also demonstrate other ways the baby can explore an object through touch, such as by patting it or using a single finger to examine it. This joint attention will increase parent-baby connectedness. Other games can also help a baby learn skills for social peer connectedness. A game such as modified peekaboo (cover the parent's face with a cloth; remove cloth when baby moves in response to the question, "Where's baby?") or pretend talking on a cell phone can help a baby practice social skills such as taking turns while speaking with someone else (Fazzi & Klein, 2002).

Babies with CVI may have other sensory dysfunctions or motor disabilities that can cause them to be hypersensitive

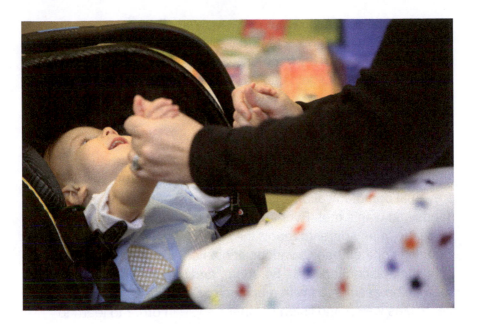

It is important to cue babies who do not see well when they are about to be picked up or moved. The mother in this photo is lightly lifting the baby's arm to signal that he is about to be moved.

and exhibit reactions of discomfort, such as fussing or leaning away when being touched or picked up, or showing sensitivity to loud sounds. To parents, these unexpected reactions to their attentions may be perceived as rejections. Teachers of children with visual impairments can help dispel these feelings by explaining how a baby's other disabilities might affect his or her responses to certain stimuli. Often massage activities and the use of firm instead of light touch are more comforting to babies with hypersensitivity. It is also important to alert babies with CVI whenever they are about to be picked up, moved, or touched, in order to avoid startling them.

Babies with CVI may also have difficulty recognizing faces, which hinders their ability to fixate on their parents' faces (Good et al., 2001). Parents can misinterpret this lack of recognition or gaze to indicate a lack of interest or affection. One solution to this problem some parents have found is to accentuate their own facial features

Babies with CVI

with dark rimmed glasses or colorful makeup. Both may help direct their baby's visual attention toward their faces. As mentioned earlier, decorating the baby's environment with face motifs such as a happy face design seems to help babies with CVI start to regard faces.

Early Communication and Language Development

The need to communicate is the basis for early language acquisition (Dutton & Lueck, 2015; Lueck et al., 2008). A baby's preverbal communication initially centers on getting his or her needs and wants met. Even though a baby cannot use verbal language, many parents report they can still differentiate the meanings of their baby's various cries. For example, feelings of hunger, discomfort, fear, boredom, and loneliness each seem to be associated with a unique cry. In the first years of life, babies watch and listen to other people in order to learn to understand words and gestures, and then use sounds and words themselves to communicate their own needs and wants. Babies who are blind or visually impaired do not have distance vision in order to study typical communication cues and do not use typical facial expressions such as smiling or making eye contact in order to communicate. They may use nontraditional bodily cues to communicate wants, needs, or interests. For example, a slight movement of the hand or change in breathing might be a baby's cue to indicate interest. Unless coached to watch for nonconventional reactions from their baby, parents may either miss or misinterpret their baby's attempts to communicate with them.

Without the ability to see a parent's behavioral cues and expressions, a baby may also become easily frustrated and fussy; and this can also limit positive interactions and communication (Fazzi & Klein, 2002). A teacher of children with visual impairments can help parents interpret their baby's different communication cues more accurately and learn alternative ways to communicate successfully with their child. Strategies to increase understood (receptive) and expressed (expressive) language are discussed in **Chapter 5.**

For a baby with typical vision, early *receptive language*, or the ability to understand words and language, increases as the baby sees an object or action and simultaneously hears the words that denote what he or she is seeing. As already stated, babies who have CVI or other significant vision loss do not have effective distance vision, which gives them fewer opportunities to be interested in the objects and events that would increase their concept and language repertoires. They may also have coexisting nonvisual disabilities such as hearing loss that interfere with language learning. Providing environments where a variety of toys, objects, and textures are easily available for babies to explore can help a baby with vision loss or CVI have more opportunities to interact with objects and start to build concepts and learn associated words. (**Chapter 5** discusses learning environments.)

Sometimes babies who are blind or visually impaired may repeat words or phrases they hear over and over (echolalia), either to practice making the sounds, for stimulation, or to participate in social communication (Fazzi et al., 2015). Teachers of children with visual impairments and parents can model appropriate verbal interactions for a child who repeats inappropriately. Sometimes, too, children who are blind or visually impaired can discuss certain objects or events in great detail without having direct experience with them. However, if the child has never actually experienced the real object or event, that knowledge is only theoretical. Without hands-on experiences, children with CVI may develop *empty language*. Empty language is produced when a child uses language to refer to something but has no real understanding of the concepts connected to the words. (**Chapter 5** discusses the importance of life experiences for a child who has CVI.)

Babies with CVI increase their understanding of communication and language when parents and teachers demonstrate the signals or gestures a baby can use to express wants and needs. For example, when parents lift a baby's arms slightly and say "up" before lifting the baby, the baby eventually learns this gesture to signal a desire to be picked up before he or she can ask using words.

Parents and teachers of children with CVI can help provide connections and build communication by providing real-life experiences, teaching the baby to understand cues and signals, and engaging in verbal play that involves taking turns with verbalizing or babbling. (Strategies to build language, such as using scripted routines, are discussed further in **Chapter 5.**)

Maximizing Learning Potential

What Can I Do to Maximize My Baby's Vision and Learning Potential?

A crucial way parents can help their baby who has CVI maximize potential for growth, development, and visual learning is to work with professionals who are knowledgeable and

Parents who understand goals, interventions and who engage in related activities regularly usually experience the most success in helping enhance their baby's development. To address one of her baby's language goals, the mother in this photo is cuddles her baby and says some key words such as "look" as her baby looks at the sparkly beads.

experienced about vision, CVI, and early childhood development to implement important interventions. As mentioned previously, even when a baby has additional health and developmental needs such as respiratory distress or muscle weakness, being sure to make time for early visual intervention is vital to successful outcomes of visual goals (Catteneo & Merabet, 2015; Pogrund, 2002b) because of the critical and sensitive period of brain plasticity during early life (Catteneo & Merabet, 2015).

Consistent and creative interventions, especially those that stem from a baby's specific interests, are the key to early learning success for babies with CVI. However, this is possible only when parents and professionals work together. Sometimes overwhelmed parents may mistakenly conclude that the periodic, face-to-face interactions between their baby and teachers or specialists is sufficient time for learning intervention. However, experience confirms that daily and consistent interventions included within routine activities are paramount in helping a baby with CVI develop. In the author's experience, parents who know which goals to address, who understand an intervention's purpose, who consistently repeat the intervention as suggested, and who engage in related activities that address the same developmental goals are usually the most successful in helping their baby experience a notable growth in visual skills and development.

CONCLUSION

A diagnosis of CVI raises many questions. It is important for parents and professionals to understand how vision loss and CVI can affect early development and vision so they can plan appropriate goals and strategies to help a baby with CVI. A broader understanding of CVI includes the history and rationale behind its changing names, how it is identified, and the different implications of the diagnosis. That understanding can empower parents and reinforce their awareness of the critical importance of early and appropriate interventions to increase development and visual skills.

CHAPTER 4

Creating a Home Action Plan

HOME ACTION PLAN

As discussed in the previous two chapters, the most critical or sensitive period of visual brain plasticity takes place during infancy and early childhood, although brain plasticity continues throughout an individual's lifetime (Catteneo & Merabet, 2015). During this early period, other areas of the brain responsible for visual functioning can more easily reorganize and rewire in order to process the neural activity that would normally be handled by damaged areas of the visual pathways and primary visual cortex (Catteneo & Merabet, 2015; Tychsen, 2001). When other parts of the brain reorganize and rewire, increased visual capabilities can result.

It is important to emphasize this critical point once again: *Since the brain is especially plastic in early childhood, early exposure to visual activities during this period is extremely important.* Unfortunately, for a number of reasons discussed previously, parents may have difficulty finding time each day for the recommended vision interventions. Parents may be grieving over their baby's diagnosis or trying to keep track of medical appointments, and may feel disorganized, tired, and overwhelmed as a result. A parent's state of mind may cause their baby to miss valuable opportunities to increase visual ability. Teachers of children with visual impairments can help families feel more in control by helping them establish a *home team.* This team, which includes the parents, gathers information about the baby's skills and uses that information to create a home action plan. Teachers can help parents organize the following:

- A **home team** of professionals, family, friends, services, and resources that can uniquely help the family

Regular and planned exposure to visual activities is extremely important for a baby with CVI because of the sensitive period of early childhood brain plasticity. In this photo, a teacher of children with visual impairments works on a visual goal by using a light toy to encourage the child to look down and sideways, thereby expanding her visual field.

- A **home file** of pertinent information used in setting goals and planning interventions
- A **home action plan** of goals and strategies to help the baby achieve objectives, enhance skills, and stimulate development

THE HOME TEAM

The *home team* consists of individuals, both professional and lay, who can energize and support the family of a baby with CVI. The team provides knowledge and guidance and helps the family gain confidence and feel hope. As discussed, just like any major diagnosis, a diagnosis of CVI can be a traumatic event for a family. At this point, it is vital to provide the family the guidance they need to feel a greater sense of control. Once a family gains this sense of control, they can better plan goals and interventions. A positive and knowledgeable home team can help a family gain this sense of control.

Members of the Home Team

A home team is usually assembled by the parents of a child with CVI. The parents are ideally the leaders of this team, which also includes professionals, friends, and family who are able to provide positive, knowledgeable input, and guidance. The team can include relatives, caregivers, friends, and others who can help serve as family advocates. Professionals on the team include a teacher of children with visual impairments (ideally one specializing in early childhood and CVI), and can also include a social worker or counselor, an early interventionist, an orientation and mobility specialist, a physical or occupational therapist, a speech and language specialist, a school district representative or members of other participating agencies, a nurse, and anyone else involved in working with the baby and the family. Although many people may want to help at this sensitive time, it is important for parents to realize that not everyone will be able to meet the family's needs.

Home team members should have particular knowledge and abilities, which may include the following:

- Knowledge about CVI
- An understanding of child development in general, and strategies for working with babies with CVI in particular
- A familiarity with ways parents can help their baby
- The ability to train parents and daycare personnel to use effective strategies to increase development and vision abilities
- The ability to help parents lead the family's home team
- Familiarity with the stages of grief and how grief can affect parents of a baby with CVI
- Being capable of building parents' confidence to care for and help their baby

- The skills needed to communicate with the family in an emotionally sensitive manner
- Awareness of how to foster *realistic* hope

Erica and Keith had their first baby, Sealy, who was born prematurely at 34 weeks gestation and weighed just 4.5 pounds. Erica began to grow concerned about Sealy's vision. When Sealy was 3 months old, the pediatrician referred him to a neuro-ophthalmologist who ordered an MRI. The MRI indicated that Sealy had damage in the brain's occipital lobes, which led the doctor to conclude that Sealy might have a cerebral visual impairment. The family was understandably shocked.

Erica and Keith were referred by the doctor to several programs, professionals, specialists, social workers, support groups, references materials, and websites—all of which were intended to help them. However, the couple quickly found that some of the resources the doctor recommended were actually not very knowledgeable about CVI. They also found that while some resources had accurate information, what they had to say seemed discouraging. In response, Erica and Keith realized that they themselves needed to select the professionals, people, programs, and resources that could help them aid Sealy, and who could also give them the hope and confidence they needed. They began to understand that they needed to work with people who communicated well, were emotionally sensitive, and had experience working with babies with CVI. Sealy's family was learning the essentials of organizing a home team.

Communicating With the Home Team

Once the members of the home team are identified, a parent or other designated leader of the team must regularly communicate with other team members in order to stay organized and collaborate on the baby's goals, interventions, schedules, needs, and progress. The leader can facilitate communication among the team members by making a *home team form* similar to the one shown in **Figure 4.1,** which lists contact and professional

A strong parent-professional team is one in which the parents are supported by people who communicate well, are emotionally sensitive, and have experience working with babies with CVI. In this photo, a parent and teacher of children with visual impairments review ideas about working together to help build the baby's growth and development.

information about each team member, to distribute to each member in order to help the team stay connected.

In addition to face-to-face meetings, group communications can take place by phone, email, text, or social media groups. Another way to share information among team members is to maintain a readily available diary or notebook about the baby that records pertinent daily or regular notes, archives printouts of emails sent among team members that highlight their sessions with the baby, and quarterly updates of the child's progress.

Trying to organize communication from both the home team and various specialists is often daunting for parents, yet it is an important and worthwhile effort. Sending group emails addressed to the team can allow each member to keep current

Figure 4.1
Sample Home Team Form

Home Team Form

Child's name: _____   DOB: _____

Team leader: *Tom Smith*

Team Members

Name	Role or Profession	Program or School	Phone	Email	Notes
Tom Smith	*Father/team leader*		*xxx-xxx-xxx*	*tsmith@email.com*	
Susan Grand	*Teacher of children with visual impairments*	*Early School*	*xxx-xxx-xxxx*	*sgrand@email.com*	*CVI specialist*
Dr. A.Son	*Pediatric Ophthalmologist*		*xxx-xxx-xxxx*	*ason@email.com*	*Jennifer Grand, great Physician Assistant- good contact*

with a child's progress. It can also provide helpful strategies for the team to adopt and can help members integrate other specialists' goals into their own planning and interventions. To mitigate concerns over confidentiality, the parents can start by sending an explanatory email to all members of the home team. In this first email, parents invite members to reply, specifying that all persons copied may share information about the child with each other online but that this information is confidential to members of the team only. Parents should ask members to respond with an email introducing themselves and listing their particular specialty. In addition, members should list goals for the child, describe the high points of a particular work session, and mention any activity or strategy that seems especially effective for the home team to reinforce.

Another way for team members to meet and stay connected is to share videos taken of the child during an appointment with a particular member demonstrating a particular activity. In addition, both audio and video conference calls help team members better collaborate with one another and keep everyone informed of the child's updated goals. Creating a discussion forum for the team using web applications such as Google or Facebook enables parents to set up an online page with information about their baby along with any goals or interventions they would like to share. Most importantly, group sites allow all team members to have access to and share the same information in one common place.

Training the Home Team

Training about CVI and information about the baby will ensure that members of the home team understand the child and his or her needs. **Appendix C** offers a guide for training home team members who are not vision specialists, such as caregivers and other professionals. The guide presents general information about visual impairment and CVI, along with strategies and suggestions for interventions. It will help team members learn more about the specific details of that baby's CVI diagnosis as well as that child's unique teaching and learning needs. Parents can increase member engagement by personalizing the guide; they can add pictures of their baby, include the baby's name, and provide information about their baby's likes and dislikes.

The Family Questionnaire

Parents should complete a family questionnaire (see **Figure 4.2**), a tool to help the home team learn as much as possible about the baby. The questions chosen should be pertinent to the specific cluster of CVI characteristics that the baby possesses, and the answers to these questions can help team members plan and then support interventions and strategies tailored to the needs of the baby and family. The questionnaire also facilitates early communication between the team and the family about the needs of the family and the baby. It is helpful to keep a copy of the completed questionnaire in each family's home file. The Family Questionnaire included in **Figure 4.2** is one example of such a form. However, many teachers and early childhood special needs programs may wish to design their own forms to best suit their particular needs.

Meg was 3 months old when she and her family met with Julie, a teacher of children with visual impairments, at a center for children who have visual impairments. Meg's family shared information with Julie at their meeting including contact details from doctors and other professionals with whom the family had been working. Meg's medical reports indicated that she had a cerebral visual impairment as a result of being shaken by a babysitter when she was just 1 month old. The shaking caused bleeding within the brain that resulted in brain damage.

The family's second meeting with Julie took place at their house. After the family provided more details about Meg's early history, they said they wanted to learn more about her vision impairments in order to be able to help Meg use her vision more effectively. They also wanted to learn how to help her build development and increase her visual abilities. Julie explained that whatever specific goals they had for Meg would provide the basis for their work together. During their next meeting, Julie provided more in-depth information about Meg's CVI diagnosis. She also answered questions regarding behaviors Meg displayed

Figure 4.2
Sample Family Questionnaire

Family Questionnaire

General Information

Date: _____

Child's name: _____ Date of birth: _____

Visual diagnosis: _____

Parents' names: _____

Siblings in the home (names and ages): _____

Adults in the home (names and ages): _____

Language(s) used in the home: _____

Pediatric ophthalmologist: _____ Phone: _____ Email: _____

Date of last appointment: _____

Pediatrician: _____ Phone: _____ Email: _____

Date of last appointment: _____

Other medical professional(s): _____ Phone: _____
Email: _____

Date(s) of last appointment: _____

Medications: (name and frequency of dosages)

_____

Other difficulties: _____

Surgeries (past type and date): _____ (upcoming): _____

Do you have any questions about the information provided by any of the doctors?

Questions about Your Baby

1. What makes you happy about your baby?
2. What about your baby worries you?

Figure 4.2 (continued)

3. Do you have a nickname(s) for your baby?

4. What are your baby's strongest abilities?

5. What are your baby's most difficult problems?

6. Does your baby use special equipment for support (e.g., wheelchair, foot brace, cane)?

7. Does your baby have difficulty sleeping or distinguishing day from night?

8. Does your baby cry? A lot _____ Not very often _____ Only when uncomfortable _____

9. How would you describe your baby's personality (e.g., easygoing, fussy, nervous, calm, cuddly, stand-offish)?

10. What do you think your baby sees?

11. What do you want to learn?

12. How does your baby react to the following?

	Likes	Does Not Like	Neutral
Objects			
Sounds			
Touch			
Foods			
People			
Environment			
songs			
Other			

that the family found confusing. Julie gave them a family questionnaire to complete after the visit. She said that during her next visit, they would review the questionnaire. The parents' responses, she said, would be the first step towards building a home file of information related specifically to Meg.

THE HOME FILE

The *home file* contains the information needed to organize a home action plan. The *home action plan* is the master plan of identified developmental goals and intervention strategies for that particular baby and his or her family. The home file should be portable: kept in file box, a large binder, a USB drive, or online. This information needs to be portable so it can be readily shared when doctors, professionals, or agencies provide services to the baby.

The home file should include the following data:

- Information about the baby, including details about the baby's history and diagnosis; information received from doctors and specialists (such as assessment findings and copies of specialists' reports) as well as a calendar of the baby's appointment dates and times

- Information about the baby's family, such as the number of family members and the language usually spoken at home

- A list and description of the baby's other educational and caregiving programs

- A home action plan listing the family's goals along with the strategies to achieve them

Information About the Baby

A family history, along with medical information, assessments, and observations, provide important details about the abilities and requirements of a baby with special needs. Each assessment or observation provides different details about a baby's developmental requirements. Medical evaluations, family observations, functional vision observations, functional vision assessments, and developmental inventories together provide an inclusive record of information about the developmental needs and visual abilities of a baby whose vision loss is related to CVI.

Family Information About Baby

Family information and observations are critical to understanding a baby's abilities and needs. The family knows the baby intimately and observes the baby in a variety of situations. Family information and observations include some of the following:

- Perceptions about their baby's developmental abilities and needs

- Details about interactions with and the parents' level of bonding with their baby

- Information about the baby's personality and behaviors (e.g., is he or she easygoing and happy or easy to soothe;

Important information about the baby's needs and abilities is gained through a parent questionnaire which is greatly enhanced with face-to-face family meetings as seen in this photo.

does he or she sleep frequently, have difficulty eating, or cry a lot)

- A list of the baby's particular likes and dislikes, which are helpful in planning appropriate activities and strategies

While some of this information can be obtained from the family questionnaire, more can be acquired through team-family interviews and observations of the baby and the family dynamics. **Sidebar 4.1** offers some suggestions of ways to obtain this data from the family.

Medical Information

The baby's medical history can be gathered from intake forms from a hospital or program registration. Whenever a baby is released from the hospital, parents receive a written medical discharge summary, a document that identifies diagnoses and areas for medical or therapeutic follow-up. Current medical information can also be obtained through medical reports. If parents do not already have copies of these, they can request them from the baby's pediatrician, pediatric ophthalmologist, or other doctor. Medical reports typically provide information about the following:

- The child's visual diagnosis as well as related diagnoses and their implications
- The baby's general state of health along with his or her current medical needs
- Medications prescribed for baby and their possible side effects, especially side effects that are vision-related; for example, some anti-seizure medications can affect how a child uses vision (Topor, 2014)
- The child's known allergies or food sensitivities
- Any scheduled or anticipated surgeries

Information about a baby's functional vision can be gathered from observations made by the teacher of children with visual

Suggestions for Home Visits

A home visit increases the likelihood of a family being at ease because they are in a familiar environment. In a home visit, a teacher of children with visual impairments needs to combine the role of consultant with that of a guest. It is important that the teacher be perceived as knowledgeable and professional. A teacher during a home visit can do the following:

- Answer questions clearly and show expertise about CVI
- Explain or interpret information provided by doctors
- Describe possible characteristic behaviors of CVI and explain why a baby with CVI may display those behaviors
- Build hope realistically
- Respect the knowledge of the parents
- Ask what concerns the parents may have about their baby and what information they can provide about the baby's behaviors
- Include the family in discussions and decisions
- Show positive interest in the baby
- Touch or interact with the baby as soon as the baby is ready
- Make positive comments about the baby and provide encouragement
- Show interest in the family's history and the baby's story and listen with sensitivity
- Help build the family's self-confidence and self-respect
- Respect home customs and rules
- Include parents in discussions if other professionals are present

(continued)

- Ask permission to interact when managing a baby's behavior

- Include other family members (siblings, grandparents) when possible and appropriate

- Teach by example and by providing easy explanations

- Explain why an activity or suggestion helps their baby

- Give regular, positive feedback about growth and functional vision skills

impairments or the baby's parents. Other sources may include anecdotal reports, collaboration with other professionals and day care providers, and functional vision assessments, which provide specific information about the baby's visual capacity and other developmental needs as discussed in **Chapter 2.**

Functional Vision Observation Questionnaire

Figure 4.3 provides a sample functional vision observation questionnaire. This questionnaire alerts members of the home team to take note of a baby's specific visual abilities. The questionnaire is intended to be completed independently by the family as well as those who spend time treating or diagnosing the baby. Taken together, these multiple perspectives provide a complete understanding of the baby's visual and developmental needs across a variety of settings and situations. The replies of parents, teachers, professionals, and care providers will add to information about the baby's visual abilities gathered during a functional vision assessment.

Functional Vision Assessment

A *functional vision assessment* (FVA) gathers information about a child's current visual ability. An FVA, as defined in **Chapter 2,** is an evaluation of a child's capacity to use vision in

Figure 4.3
Sample Functional Vision Observation Questionnaire

Functional Vision Observation Questionnaire

Date: _____

Name of individual completing the form: *Jane Taylor*

Role: *Teacher of children with visual impairments*

Baby's name: *Emmy*   DOB: _____

Parent's name(s): *Jack and Stacy Miller*

Questions about Emmy's vision:

1. Do you think Emmy has some ability to see?   Yes   No

   If yes, what behaviors make you think this? (describe in detail)

2. Do you think Emmy has a favorite toy?   Yes   No

   If yes, can you describe it, including its color, size, and if it makes sounds or moves?

3. Does Emmy:

	Yes	No
Keep her eyes open when awake?		
Tolerate visual activities?		
Exhibit unusual eye movements (e.g., wiggling, blinking often, eyes closed most of the time)?		
Have eyes that look straight (i.e., do not cross or seem to move in different directions)?		
Hold her head in one particular position (e.g., to one side or chin-on-chest)?		
Seem to look at lights a lot?		
Avoid looking at lights or squint in bright light?		
Blink when something quickly moves toward her face?		

(continued)

Figure 4.3 (continued)

	Yes	No
Appear to react to objects of a specific color?		
Alert to a target using peripheral vision? (If so, from which location?)		
Alert to a new item presented nearby?		
Appear to gaze toward a moving ceiling fan?		
Seem more visually alert at night?		
Seem more visually alert during the day?		
Seem more visually alert outdoors?		
Seem more visually alert indoors?		
Alert to light in a dark environment easily?		
Alert to light in natural room light?		
Show interest in items with certain characteristics? If so, please describe them.		
Look at a favorite item that is nearby without visual delay?		
Look at familiar face(s) when nearby? (How near?)		
Establish brief eye contact with a familiar person?		
Shift gaze (left to right, up and down, or near and far) to locate a favorite item nearby? How near must the object be?		
Reach or try to contact favorite items?		
Look at items that are not visually interesting (e.g., plain in color, no pattern)?		
Fixate on a desired item within a cluttered background (e.g., a specific toy in a toy box)?		
Maintain gaze while reaching for an object?		
Look toward an object or person to achieve a result (e.g., gaze at an adult to be picked up or gaze toward an item, such as a bottle, to get it)?		
Change position to improve view of a favorite target (e.g., roll slightly to view a moving pinwheel)?		

Babies with CVI

Figure 4.3 (continued)

	Yes	No
Move slightly to improve the ability to activate an object (e.g., move forward to reach a chime toy)?		
Look toward a named object located among two or three others?		
Smile spontaneously in response to an adult's smile?		
Look at high-contrast photos of known items or people?		
Look toward a photo of a very familiar person (e.g., Mommy) when the photo is named or when asked ("Look at Mommy's picture")?		
Imitate adults' simple gestures (e.g., waving, touching nose, clapping)?		
Visually notice movement (e.g., an adult or animal walking by) across a room (beyond 4 feet)?		
Look toward a named item or person beyond 6 feet?		
Move toward a named item or person beyond 6 feet as physically able?		

a variety of tasks and settings, or the child's potential for visual function (Topor, 2014; Topor, 1999). It collects details about near and distance vision, visual fields, eye movements, and responses to environmental characteristics such as light and color. An FVA for a baby who is suspected to have CVI can also include more specific details related to the characteristic behaviors shared by most children with CVI (Roman-Lantzy, 2018). An FVA can help determine how damage to the brain affects vision, and whether observed visual behaviors may also indicate the presence of additional neurological involvement. In addition, it helps determine how a particular visual impairment may affect a child's specific learning needs, which is essential for establishing developmental goals and the interventions needed to attain them, making it critical to the development of an effective home action plan. If a diagnosis has not already been made, the FVA may simply conclude that a baby should be referred to a pediatric ophthalmologist for a full medical exam to confirm a possible diagnosis of CVI.

Information gathered from an FVA includes the following:

- Evaluation of a child's current visual functioning under optimum conditions
- Identified areas of visual difficulty
- Bodily positions or the sorts of objects that appear to enhance the child's ability to use vision
- Environmental factors that enhance or detract from the child's visual ability

If a child uses any special optical devices such as prescription eyeglasses, an eye patch, or prescribed positional equipment, the child should also use them during the FVA.

Conducting an FVA with a baby is different than conducting one with an older child. Babies may be more sensitive to factors that do not affect older children, such as shyness around strangers; thus, babies may respond by displaying inhibiting behaviors. Since babies are preverbal, keen observation of a baby's subtle or unique reactions and muscle movements is necessary to accurately determine a baby's visual abilities. Taking the time to put a baby at ease and making efforts to encourage natural behavior can help in obtaining more accurate assessment information. For example, babies may need adequate warm-up time before they are comfortable engaging the assessor, and may benefit from an introductory activity such as playing with a familiar toy with the assessor. Additional needs to consider when conducting an FVA of a baby with CVI are presented in **Sidebar 4.2.**

Suzy is 9 months old. She has CVI resulting from brain damage as a result of loss of oxygen during birth. During a clinical eye exam, Suzy's pediatric ophthalmologist found no reason for the unusual visual behaviors her family reported, and referred Suzy to a neuro-ophthalmologist who then identified damage

Conducting a Functional Vision Assessment with a Baby

Conducting a functional vision assessment (FVA) with a baby is different than with an older child. Therefore, specific needs and considerations should be taken into account. Keys to conducting an effective FVA with a baby include the following:

- Choose a setting that takes into account lighting, positioning, and distractions
- Pace interactions to accommodate the baby's interests and energy level
- Plan an appropriate and specific number of targets to use throughout the assessment
- Identify who interacts with the baby

Choosing the Setting

Certain aspects of the assessment environment may influence the baby's behavior.

- The timing of the session is important. A baby may be more alert and receptive at certain times of day, so the assessment should be planned for those times.

- Before an assessment, the parents and teacher should try to maintain a calm and relaxed demeanor. Babies are very alert to their parents' emotional states. Consider starting the assessment while the baby is held in the parents' arms or on a lap in order to provide emotional support.

- Sounds and movements can distract a baby from trying to alert to visual stimuli; so as much as possible, the assessment should take place in a location with minimal auditory or visual distractions.

(continued)

- Sometimes babies may not respond well to a certain individual and will shut down when interacting with that person. In this case, a different person might be substituted or the session postponed until the baby feels more comfortable.

- A baby's physical position can affect the use of visual skills, so ask parents about the baby's favorite positions and try to place the baby in those positions during the assessment. (Remember that children with CVI may have additional difficulties, such as cerebral palsy, and may need additional support.)

- When babies are lying down, they are fully supported and can concentrate better on alerting to visual stimuli. Adapting to a different supported position, such as sitting or side-lying, should be made slowly with cues as this is less likely to disrupt the baby's visual alerting. Providing any positional equipment the baby typically uses, such as a special support chair or infant seat, may also help the baby alert to visual stimuli.

- Slightly dimmed and relaxed lighting can help calm the baby and parents before the start of the assessment. Lighting can then be adjusted during the assessment to the appropriate amount and type of light to enhance the baby's visual ability.

Pacing Interactions

Babies with CVI often visually respond after a delay (visual latency); and their attention can be brief, so pacing interventions is important.

- Wait for a visual connection or behavior from the baby without talking or touching.

- Allow an appropriate wait time for a visual reaction.

- Change interventions smoothly to help a baby maintain interest. A verbal or tactile cue may help prepare the baby for a change.

Planning Targets

Babies with CVI often respond better to familiar objects than to novel ones. Using a familiar item at the beginning of the assessment may enhance the baby's level of comfort.

- Have objects ready to present to the baby.

- Helpful targets may include a pacifier, favorite blanket, or toy.

- Use objects with characteristics that appeal to a baby with CVI, such as an object of a preferred color or one with movement properties.

Interactions

Babies often do not feel relaxed with strangers, such as a teacher they may only have met a few times. Once a baby has had time to become familiar with a teacher, the baby's reactions and behavior may then become more natural.

- A teacher of children with visual impairments may get more accurate assessment results by allowing the baby time to get comfortable before starting the assessment.

- If the teacher does not directly approach a baby at first and talks to the parents for several minutes, the baby may have time to become comfortable with the adult and may show greater comfort by turning toward the teacher or beginning to relax his or her muscles. These behaviors indicate an interest in interacting and suggest that it might be time to begin the assessment.

(continued)

- Some subtle behavioral changes that might indicate a baby is still uneasy include the following:
- breathing patterns
- yawning
- holding his or her breath
- tightening muscles
- turning away
- hiccups
- gas
- having a bowel movement
- sleeping

involving visual areas in the brain. The neuro-ophthalmologist's office referred Suzy's parents to Jan, a teacher of children with visual impairments, for a functional vision assessment. Jan interviewed the family by phone and then sent them a family questionnaire to help her learn more about Suzy and her parents.

Suzy's parents promised to have a few of Suzy's favorite toys and objects available for Jan's first visit. After entering the family's home, Jan took time to make sure Suzy's parents felt relaxed, and also to give herself the opportunity to review the responses to the family questionnaire. Jan also casually observed Suzy while she continued to chat with the parents before starting the formal assessment.

Before starting her assessment, Jan adjusted the room lighting to prevent glare. Next, she prepared Suzy for a change by telling her that they were now going to play on the floor. In order to get Suzy ready for vision play, Jan gently massaged her and talked about each body part as she massaged them. She then rolled Suzy onto a blanket to help her stretch, and then she and Suzy's mother picked up the blanket together and created a makeshift swing for Suzy. These actions ensured that Suzy's brain and body were sufficiently warmed up and prepared to begin her session. Her brain had been stimulated by touch and movement, and she now felt relaxed with Jan. They played together with objects of different colors and sizes, and with other items that moved in different ways or made various sounds. Jan held each object at different distances and in varying locations in relationship to Suzy. During their session, Suzy was placed in several positions, such as lying down, propped on her stomach, sitting up, and being held.

When vision play was finished, Jan reported her observations about Suzy's functional vision to the family. She also explained to them about a functional vision questionnaire that would be completed by them and anyone else working closely with Suzy. The responses from the functional vision questionnaire and her own observations during the FVA would help them create a plan for regular, strategic interventions that could help Suzy learn to use her vision more effectively. Jan explained that during each visit she would teach the family ways to include activities intended to improve Suzy's visual ability and development into their daily routines. Together, Jan and the family would focus on improving Suzy's development. With each visit, the family would continue to learn more about CVI and any available resources for support. Jan and Suzy's parents made a commitment to work together as a team.

Checklists, Inventories, and Guides

Developmental checklists and inventories list incremental behaviors by major category of development. They identify information about a baby's achieved developmental ability as well as areas of developmental need. Developmental checklists (see **Figure 4.4**) are essential instruments to include in the home file and are used to plan a baby's goals and the interventions required to meet them. These documents are not, however, formal assessment instruments, and should be used only for planning. The Developmental Skills Checklist in **Figure 4.4**

Figure 4.4
Sample Developmental Skills Checklist for Babies

This sample checklist identifies early developmental skills which are the foundation of ongoing development. Activities to address these skills are most effective when embedded within other visual or skill activities. The list is intended as a guide for planning goals and interventions. Specific skills can be included or removed based on the needs of the baby. Skills that are not fully accomplished can be identified as goals on a home action plan.

Developmental Skills Checklist

Directions: Mark each skill with a + for accomplished and a—for emerging. Any skills that are not accomplished or emerging should be left blank.

Social Connectedness

_____ Shows attachment to primary adults

_____ Leans into the adult when being held

_____ Tolerates or enjoys being played with

_____ Tolerates or enjoys parent-initiated games and songs

_____ Exhibits ability to calm self

_____ Calms to the primary adult's voice or when being held

_____ Follows simple directions (e.g., "Open your mouth")

_____ Shows an awareness of parental limits (e.g., stops an action in response to "no")

_____ Engages in play with an adult or another child

_____ Begins turn-taking activities

Sensory or Tactile Awareness

_____ Tolerates or enjoys being touched by an adult

_____ Tolerates a variety of tactile stimuli

_____ Typically holds hands open

_____ Tolerates messy play such as finger painting

_____ Willingly allows hands to be guided toward objects and during activities

_____ Initiates use of feet to interact with objects

_____ Initiates use of hands to interact with objects

_____ Uses the whole hand to feel objects

Figure 4.4 (continued)

_____ Moves hands over a target in active exploration

_____ Splashes in water

_____ Explores tactile books with pads of fingers

_____ Identifies a favorite toy, device, or book using a tactile cue, such as a sticker

Auditory Awareness

_____ Mild or no startle response to soft moderate sounds

_____ Alerts to the sound of objects by stopping action

_____ Alerts to a parent's voice by stopping action

_____ Looks toward the sound of an object

_____ Looks toward adult when hearing his or her voice

_____ Shows anticipation of a routine when hearing a familiar sound (e.g., going into a car after hearing keys jingling)

_____ Calms to a familiar adult's voice

_____ Calms to instrumental music

_____ Slightly moves hand or foot o a familiar song

Visual Awareness

_____ Changes behavior in response to a lighted stimulus in a dark environment

_____ Show awareness of whether lights are on or off

_____ Changes behavior when shown a lighted stimulus in a dim environment

_____ Fixates on a lighted toy in a dark environment

_____ Fixates on a lighted toy in a dim environment

_____ Fixates on a lighted toy in normal room light

_____ Locates or touches lighted objects in a dark environment

_____ Locates or touches lighted objects in a dim environment

_____ Locates or touches lighted objects in normal room light

_____ Fixates or reaches toward moving objects

_____ Shows awareness of shiny objects illuminated by a flashlight

_____ Shows awareness of shiny objects in normal room light

(continued)

Figure 4.4 (continued)

_____ Shows reduced delayed fixation to known objects

_____ Regards non-lighted objects with interest

_____ Fixates on up to 10 visually motivating objects

_____ Reaches for visually motivating objects

_____ Spontaneously reaches to repeatedly bat, grasp, or operate objects in a play box

_____ Uses eye contact to signal intent to be picked up

_____ Shifts gaze between two visually motivating targets

_____ Moves an arm toward a visually located nearby target

_____ Visually locates dropped objects that are touching the body

_____ Visually locates dropped objects near the body

_____ Visually localizes objects located on the side

_____ Maintains fixation while reaching for a visually motivating target

_____ Maintains fixation while reaching for a desired object

_____ Selects a desired object (visually or by reach) in group of three or four known objects

_____ Responds primarily to one or two preferred colors

_____ Chooses visually between two objects

_____ Responds to simple observed gestures, such as a wave

_____ Views a smile or other facial expression and responds

_____ Maintains fixation on a slowly moving visually motivating target in near visual field

_____ Names or identifies viewed and known objects in near visual field

_____ Selects objects representing items in a story or book

_____ Gathers scattered objects as much as 4 feet away

_____ Scans a lighted surface to find an object

_____ Scans a lighted surface to find a named object

_____ Moves across a room toward a light source

_____ Watches the movement of a large target more than 10 feet away

_____ Identifies a large target from 12 to 20 feet away

_____ Show recognition of primary adults and self in a clear photo

Figure 4.4 (continued)

Gross Motor Development

_____ Keeps head at midline much of the time

_____ Typical muscle tone in upper extremities

_____ Typical muscle tone in lower extremities

_____ Maintains straight back for 3-5 minutes in supported sitting

_____ Shows head and neck strength in supported sitting

_____ Bears weight on legs momentarily

_____ Holds arms at mid-level much of the time

_____ Tolerates tummy-time activities

_____ Rolls front to back

_____ Rolls back to front

_____ Moves forward when on tummy

_____ Holds position on all fours

_____ Plays with objects while in all-fours position

_____ Stands at furniture when occupied for a few minutes

_____ Moves laterally along furniture

_____ Returns to sitting from standing

_____ Takes several steps using equipment or holding hands

_____ Stands independently for several seconds

_____ Takes several steps independently

Fine Motor Development(Grasp, Manipulation) and Object Use

_____ Keeps hands open when relaxed

_____ Maintains equal strength and dexterity in left and right hands

_____ Bats at objects

_____ Holds an object placed in one hand

_____ Pulls cloth from face when playing "peek-a-boo"

_____ Voluntarily grasps objects

_____ Releases objects

_____ Holds objects in both hands simultaneously

_____ Brings hands to mouth

(continued)

Figure 4.4 (continued)

_____ Brings both hands to midline

_____ Transfers objects between hands (left to right and right to left)

_____ Makes up to five movements with an object (e.g., shakes, bangs, turns)

_____ Moves to operate a simple cause-and-effect toy after demonstrations

_____ Claps hands in response to a song

_____ Takes objects out of containers

_____ Puts objects into containers

_____ Uses an emerging pincer grasp (holding an object between thumb and index finger)

_____ Opens a simple container

_____ Closes a simple container

_____ Operates a switch to achieve a desired result

_____ Operates simple fasteners (e.g., zippers, snaps, Velcro)

Personal Independence

_____ Holds bottle independently

_____ Begins to pull shirt over head with help

_____ Helps to hold spoon during feeding time

_____ Begins to finger feed

_____ Participates in diaper routine by holding wipes

_____ Removes clothes independently

_____ Participates in some chores (e.g., throwing trash in a container)

Concept and Language Development

_____ Shows awareness of major body parts (i.e., hands, feet, head)

_____ Makes verbal sounds in play

_____ Imitates simple gestures when modeled

_____ Uses a few gestures to express wants

_____ Responds appropriately to up to five verbal or gesture requests

_____ Participates in regular lap story time involving music, a story box, or a book

_____ Participates in scripted routines with identified vocabulary

_____ Shows understanding of vocabulary of up to 20 words or signs

shows a sample skills checklist. It is used to identify which developmental milestones a baby has already achieved, and which skills need to be focused on during upcoming activities and routines. The steps in the checklist need not be followed sequentially.

Psychologists, diagnosticians, and early interventionists each have specific scales to help them identify age ranges of development for children with typical vision. These instruments are problematic, however, when used with children with visual impairments such as CVI because these children may develop certain skills at later ages than sighted children (Anderson et al., 2007). When employing any scale, it is therefore important to consider and report about how a child's visual impairment may have affected the results of the evaluation.

There are, however, developmental guides created to inventory the specific needs of very young children who are visually impaired or who have CVI. These guides can also provide data to help the home team establish goals and required activities that consider a child's specific visual impairment. Two guides used extensively with babies with CVI include the following:

- The *INSITE Developmental Checklist* (Morgan & Watkins, 1989), which evaluates many domains of development

- *The Oregon Project for Preschool Children Who Are Blind or Visually Impaired* (Anderson et al., 2007), which evaluates developmental levels of children with visual impairments in areas including gross and fine motor skills as well as concept development. It also guides the selection of goals and documents the acquisition of skills.

Information From the Family

Family and Household Information

Information about the family is usually gathered from registration data, family questionnaires, observations, and parent interviews. It can also be collected from discussions with family members, specialists, and social workers. The following topics are important to include when obtaining information about the family:

Need for Support. The strength of a family directly affects their ability to help their child learn and grow. Finances, available time, and support from others are all resources that either help or impede parents' ability to carry out appropriate plans and suggestions.

Language. Families who speak a language other than English may need a translator when interacting with professionals. Since older siblings or English-speaking relatives sometimes serve as translators, parents may become uncomfortable when these other family members are asked to translate sensitive information. Parents might appreciate being given the choice between using a professional translator or a family member. Non-English-speaking families may also wonder whether they should speak their native language or English to their baby. Questions about dual-language households should be referred to a speech and language specialist.

Customs and Rules. Understanding and respecting a family's customs and household rules can enhance the relationship between parents and professionals. For example, if the family does not wear shoes in their house, teachers and other professionals should respect the family's customs and remember to remove their shoes upon visiting.

Siblings. Parents may feel guilty about not giving their other children enough attention when they have a baby with CVI. They may also be concerned about asking older children to assume adult responsibilities, such as participating in interventions with their younger sibling. **Sidebar 4.3** provides information about addressing the specific needs of the siblings of a baby with CVI.

Grandparents. Parents sometimes express frustration about grandparents and other extended family members who they feel do not fully understand the challenges of raising a baby with CVI. In actuality, just like the baby's parents, grandparents may also be grieving or experiencing denial themselves. Both feelings can make

Siblings

Babies with CVI require therapies and extra attention. It is therefore important for parents to give attention, time, and energy to their baby with a visual impairment. While siblings may understand that their brother or sister requires extra time and attention, they may still feel left out or confused. Parents have a variety of support and educational groups they can access. Siblings, in contrast, generally do not have the same outlets for support which may put them at risk for depression. They also may try to overcompensate for their sibling's perceived shortcomings by acting more responsible or achieving more. They may hide negative emotions so as not to put stress on their already overwhelmed parents (Fazzi, Klein, Pogrund, & Salcedo, 2002). Age can also affect their feelings toward their sibling with a visual impairment. Preschoolers, children of elementary school age, and adolescents have a less mature understanding and response than older siblings.

Some common emotions and reactions that siblings may experience include the following:

- Fear (Can I catch this?)
- Jealousy (My parents spend more time with my sibling than with me.)
- Anxiety (What about my own future and relationships?)
- Worry (Will I be able to have a typical child when I get older?)
- Concern (What is my responsibility for my sibling when my parents are no longer able to care for him or her?)
- Pressure (My parents expect me to be perfect.)
- Loneliness (I feel different from my friends and often feel alone.)

- Anger (The rules for me are different than those for my sibling.)
- Guilt (I feel guilty that sometimes I don't want to protect my sibling.)
- Mixed feelings (I don't like that I can do things that my sibling cannot.)
- Embarrassment (Sometimes having a sibling with special needs embarrasses me.)

Sibshops are positive resource for siblings (Sibling Support Project, n.d.). These local groups provide opportunities for siblings of children with visual impairments and other health, developmental, and mental needs to obtain peer support and participate in programs and activities in a recreational setting. They reflect a commitment to the well-being of the family member who is likely to have the longest relationship with the individual with a visual impairment.

Many siblings exhibit great pride in the accomplishments of their sibling, as well a strong bond and love. In fact, in this teacher's experience, many siblings grow up to become teachers or specialists of individuals with special needs.

it seem like a grandparent is dismissing circumstances around them. For example, a grandparent might say of their grandchild, "Oh, I think she sees fine," even though they may be struggling to come to terms with the situation. Although grandparents may intend to help by providing parents with resources, or by offering suggestions and advice, sometimes these well-intentioned actions cause parents to feel inadequate about caring for their child or question whether they are capable to meet their child's needs. The teacher of children with visual impairments should take note of what other relatives live with the child and how each person relates to the child. Grandparents may benefit from support sessions with a knowledgeable social worker or by participating in a support group with other people whose grandchildren have CVI or other visual impairments. **Sidebar 4.4** has additional suggestions for addressing the needs of grandparents.

Family Meetings. Whenever individuals other than the baby's parents—including grandparents, daycare providers, and adult siblings—act as caregivers, communication between these caregivers and the baby's family is especially important. Caregivers should report to parents about their participation in intervention sessions, as well as daily experiences, goals, current interventions, and progress. Collecting information from all the child's caregivers in a notebook or diary is a good way to keep everyone on the home team up-to-date.

A grandparent's role in supporting the parents of a baby with CVI is tricky. Family support is often more helpful than suggestions and input. This photo shows a smiling and approving grandmother who admires her granddaughter and thereby supports the baby's parents and their efforts to help their child grow and develop.

Grandparents

Grandparents of a child with a visual impairment are in a difficult position. They are grieving for their grandchild with serious problems, for their own child's difficult situation, and for their own feeling of confusion and loss. As parents themselves, they have always been the ones to provide solutions; but they may feel helpless in this situation. Below are some helpful suggestions teachers might offer to grandparents.

- The situation is real, and it is difficult for everyone involved. Diminishing the seriousness of the situation or the baby's difficulties will not be supportive to parents.

- It is very important that parents are allowed to be the specialists regarding their child's development and needs.

- Parenting a child with a visual impairment requires extensive and continued research. While parents need to be in control, they might appreciate offers from grandparents to help with research and tracking down information.

- Since they have experience being parents themselves, it is only natural for grandparents to want to offer advice. However, grandparents should be careful to make sure advice does not come across as criticism.

- Grandparents should show love and warmth to their grandchild, even if it may be difficult for them to do so. Pain and sadness will not be helpful to either their child or grandchild, but their love will be.

- Each parent must find their own way to work with their child. Support in this process from grandparents will be important to the baby's parents.

- If their child trusts them with their feelings about their baby with CVI, grandparents should make every effort to really listen to hear what their child is expressing.

Space and Lighting. Babies with CVI may have additional sensory sensitivities; therefore, familiarity with the layout and features of a family's house will help when teachers prepare areas for use. The baby's sensitivities can easily cause him or her to become overwhelmed or unfocused if an area has too many distractions. For example, babies with CVI may be especially light sensitive, or they may gaze at lights. While parents can reduce lighting in an effort to accommodate their baby's light sensitivity, remind them that adequate lighting is essential for effective use of vision. Using side lamps instead of overhead lighting and reducing glare in a room by repositioning lamps and adjusting window blinds will help a child with CVI use vision more optimally. Although families may reduce lighting in their homes to help babies use vision better, sometimes continual dim lighting in a home may offer clues to a family's emotions, and may indicate that the family could benefit from grief support.

Noise and Activity Level. Babies with CVI may have difficulty maintaining attention. As a result, distracting noises and high levels of activity in an area can hamper a child's ability to attend to visual activities. It is important for interventionists to become familiar with the family's home schedule so they can schedule visits for times when there is less activity in the house. Other strategies may also be needed to help reduce noise and commotion, such as using a study carrel, trifold board, or play box.

Daily Routines and Household Objects. Routines are an important part of the teaching strategy for children with CVI since they learn better from experiencing planned repetition. Children with CVI visually respond to objects that are known to them. Using familiar toys, books, and even kitchen items in activities, play, and practice will help a baby with CVI be more visually alert to those objects. (Use of routines and adapting toys and objects to be more effective visual targets are discussed in **Chapter 5.**)

Information About Other Programs

Educational Programs

Information about other programs in which a baby with CVI participates is an important component of the home file because these programs will affect schedule planning, goals, and interventions. Other programs might include the following:

- School and state early intervention programs
- Private centers that serve children with special needs
- Centers or programs that provide specialized therapies
- Private preschools and caregiving programs
- Individual home educational or therapy services

It is helpful to include information in the home file about these other programs including their purpose and primary goals, whether they are home- or community-based, and whether they are public or private. It is important to note when the sessions (individual, group, or a combination of both) are scheduled, as well as a description of the program staff's experience with CVI. Additional questions the parents should consider when choosing a program and discuss with their home team can include the following:

- Does the program understand how CVI-related issues can complicate a baby's ability to accomplish other goals, complete activities, and achieve maximum potential? If not, does the staff welcome additional training?
- Does the program have a history of collaboration with other professionals and programs?
- Is the program able to synchronize schedules and coordinate goals with other programs and professionals?
- Does the program have both the ability and intent to make accommodations for vision loss and CVI behaviors and needs?

A shared calendar will facilitate collaboration among all parties since it can help to manage schedules and multiple appointments. A digital, color-coded calendar allows for information to be shared with other professionals and programs. Additionally, it is useful to include a paper calendar in the baby's diaper bag so it is always available to help coordinate appointments.

Caregiving Programs

Many children attend a caregiving program or spend time with a nonrelated caregiver for a majority of their day. Group caregiving, which can take place in either a private home or formal facility, will include several other related and nonrelated children. Private home caregiving, in contrast, may take place in either the caregiver's or child's home. If private care takes place in the home of a baby with CVI, that baby is usually cared for, along with their siblings, by one individual. It is important to consider a baby's caregiving program when planning goals and interventions. While some caregiving facilities support any special learning needs of their enrolled children by offering and providing support for interventions carried out on site, other programs do not. It is also important to determine whether caregivers are capable of supporting interventions to specifically help a child with CVI develop and improve visual skills. The home file should contain information about caregiving programs that answer the following questions:

- Is the program accredited? Most states have regulations and guidelines for accredited early childhood caregiving programs. The National Association for the Education of Young Children (NAEYC) maintains a list of accredited programs to help families find one in their area (n.d.).

- Does the person or the program have sufficient childcare experience? Beyond that, does the caregiver or the facility understand the needs of working with a baby with CVI? Do they have the time and skills to implement important suggestions? If they need specific training, are they willing to partake in it?

- What rules has the caregiver or program established for their facility? Will the baby be allowed to bring favorite toys? Will they allow a baby to play on the floor? It is possible that a program's rules may limit the ability to carry out specific interventions required by babies with CVI.

- What is the caregiver or program's daily schedule? When are meal times, and when is outside playtime scheduled? Based on this schedule, when is the best time to set up intervention appointments?

HOME ACTION PLAN

A *home action plan* lists current goals along with recommended activities and strategies identified by the family, professionals, and the home team intended to help the baby improve visual skills and maximize learning opportunities. The home action plan should be revised as skills improve or whenever a baby's health or the family's needs change. Information collected in the home file identify the baby's requirements, which in turn indicate appropriate goals and the activities required to meet them. In addition, findings from the FVA are fundamental to create an effective home action plan and identify specific interventions. The home action plan also identifies strategies and activities to include in daily routines. It also specifies who is responsible to conduct each intervention. A home action plan should be concise enough not to overwhelm the family, but robust enough to adequately identify goals, activities, and strategies to help develop the baby's visual skills. Plans remain current only from two to six sessions with a teacher of children with visual impairments. Therefore, the plan needs to be updated frequently in order to continue to be effective in planning the baby's learning.

A leader should be selected to oversee the home action plan just as was done for the home team. Since one or both parents are usually the leaders of the home team, they usually direct the home action plan as well. However, sometimes parents will co-lead the home action plan with a teacher of children with visual impairments or a social worker.

The home team develops a home action plan by identifying the baby's needs as outlined in the FVA, as well as sharing strategies for interventions with team members and the family, and by consulting developmental checklists. Goals can then be set to address visual abilities, concept development, and early developmental skills. One way to compile a list of goals is to ask each home team member to contribute one goal to address on the home action plan, along with necessary strategies and suggestions to meet that goal. It is suggested that the home team limit the number of goals on the home action plan because a family can easily become overwhelmed if there are too many goals and interventions. If parents feel overwhelmed, it can negatively affect the plan's implementation.

If the family has an individualized family service plan (IFSP) through a public school program, the home action plan can share the list of goals from the IFSP. In that case, a copy of the IFSP should be included in the home file. **Figure 4.5** offers a sample home action plan. Methods for creating specific strategies to address goals on the home action plan will be addressed in **Chapter 5.**

A home action plan provides a focused course of action for implementing interventions at the family's home. While it provides the current directions and information required to reach identified goals, the home action plan should always be considered a work in progress. Since it is a fluid document, the contents of the home action plan should continue to be discussed by the home team at regular intervals and then updated as needed.

Some additional suggestions to keep in mind when working with a home action plan include the following:

- The plan is most effective when the family can readily see it; it should be posted on a refrigerator or on a bulletin board in a busy area of the house.
- The plan needs to be current in order to be useful; frequent review and communication with the home team is necessary to keep the plan up-to-date.

Figure 4.5
Sample Home Action Plan

Home Action Plan

Baby's name: Robbie   DOB: _____

Plan dated: _____

Sessions dates (Visit 1 to Visit 4):

Plan: #1 Starting Program

Team Member	Name	Goals	Strategy	Person(s) Responsible	Suggestions
Mom	Kathy	Increase social responsive-ness (looking toward parents' faces)	Put face motifs around crib area close to Robbie	Mom, dad, grandmother	Happy-face plates are good décor to include in the crib area.
			Shine light on parents' faces while singing or talking after diaper time.		Include flashlight play after diaper time.
Teacher of children with visual impairments	Ms. Smart	Increase visual awareness	Use objects identified in the FVA to create a stimulating visual play environment. Robbie can relax in this small space several times a day.	Mom, dad, older brother	Review suggestions for creating a Little Room (Nielsen, 1992). Create a small space for Robbie's quiet time. Try not to intervene.

Figure 4.5 (continued)

Team Member	Name	Goals	Strategy	Person(s) Responsible	Suggestions
Orientation and mobility specialist	Mr. Howe	Increase awareness of body parts	Add rattles or sound-making bracelets to wrists and ankles for short amounts of time during the day.	Mom, dad, grandmother, older brother	Periodically rotate toy from left wrist to right and then to each ankle. Create homemade wrist toys that are fun, colorful, and can be changed often.
Physical therapist	Mr. Strong	Increase head and body strength	During tummy time, include sound and visual objects near Robbie's head. Include a rolled towel under chest for support. Repeat several times a day.	All	Use a plain quilt and put 3-5 objects near Robbie's head. At certain times, hold Robbie facing away from the adult who is carrying him.
Occupa-tional therapist	Ms. Lee	Increase ability to hold small objects	Have Robbie hold a favorite small item in one hand and gently shake that hand during bath time.	Mom, dad	Small items, such as a plastic ring and bell or soft squeak toy, are good objects for holding activities co-active movement may help Robbie increase his grasp.
Speech and language pathologist	Mr. Good	Increase attention to voices of adults	During routines, such as before naps or bedtime, sing and talk to Robbie.	All	Try to routinely repeat Robbie's favorite songs.

(continued)

Figure 4.5 (continued)

Team Member	Name	Goals	Strategy	Person(s) Responsible	Suggestions
Pediatrician	Dr. Martinez	Attend all medical appointments		Mom, dad	
Pediatric ophthal-mologist	Dr. Conrad	Attend all medical appointments		Mom, dad	
Caregiving provider	Nanny Fiona	Increase tolerance to touch	Provide Robbie with a short massage after diapering and incorporate a variety of textured toys and blankets.	Mom, dad, grandmother, older brother	Provide fun tactile exposure to Robbie including having short massages regularly
Social worker	Ms. Thompkins	Increase positive awareness of parents	Use a cue, such as a cheek touch or an identifying piece of jewelry, especially during bonding activities.	Mom, dad	Help Robbie touch identifying jewelry, such as a watch or ring. Use cue consistently.

- The plan must be simple. Too much detail in a home action plan can make the plan appear daunting.
- When applicable, the plan might include links to websites and information about other resources.

Families who consistently use a home action plan to organize daily activities often end up feeling that they have a greater influence over their baby's growth, making them feel more confident that their baby's needs are being met. Additionally, the babies of families who consistently use a home action plan reach developmental goals more easily than babies whose families rely solely on professionals to implement activities and suggestions. Planned, regular, and frequent participation in recommended, strategic activities can help a child with CVI achieve his or her visual and development goals.

The local chapter of a national parents association was holding its annual conference for parents, grandparents, and siblings of children with visual impairments. Meg's and Sealy's parents, siblings, and grandparents were all attending this conference for the first time. Each family had invited some members of their respective home teams to join them.

During dinner, Meg's and Sealy's families and teachers were seated at a table with other parents of children with visual impairments. They discussed how critically important—but sometimes daunting—it was to implement activities to address goals at home. Meg's and Sealy's parents talked about how they organized all the information required to plan goals and activities by creating a home file with pertinent information. They shared how helpful the formation of a home team consisting of specialists and supporters had been to them. Collaborating with their home teams, both families had developed home action plans for goals and activities to work on daily to help their baby. Both families agreed that their plans had helped them feel more confident and organized, not to mention more in control, during this difficult time.

CONCLUSION

Exposure to visual interventions in the first years of life is extremely important to developing early visual abilities in babies with CVI. Parents who struggle with feelings of grief or are confused by the great amount of information they receive about their baby's diagnosis can easily start to feel overwhelmed by a schedule full of appointments and by the worries they have about their baby's diagnosis and development. Feeling overwhelmed can cause parents to neglect implementing interventions at home. Teachers of children with visual impairments can help parents feel better organized by assisting them to assemble a home team of family members and caregivers, along with essential professionals who can provide them with pertinent information in a sensitive way. Keeping this information organized in a home file can help parents become better able to collaborate with the members of their home team and feel more confident to implement suggestions, activities, and strategies each day to help their baby reach planned developmental goals. Parents who work with their home team to create a home action plan of goals, activities, and strategies are more likely to implement interventions consistently, with less confusion, and without feeling emotionally overwhelmed.

CHAPTER 5

Developing Visual Skills

As discussed throughout this book, early intervention is the key to developing visual skills in babies with cerebral visual impairment. This chapter provides an overview of several types of interventions designed to help babies attain planned goals. It emphasizes the importance of pre-intervention preparation and introduces the concept of the *intervention readiness chart.* This chart presents factors that increase the chances that interventions undertaken will yield success as well as being a tool to help both parents and professionals prepare for appointments and interventions.

INTERVENTIONS

The *interventions* explained in this chapter include exercises, activities, planned daily routines, controlled learning environments, and life experiences designed to increase a baby's visual abilities and general development. Interventions employed for a baby with CVI address the development of visual abilities and the baby's individual goals as identified in the home action plan (see **Chapter 4**). Interventions to address visual ability and development are not presented in isolation once a baby starts to show awareness of vision (Hyvarenin). Rather, interventions are integrated into daily events, activities, and routines.

For example, while bathing a baby, a parent can present an item such as a squeaky rubber duck bath toy to the baby and announce, "Look, here's your bath duck." They can then squeeze or shake the duck so that the combination of sound and movement can attract the child's auditory and visual awareness. Next, the parent can guide the baby's hand to touch the duck as it becomes immersed in the water, perhaps also verbally prompting the baby by saying, "Look! Your duck is having a bath!" This intervention integrates several areas of development into the everyday experience of bathing. These include vision, language, listening, and touch stimulation. The intervention of motivating the baby to visually look toward an object like the rubber duck is blended or embedded into the process of bathing the child along with other planned stimulations.

Types of Interventions

Five types of interventions are noted here that are especially important to help a baby achieve the goals proposed in the family's home action plan. These are exercises, activities, daily routines, controlled learning environments, and life experiences.

Exercises

Exercises are interventions that stimulate either a targeted reaction or an area of development. In most cases, an exercise is carried out specifically to sustain or improve a *single* targeted

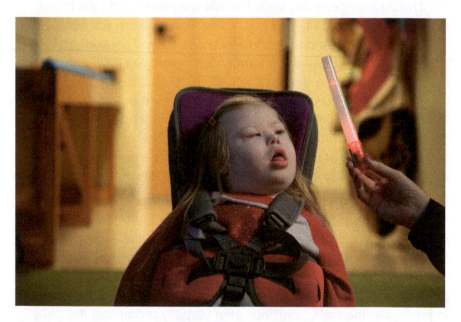

Presenting a light or lighted object to initiate a baby's initial visual awareness can be beneficial to help a baby start using vision. In this photo, the child is turning her head to gaze at the light an adult is holding that peeked her visual interest.

reaction, such as learning to move and strengthen a particular body part or to increase hand dexterity. Exercise interventions are not intended to address multiple issues, but to provide focused opportunity for the baby to learn or to practice a targeted skill. Exercises are often one of the early interventions employed by physical and occupational therapists or by speech and language specialists. Since teachers of children with visual impairments are not vision therapists, they rarely use isolated exercises as one of their early interventions. However, vision exercises such as presenting a light or lighted object to initiate a baby's beginning visual awareness can be a beneficial intervention to help a baby start to use vision.

Activities

Activities are planned interventions that are introduced sequentially in order to help accomplish a particular goal. Unlike an exercise, which focuses on a single reaction, an activity is

Daily routines are frequent and familiar times to practice a skill or work on vocabulary. In this photo, the baby and his parents are preparing to go in the car, a daily routine. They are also rehearsing the 'go for a ride' routine vocabulary.

multifaceted. It builds developmental skills and integrates visual skills, vocabulary, and activity-related concepts such as size, color, shape, or spatial awareness. Activities are most effective if they take into account a child's specific interests and incorporate elements that build upon one another with a functional purpose to motivate a child's reaction.

Daily Routines

Babies with CVI learn more easily when interventions are repeated frequently and at predictable times. Since daily routines fit this description, these present convenient times to teach concepts, language, and visual skills (see **Sidebar 5.1**). Daily routines can help babies with CVI anticipate events, integrate their use of vision, associate words with events and objects, and experience other sensory stimuli consistently.

For example, preparing a baby to ride in an automobile offers a daily opportunity for parents to use language that relates to transportation, such as the word *car* and the phrase concept *go for a ride,* while the baby simultaneously experiences the sound of the car's engine and the visual experience of looking at related objects such as a shiny door handle or side view mirrors.

Sidebar 5.1

Learning Through Daily Routines

Structured daily routines can reinforce cues, actions, words, and concepts through repetition.

- Select a few routines (e.g., bath time, feeding time) to become opportunities for learning.

- Identify which actions a baby can experience independently, and which need to be performed with a parent's help, such as moving a washcloth together during bath time.

- Develop key words or cues to use each time the baby is engaged in that same routine.

- Identify which objects a baby is going to touch regularly and what they are going to be called.

- Include a cue to start and end each routine, such as a gesture, touch, or sound.

The following steps will assist in preparing a daily routine for learning.

1. Identify up to four daily routines to be teaching routines for the baby and family member to experience together (e.g., bottle time, bath time, diaper time, or nap time).

2. For each routine, create a simple script of the event. Identify who does what, when it happens, and where it takes place. Keep it simple. For example, an adult might pick the baby up five times a day to carry the baby to the diaper station. This would be an excellent learning routine.

3. For each script, identify the core vocabulary, or the words and signs to use consistently during the routine. For example, the adult might say "up" as the baby is picked up. The adult then says "diaper" and hands a diaper to the baby to feel. The adult says "cold" as the baby is wiped clean after the diaper change. Finally, the adult both says and signs "all done" by moving the baby's arms apart to indicate when diapering is complete.

4. For each routine, plan one or two opportunities for the use of vision. For example, before picking up the baby, the adult might get close to the baby and remind the baby to look at his or her face using a gesture such as pointing to the face. The adult then shows the baby the diaper and helps the baby touch the material. Finally, the adult shows the baby the baby wipe container and helps the baby touch it.

Controlled Learning Environments

Controlled learning environments are specific areas or spaces that are strategically enhanced with objects, textures, switches, or devices intended to engage a baby's full range of sensory experiences (see **Sidebar 5.2**). These enhancements make the learning environment "controlled." Such environments can capture a baby's interest and curiosity while also encouraging use of vision. They can also motivate a baby with CVI to use thought, learn concepts, and physically move his or her body to investigate an object. The idea of controlled learning environments has its roots in the practice of *active learning*, an approach to intervention based on the work of Lilli Nielsen and her concept of the "Little Room" (Nielsen, 1992).

interactions with objects in the same space, concept development, curiosity, time to think, experimentation, and opportunities for object manipulation.

A controlled learning environment is most effective when a baby's interests and developmental level both guide the design of the environment. Safety is the first consideration when creating a controlled learning environment; babies should not be left unsupervised in this area. Areas that can serve as controlled learning environments may include a baby's body space, close space, near and familiar space, or slightly novel space.

Body Space

Body space can be an effective learning environment because children are interested in their own bodies.

- Provide items that can be worn on the body, such as wrist rattles, bells, beads, bracelets, or headbands. These encourage object exploration.

- Attach objects to a body vest or bib, making them immediately available in order to generate interest and play.

Close Space

Close space can be an effective learning environment because children are interested in exploring objects and people within their arm's reach.

- Introducing tactile blankets that have different textures and objects attached can add interest during play and relaxation time.

- Add crib toys and objects to an inflatable pool, creating an interesting play space.

(continued)

- Use tactilely and visually stimulating burp cloths to increase interest when resting on a parent's shoulder.

- Attach socks, sweat bands, toys, or lights to a bottle or to the baby's arms, enhancing bottle time.

Near and Familiar Space

Near and familiar space can be an effective learning environment because children are interested in household objects and caregiving routines.

- Place bath toys, tub stick-ons, or the regularly-used sponge or washcloth near the tub in the same place each time, turning bath time into a learning environment.

- Use a changing table mirror, powder box, or small object board demonstrating ointment, diapers, and wipes. These can enhance diaper time, or be used as subjects in a story about diaper time.

- Connect toys to a highchair, placing black or white mats on the eating tray to provide contrast, providing an object board of foods or utensils, or placing textured slip covers on the tray enable a baby to explore during mealtime.

- Attach a steering wheel toy or a tactile book to a car seat, or a toy to the backside of the front seat, enhancing car time.

Slightly Novel Space

Slightly novel space can be an effective learning environment because children are always interested in their homes and familiar areas, and modifications can encourage learning by turning those areas into slightly novel spaces.

- Attach a favorite rattle or cause-and-effect toy to a consistent place in the home. This can be motivating and interesting for the baby, and serve as an orientation landmark.

- Provide object boards in frequently visited areas, such as the bathroom, with themed bath time items, helping to build understanding of concepts.

- Place motivating objects in an inflatable pool in order to attract a baby's interest. The child can also crawl into and out of the pool for fun and movement practice.

Some additional items that can be used in a controlled learning environment include:

- CDs, springs, funnels
- Baby rattles, cat and dog toys
- Plastic and rubber soap dishes
- Christmas decorations, aluminum foil, pom-poms
- Bottle brushes, hair brushes, or other stiff brushes
- Beads, measuring spoons, keys
- Pot cleaners, sponges
- Straws, combs, forks, spoons
- Strips of Mylar tied into knots
- Bells, castanets, chime toothbrushes
- An ear syringe, a small colander
- Squiggle pens
- Purses
- A net with several different-sized balls (large and small)
- Nuts and bolts
- A rubber glove with cornstarch inside

Life Experiences

Life experiences are daily opportunities for babies with CVI to learn new concepts and skills. They can also offer babies a chance to practice concepts and skills that are already emerging (see **Sidebar 5.3**). Examples of life experiences can be a family outing, a visit to a park, a ride in the car, a trip to the grocery store, or a visit to a relative's house. Any life experience can be enhanced by providing babies with related vocabulary, concepts, and opportunities to practice visual skills. The greater the variety of life experiences babies with CVI encounter, the broader their knowledge and concept base will become.

Factors That Influence Success

The success of each intervention in an early intervention program depends on several factors. These include the parents, the environment, the baby, and the baby's readiness for

A teacher of children with visual impairments is showing the parents how to use the baby's loved sippy cup to motivate visual response and eye-hand co-ordination.

Life Experiences

Life experiences are regular life events that are given special attention as opportunities for learning. Experiencing life is an effective way for young children with CVI to accurately build concepts about life in general and things in their world specifically. The richer the variety of experiences, the broader their knowledge of the world will become.

During a life experience, a baby's attention is intentionally drawn to sensory aspects of a particular experience. Any part of the experience can be given special focus, including an object, a sense, an action, or an idea. For example, touching and describing the leaves of a plant, the difference between a big and a small ball, or the softness of a pet's fur can all be learning opportunities.

Without hands-on experiences, children with CVI can develop *empty language:* words that do not relate to actual concepts or objects (see **Chapter 3**). Planned life experiences are important for avoiding empty language.

Typically sighted children understand a vast majority of concepts and information about the world just by looking around and observing. They can learn from observing objects and events that are close or far away. In contrast, babies who have CVI cannot gain accurate information through distance vision. Life experiences can compensate for this lack of incidental distance learning.

Planned life experiences for babies with CVI are most effective when

- There is plenty of time to engage in the experience, so that discovery and exploration are not rushed. An effective life experience can happen anywhere, but sufficient time is required for a baby to learn from it. This includes time for a baby to react to and process the

(continued)

experience. In addition, the baby needs time for the brain to process what the hands are experiencing. A baby can also benefit from having time to use available vision to look closely at objects.

- There is a parent or teacher available to coach the baby. Coaching requirements are different for children of different ages and learning abilities. Effective coaching for infants likely involves providing vocabulary (ball) by using core words in simple sentences ("This is a ball.") and encouraging touch exploration as appropriate. Coaches of older babies might ask a few questions to encourage the child to think about what he or she is experiencing. For example, saying, "I wonder what this is" could entice the baby to think, respond, and explore.

- The learning experience is fun. Children naturally engage when they are enjoying themselves. Building learning opportunities into life experiences and repeating them often make them meaningful to the baby. Adults can make situations more engaging by being a little silly, singing a song, or reciting a rhyme—but the adult should be engaged for this learning experience to be effective.

intervention. The design of a successful intervention is discussed later in this chapter.

The Parents

Parents and other family members are key in a baby's early intervention success. Their readiness and commitment to participate in interventions can affect successful outcomes. Parents begin to learn early intervention strategies from their baby's teacher of children with visual impairments and become partners with the teacher and their home team (see **Chapter 4**).

Information and support provided to parents as early as possible increases the parents' readiness to help their baby.

When introducing interventions to parents, the teacher of children with visual impairments can begin by asking questions designed to gauge parents' readiness and needs.

- *Does the family understand the importance of early intervention?*

  Babies' brains are very adaptable. Interventions introduced by their teacher of children with visual impairments, when provided early enough, can help the brain reorganize itself, allowing it to improve visual and developmental skills. As discussed in previous chapters, initiating planned interventions as early as possible is important to increasing the visual ability of babies with CVI.

- *Do the parents want to implement interventions at home?*

  Some parents may not have time for or feel comfortable implementing interventions that could help develop their baby's visual abilities. Some may prefer that professionals manage and implement interventions. However, when an intervention is conducted less frequently, it will undoubtedly be less effective in helping a baby reach goals than those repeated frequently at home. Parents sometimes hire others to carry out interventions, or arrange for friends or other family members to help.

- *Do the parents know how to replicate and expand on suggestions and demonstrations presented by the home team?*

  Be sure to give parents specific and clear instructions about how to implement an intervention presented during a home visit or appointment in order to ensure that parents can replicate the steps without your presence. Parents benefit from suggestions about how to expand interventions by adding additional content like vocabulary, sensory experiences, and interesting objects. The sample individual visit review sheet in **Figure 5.1** is intended to be filled out at each visit and remain in the home in a prominent place to remind parents about the important information shared during the visit and as a reminder to conduct these interventions themselves at home.

Figure 5.1
Sample Individual Visit Review Sheet

Individual Visit Review Sheet

Directions: During an intervention appointment, complete a review sheet of important points. Use one review sheet for each goal identified and include two or three activities. Review each activity at the next visit and mark each one with a + for those accomplished and – for those emerging, along with the date. If there is no change, leave it blank. Write the date and time of the next appointment at the top of the sheet.

Baby's name: *Tommy*   Date: _____

Session #:*1*   Goal: *Increase interest in objects**

Next appointment: _____

_____ **Activity 1: A moving pinwheel**

- Show Tommy a *moving* pinwheel 4-6 inches in front of his face when he is comfortably on his back.

- Wait for any behavioral change suggesting that he is visually alerting. Shake the pinwheel slightly to continue the activity.

- Expand the activity by adding vocabulary (e.g., "look," "see," and "pinwheel").

- Encourage Tommy to touch the pinwheel, perhaps by guiding his hand by placing it under or over a parent's hand.

- When Tommy alerts to the pinwheel's motion, try holding it steady for a moment before moving it again.

- Repeat the activity several times during every bedtime and nap routine. Allow sufficient time for Tommy to react.

Teacher's follow-up comments:

_____ **Activity 2: Controlled environment**

- Create a Little Room (Nielsen, 1992) for Tommy that includes his quilt and other interesting objects hanging from elastic.

- Include vocabulary (e.g., "toys," "your space") as you place Tommy into the room.

- Once he is comfortable, allow him quiet time and space for interaction with the objects without additional language or interactions.

- Repeat the activity regularly, providing about 15 minutes in the area after each nap.

Teachers' follow-up comments: _____

Babies with CVI

- *Does the family understand the importance of completing interventions at home?*

     Parents can become overwhelmed when they try to incorporate the various intervention recommendations that they receive from different professionals working with their baby. If parents already feel like they have too much to do, explain how they can integrate interventions into their daily routines. When they are incorporated into daily activities, parents are more likely to consistently complete them.

- *Does the family have access to the items needed to complete the interventions?*

     While specialized toys or equipment may provide the most efficient way to teach babies with CVI a particular skill or concept, such tools may not be readily available for all families. Whenever possible, try to use common objects that are available in most homes. However, if an intervention must be conducted using a specialized item, be sure it is something you can leave with the family in between appointments. Experience suggests that if an intervention uses an item that needs to be constructed, such as a study carrel made from boxes or an object hanger assembled from PVC pipes or a box (see **Appendix A**), it is less stressful for the parents if you provide the finished item for them or make it with their help during a session.

The Environment

     Any environment, whether a home or a professional or group setting, can affect a baby's ability to use vision and be engaged during interventions.

Home Environment

     Many early intervention programs are based in a home, either that of the baby's family or that of a daycare provider. The home environment is a known, comfortable, and convenient environment for both parents and child, which allows them to engage more readily and comfortably with a teacher of children with visual impairments and participate in interventions. Some issues to keep in mind related to the home environment include the following:

- Phone use and family interruptions during a home visit are distracting and awkward. Providing an information sheet that outlines how families can prepare for a home visit (see **Sidebar 5.4**) can better establish expectations about managing interruptions and distractions.

- While the teacher of children with visual impairments is a guest in the home, they are also an educated and skilled professional. Finding the right balance between these two roles can be a delicate process. Although the teacher often attains the status of an honorary family member, too much familiarity can detract from the family respecting and following the teacher's professional knowledge and advice.

- Some babies with CVI have learned from experience that some adults do not expect much effort from them during a home intervention. For example, babies may feel it is acceptable to put forth less effort when working with people with whom they are familiar. Fortunately, it is possible to teach babies that intervention time is a different form of playtime, and effort is expected but rewarded during these times. In order to help babies distinguish intervention time from other activities in the home, the teacher of children with visual impairments can reserve specific cues, strategies, and toys that are used only during these intervention times. They can also teach other adults who live at the family's home how to encourage effort from babies during an intervention. **Sidebar 5.4** provides information on how to help parents prepare for a home intervention visit.

Professional Environment

Professional environments include individualized teaching spaces that are within centers, schools, or hospitals, but not a child's or care provider's home. They have several advantages over home environments:

Maximize Home Intervention Visits

Being prepared for a home intervention and follow-up visits helps to increase success of each visit. Teachers of children with visual impairments can help parents prepare by doing the following:

- Make sure parents prepare for your visit by feeding and diapering the baby. They should also put the baby down for a nap prior to a visit. Participating in massage and exercise play can also help a baby get ready for a visit.

- Keep interruptions to a minimum. Visits are intended to share information, and any interruptions can negatively affect available teaching opportunities.

- Reduce or eliminate background noise in the home. These can distract not only the baby, but parents and teachers as well.

- Ask questions and offer observations about the baby.

After the visit, the teacher should explain the interventions conducted to family members, so they will know how to continue them at home. The teacher can post the visit review sheet on the refrigerator so that all family members remember to reinforce the activities through their daily home routines.

- There may be fewer distractions in the professional setting than in the home.

- A teacher of children with visual impairments may have more control over the design of the teaching environment.

- Professional environments can be better prepared for interventions before a teacher's session.

- There is typically more specialized equipment available and access to other professionals who can assist with interventions.

Sessions conducted in professional environments can be more efficient since the teacher does not have to travel to the home. The travel time saved may allow time to serve more clients. However, professional environments can also have disadvantages over home environments.

- The family may have difficulty reproducing interventions learned in the professional environment in their own home. A visit review sheet (**Figure 5.1**), however, can help remind parents of the activities and steps discussed during the session

- The family and baby may feel intimidated by a professional setting. First, they must decipher travel directions to the session. Next, they must meet strangers and experience unfamiliar sounds and events in a professional environment. They may also be anxious about what might be expected of them and how their baby will be received by these heretofore unfamiliar professionals. Efforts to make the setting feel more home-like and welcoming may help families feel more comfortable. Providing furniture that is homier and more comfortable and less institutional, decorating the space with pictures of families, and offering a beverage to families when they visit can help put parents at ease.

- Depending on their economic circumstances, some families may find travel to appointments outside of their homes to be inconvenient and expensive. In those cases, it may be worth investigating whether any local organizations or professional groups offer funding or grants that can cover all or some of a family's travel expenses.

Group Environment

Group environments are settings in which several children may all participate in interventions within the same space. These may include classes in a center or preschool, or in a group caregiving setting. While these group settings may offer the benefit of providing the parents and baby with enriching social experiences, they too can have their shortcomings.

- Just like a home, a group environment can have its own distractions and interruptions. However, the use of a smaller space within the environment or employing a study carrel may help reduce distractions.

- When a baby participates in interventions within a group environment, the family may not be able to directly take part; therefore, the family may have limited opportunities to observe or practice these interventions themselves. Without the time spent practicing interventions with the help of a professional, families can subsequently find it challenging to reproduce those interventions by themselves in their homes. One way to help parents reproduce interventions provided in a group environment at home is to provide them a list of written instructions along with information about how their baby responded during various activities while at a group center.

- The baby or family may feel intimidated in a group setting because they are not in a familiar environment. They may also feel shy or be insecure because they are unsure what a center's staff expects of them. The teacher of children with visual impairments, social worker, or other parents in the group can support a new family and their baby by taking the time to socialize with them before the actual session and interventions begin. This pre-session time can also be used to ensure parents trust their baby is being well cared for and attended to by professionals and staff. For example, staff can demonstrate how to make a child comfortable by providing adequate body support and minimizing distractions or possible irritants such as light glare and intrusive noises. Parents can help their baby feel more comfortable in this setting by bringing a favorite toy or another familiar object from home

- As was the case with professional environments, travel to a group center away from home may be inconvenient and financially difficult for some families. If that is the case, the center or facility may be able to suggest community funding or grants that support travel and program expenses.

- Interventions conducted within a group environment may appear more formal and less intimate to a family than those performed at home because they may not always be conducted directly with the parents and baby. However, these settings have the added benefit of giving both parents and child an opportunity to become accustomed to a classroom-like setting before the child starts school in a few years.

The Baby

Successful interventions require that a baby is both prepared and engaged. One of the most important skills of a teacher of

Parents can enhance their baby's comfort in a setting by having a favorite toy or object nearby. In this photo, the plush toy figure is eliciting big smiles from the baby girl.

children with visual impairments should possess is an ability to create *a teachable moment*. A teachable moment is one in which the baby's needs, the external factors which may affect his or her behavior, and whatever is currently engaging the baby's attention can all be merged into a learning opportunity. The teacher of children with visual impairments can evaluate how an intervention will affect a baby by considering a situation from the baby's perspective. For example, a teacher might consider such aspects as how well the baby's body is supported, or whether they seem especially tired or unhappy. The teacher should also consider whether the baby would feel more comfortable being physically closer to his or her parents. Teachers should also be aware of any distractions in the environment that seem to be overwhelming the baby. Taking the time to consider a baby's perspective can help increase the baby's comfort, interest, and engagement in the intervention.

Babies indicate they are ready to participate in an intervention in several ways. Some of these include breathing in a regular rhythm, remaining awake, attending to or gazing toward the teacher (as able), reaching toward the teacher (as able), making verbalization efforts, smiling (as able), and showing heightened energy. A baby is most likely to show these signs when they feel comfortable, well positioned, safe, content, and after participating in alerting activities intended to stimulate them such as tactile massage and movement play. Unlike younger babies, in order to engage fully in an intervention, older babies may also need to feel connected with the teacher and be interested in the activities conducted.

INTERVENTION READINESS CHART

The *intervention readiness chart* identifies factors that enhance the baby's willingness and ability to participate in and benefit from an intervention. The more prepared the baby is, the more likely the intervention is successful. The items in each readiness area are not sequential but are instead a list of factors performed in any order to enhance readiness in that

Babies indicate they are ready to participate in an intervention in several ways such as regular breathing and smiling. In this photo, the big smile on the little girl's face shows her readiness to participate in an activity with her mother.

particular area. Consideration of a baby's personal and physical readiness, the environmental features which may be adjusted or enhanced to improve a baby's attention, and the preparations that can help maximize the effectiveness of interventions are considered in more detail in the sections below. Additional suggestions for successful interventions are also provided for each factor. Activities for some of the suggestions can be found in **Appendix A.**

Personal Readiness

Babies with CVI often have concomitant neurological difficulties that interfere with their readiness to use vision (Steendam, 2015, p. 396). Sensory processing disorders such as tactile, auditory, or visual defensiveness can make touch, sound, or visual stimulation uncomfortable or stressful for a baby. While

Table 5.1
Intervention Readiness Chart

State of Readiness	Factors that Enhance Readiness
Personal Readiness	• The baby can be calmed • The baby is comfortable and healthy • The baby tolerates touching • The baby tolerates interventions from slightly familiar individuals
Physical Readiness	• The baby participates in movement activities regularly • The baby wears prescribed eyeglasses • The baby uses appropriate support devices or equipment • The baby uses devices to enhance vision as needed
Environmental Readiness	• Background noise and distractions are adjusted • Area light is adjusted • The baby adjusts to unfamiliar environments
Intervention Planning and Preparation	• The activity sequence plan is based on the baby's background information • Activity items are gathered and the environment set up in advance • The activity is planned to engage the baby's attention and interest • The activity is planned to systematically expand the baby's visual skills • The activity is part of a framework with beginning, middle, and end cues

babies cannot learn when they are upset, they can, however, begin to tolerate potentially upsetting situations gradually through the use of consistent and strategic interventions.

The Baby Can Be Calmed

Babies must be calm in order to learn. If a baby seems too distraught or sick, an intervention session may need to be postponed. If the appointment cannot be canceled, then a teacher of children with visual impairments can redirect the session from working directly with the child to providing parent support and education according to the family's preferences or needs. Suggestions for calming an upset baby include the following:

- Swaddling the baby in a blanket (see **Appendix A** for instructions)
- Holding the baby chest to chest with an adult while singing softly, swaying gently, or slowly, rhythmically dancing
- Rocking the baby gently in a crib, hammock, infant bouncer seat, or swing
- Introducing gently vibrating toys or objects which can be slowly shaken to attract visual attention
- Playing soft background music if the baby is able to tolerate auditory sensation
- Hum softly, imitating a foghorn, producing two tones, one an octave lower than the other.

The Baby Is Comfortable and Healthy

A dry, clean, fed, and rested baby can attend more successfully during an intervention. In addition, when other medical issues, such as seizures, are managed, and the baby feels healthy, the baby is ready for learning. Suggestions for making sure a baby is comfortable and healthy include the following:

- Ensure that the baby has eaten recently and has a fresh, clean diaper.

- Verify that the baby has taken all of his or her prescribed medication.
- Identify potential environmental triggers that could upset the baby and determine ways to avoid them.

The Baby Tolerates Touching

Many babies with CVI also have sensory processing disorders such as tactile defensiveness. As a result, they may become agitated when handled and resist being touched. The tolerance of a baby with CVI for tactile stimulation is important to learning. A baby needs to learn to touch and be touched in order to investigate objects and benefit from interventions, because babies with CVI will need to use touch to overcome the effects of reduced vision. Some suggestions for improving a baby's tolerance for touch include the following:

- Give the baby a massage before an intervention session. This can enhance alertness and help a hypersensitive baby begin to tolerate touch. (See **Appendix A** for instructions.)
- Use massage items with coarser textures such as terry cloth, flocked material, or a bath body scrubber in conjunction with a firm touch. A firmer touch may actually be more comfortable for the baby with CVI than a lighter one.
- Distract the baby with an activity such as singing a favorite song, or draw attention to a favorite toy or item like a blanket. This may help the baby tolerate touch that would otherwise be unsettling.

The Baby Tolerates Interventions From Slightly Familiar Individuals

While a baby with CVI can usually tolerate interactions with family members, they may find interactions with unfamiliar people to be unsettling. Most babies with extensive medical needs that have required them to spend a large amount of time in hospitals are often anxious around strangers. These babies need a gradual,

Tactile stimulation is an important part of learning for babies with CVI. In this photo, the baby and adult are snuggling while enjoying dancing-a fun way to help a baby enjoy tactile stimulation.

planned approach from professionals to comfortably connect to unfamiliar individuals until they become more familiar with them. In cases where the professionals involved are unfamiliar and seem to agitate or unsettle a baby, parents should initially be the ones who conduct any interventions as demonstrated to them by the teacher of children with visual impairments. Suggestions for increasing a baby's comfort around and tolerance for slightly familiar individuals include the following:

- Allow adequate time for parents and professionals to socialize with one another before attempting interactions with the baby. As parents and professionals communicate with one another, the baby will have time to get accustomed to the presence of the professional.

- Sing the same greeting song to the baby at the beginning of each session. This helps familiarize the baby to the professional.

- Record the professional's voice and play the recording to the baby at home in between visits.

Physical Readiness

Babies with CVI may need adaptive or prescriptive devices in order to function optimally, both physically and visually. For example, a baby may require devices such as a support chair, braces, a compression vest, or eyeglasses. Babies may become more comfortable with a device like a vest or a brace if given time to explore the item prior to having it placed on their bodies. Once the baby is comfortable using the devices, it isimportant to also have them available during a teaching session.

The Baby Participates in Movement Activities Regularly

Readiness activities of movement prepare a baby with CVI for interventions and learning. Movement stimulation can help a baby become more alert by stimulating the brain. Some suggestions of readiness movement activities include the following:

- Warm-up activities including movement stimulation, such as swinging the baby in a makeshift blanket "hammock." In order to do this, a parent and teacher can hold the opposite ends of a blanket to create a hammock, and then swing the baby sideways and up and down. Start the movement gently, slowly increasing the rigorousness of the movement. Slow down the movement prior to the conclusion of the activity.

- "Rough-and-tumble" play, but performed in a consciously gentle manner, being sensitive to the baby's reactions. Incorporate different movement with the baby so his or her brain is stimulated in a variety of ways.

- Dancing while holding the baby, using varying speeds and movements in different directions.

- Moving with the baby in a front carrier, which provides the added benefit of promoting closeness and bonding.

The Baby Wears Prescribed Eyeglasses

If applicable, parents should bring a baby's prescription eyeglasses to sessions. The baby needs to become comfortable wearing these, and a teacher of children with visual impairments can explain strategies to help the baby gain comfort with them. (**Appendix A** offers a prescriptive lens orientation plan, while **Appendix B** lists resources for eyeglass frames specifically for babies.) Suggestions for ensuring the baby is comfortable when wearing eyeglasses include the following:

- Make sure the eyeglasses fit properly, stay in place, and are not too tight on the face; otherwise, they may distract the baby. However, if the glasses are too loose and slide down the face, they can distort the baby's vision.

- When putting on or removing a child's glasses, make sure the eyeglasses are not snagging their hair. A comfortable strap made of elastic, either homemade with loops at each end to make it fit the baby's head comfortably, or a commercial glasses strap designed for children, should be able to secure the eyeglasses to the face while not snagging hair. Many parents report they prefer glasses with wraparound earpieces to help hold glasses securely. Use light-adaptive eyeglasses for babies who are especially light sensitive; however, make sure that light-adaptive glasses darken the environment only to a point at which the baby still has sufficient light to use vision indoors.

The Baby Uses Appropriate Support Devices or Equipment

It is important to use a baby's adaptive equipment during interventions in order to provide physical support and to help the baby maintain an aligned posture. When a baby's body is not aligned properly, but is instead hunched, crooked, or askew, they do not have optimal circulation, comfort, or balance—all of which can influence a baby's ability to attend visually. If a baby requires a new and unfamiliar piece of support equipment to participate in an intervention, be sure to use it for only part of an intervention. Otherwise, the time the baby needs to adjust to the new equipment may interfere with the intervention. Compression clothing may sometimes be prescribed by a doctor or physical therapist to promote body awareness and muscle support. Other suggestions of devices and equipment to support a baby include the following:

- Use cushions or travel pillows to adjust head alignment so that the baby is sitting or prone with the head directly over the shoulders and trunk and hips.

- Provide extra trunk support when sitting by wedging large car washing sponges around a baby.

- Help maintain body support and alignment by using a child's life vest that is typically used for water activities. A head support cushion on the vest can be cut off to improve head alignment and comfort.

The Baby Uses Devices to Enhance Vision as Needed

Various devices and equipment can help a baby use vision more effectively during interventions. Suggestions of devices and equipment to help a baby use vision more effectively include the following:

- Trifold panels, either purchased at office supply stores or homemade, to help the baby visually attend by filtering out distractions and glare

- Equipment with back lighting, such as a light box, computer, or tablet computer. An illuminated fish tank can also attract visual attention.

- Flashlights of various sizes, gooseneck lamps that can be adjusted, and lighted toys
- Photosensitive eyeglasses (mentioned earlier) or sunglasses that reduce light and glare, both of which should be used cautiously so that they enhance and not reduce visual ability
- Child-sized baseball caps or visors to help avoid glare
- Trays attached to adaptive chairs with interchangeable backgrounds, such as different colored place mats. These enhance visual alerting and reduce visual complexity.
- Dark markers, highlighters, and pieces of colored tape can be used to visually enhance targets and objects.

Environmental Readiness

Babies with CVI can be distracted or upset by events around them. Adjusting the area to minimize distracting noises, activities, and light will enhance a baby's ability to attend and learn in his or her environment.

Background Noise and Distractions Are Adjusted

Background noise, such as from a television, smartphone, or radio, distracts a baby with CVI from concentrating on visual tasks. Since unnecessary conversations, talking on the phone, or texting can be distracting to most anyone, they should also be avoided during interventions. If other group sessions or activities are being conducted in close proximity to the baby, or if there are unfamiliar people in the area, these can also distract a baby and interfere with his or her readiness to learn. Suggestions for reducing background noise and environmental distractions include the following:

- Use small enclosures or areas located away from others. These are likely to be less noisy and present fewer activity distractions than larger spaces that may be used for several simultaneous group activities.

- In extreme cases, have the baby wear earmuffs to reduce distracting noise. However, be very careful to make sure the baby does not become too dependent on these because they can also prevent the baby from perceiving important environmental sounds and hearing spoken language.

- Have the baby wear headphones that are playing quiet familiar music in order to help the baby adjust to other ambient noises. Gradually turn down the volume of the music over time, which will allow the baby to slowly become accustomed to ambient noise. Eventually, once music is no longer audible, the baby should be familiar enough with the ambient noise that it should no longer distract the baby's attention to learning.

- Set up a trifold panel or use a cardboard box, to shield the baby from audio and visual distractions.

- Have parents and staff limit phone use to essential calls only.

Area Light Is Adjusted

Light is essential to vision. Too much or too little light reduces the ability to use vision. Maintaining optimal lighting in teaching and home environments helps the baby visually participate in interventions. A room's lighting is adequate for interventions when the light is strong enough to cast shadows. Suggestions for adjusting lighting include the following:

- Increase the intensity of a room's lighting by increasing the wattage of bulbs, providing additional light sources, or opening window shutters or blinds in darker rooms.

- Use table or floor lamps instead of ceiling lights. Lamps provide more targeted lighting so that glare can be better managed.

- Adjust blinds or a baby's position in relation to windows in order to reduce the effects of glare from the window. Make sure to face the baby away from windows and powerful lights.

The Baby Adjusts to Unfamiliar Environments

It is important for a baby to be able to relax in the intervention environment. A baby may be uncomfortable in an unfamiliar environment, such as a professional's office or clinical setting. The baby may also become anxious if he or she hears noises such as alarms, slamming doors, or loud voices. An unfamiliar environment should be adjusted as much as possible to help improve the baby's attention and learning. Suggestions for making the baby feel more comfortable in unfamiliar environments include the following:

- Place the baby in a smaller area within a space, or in another room off of the main area in order to help reduce distractions and stress.

- If possible, conduct intervention sessions in the same space or office while the baby is becoming familiar with the people and area.

- Play the same music at the start of each visit. This allows the baby to learn to associate it with that particular environment.

- Provide familiar toys and soothing items, such as a pacifier or blanket from home, to calm the baby in a new environment.

- Follow the same routine during each interaction. For example, start and end each intervention with a particular song, which the parents can also sing during interventions at home.

Intervention Planning and Preparation

When a baby is fully engaged in an intervention, he or she is ready to learn. The most effective interventions address each baby's unique visual and developmental needs while employing objects they personally find interesting. Interventions that are **fun**, **functional**, and make the baby **feel good** (the three F's) are more likely to engage the baby, and thus, promote learning.

The most effective interventions address each baby's unique visual and developmental needs while employing objects that he or she personally finds interesting.

The Activity Sequence Plan Is Based on the Baby's Background Information

Interventions and activities should address reaching the goals listed in a baby's home action plan. Background information about the baby is collected from assessment forms, checklists, inventories, questionnaires, observations, and interviews. This information allows the home team to plan for a baby's specific needs and increase the effectiveness of an intervention by providing essential information about what activities and strategies a baby might need and enjoy. Suggestions for engaging the baby include the following:

- Take note of what objects, songs, or activities motivate the baby.
- Similarly, be sure to keep track of objects, songs, or activities that upset or <u>do not</u> motivate the baby.

It's important to organize all teaching materials for ready access when building an intervention. A teacher's bag, like the one in this photo, or a small suitcase can keep the items for teaching together and readily accessible.

Activity Items Are Gathered and the Environment Set up in Advance

Maintaining a baby's attention during an intervention is easier when there are minimal interruptions to the flow of an activity. Be sure to place items required for a session within easy reach to allow for smooth transitions, which increase a baby's ability to attend. Additional suggestions for preparing the environment for an intervention include the following:

- Create a controlled learning environment with visually exciting objects and designs (explained in **Sidebar 5.2**) to encourage the baby to use visual skills and explore.

- Keep all needed activity items, visually motivating targets, and toys in a teacher's carrying case (see **Table 5.2**) so they are easily accessible.

Table 5.2
Teacher Carrying Case

The teacher of children with visual impairments might bring a carrying case of objects that can be helpful in an intervention. Below are some suggested items that can be included in the carrying case.

Item	Use
Blankets (one baby blanket and one quilt)	Floor mat Positioning
U-shaped travel baby pillow (e.g., Boppy)	Positioning baby's head and body
Vibrating toys and pillow	Stimulation Interest object
Massage textures	Tactile stimulation
Lights (e.g., penlights with plastic or balloon covers, flashlights)	Alerting Highlighting
Small light box	Table Lighted background
Red tray with yellow placemat	Color attention Contrasting background
Cookie sheet and tin	Work surface Place to hold magnets
Wok-shaped bowl (small or medium sized)	Creating movement with objects in the bowl
Electric and duct tape in different colors	Drawing attention to items
Elastic	Hanging items
Fish tank tubing	Covering elastic
Washers or paperclips	Securing elastic
Hair scrunchie and wrist sweatband	Drawing attention to baby's wrist
Two mirrors	Visually motivating target Alerting
Bells (e.g., small teacher hand bell, desk bell, small jingle bells)	Visual alerting Cause and effect Auditory alerting

(continued)

Table 5.2 (continued)

Item	Use
Beads (shiny and red)	Visually motivating target
Checkerboard (red and black, or black and white)	Visually motivating target Alerting
Metallic and plastic pompoms	Visually motivating target Alerting\ Cause and effect
Colored ping pong ball in clear plastic tube	Visually motivating target Alerting to movement
Happy face motifs (e.g., on plates, balloons)	Visually motivating target Alerting
Balls (e.g., small metal ball, visually interesting balls)	Visually motivating target Movement
Larger rubber ball	Positioning Exercise
Two spinner toys	Visually motivating targets Shift gaze objects
Finger puppets (red and yellow)	Visually motivating targets
Baby socks (e.g., striped or wild pattern)	Stuffed for sound and grasp
Chime toy (e.g., Happy Apple)	Visually motivating target Cause and effect
Red puppet or toy (e.g., Elmo)	Visually motivating target Cause and effect
Slinky (red, yellow, or silver)	Visually motivating target Cause and effect
Party paper blow toy	Slow movement
Bubbles	Visually motivating target Alerting to movement
Mylar pinwheel	Movement Attention
Hand puppet (red or yellow)	Movement Attention Play

- On that day's intervention plan, make note of equipment to gather and songs to use during the session.

The Activity Is Planned to Engage the Baby's Attention and Interest

Properly pacing an activity and using motivating actions and items are important in engaging a baby during an intervention. Activities and sessions that are flexible and adapt to whatever seems to be engaging a baby that particular day or moment holds the baby's attention best. Session objectives can be folded into a baby's play and adapted to follow the baby's interests, as mentioned in the previous discussion of teachable moments. For example, if a baby seems interested in his or her own shoes, start a teaching session by featuring one of those shoes. Cue the baby by singing a song using the words that you are going to feature when you play with the shoe. Help the baby explore the shoe by using hand-over-hand technique. Add bells to the shoe and shake it to produce sound. Slip a hair scrunchie over the shoe to make it more visually enticing. Encourage the baby to pull the laces or closure tab of the shoe. Compare the baby's shoe with a parent's and talk about the concept of big and little. Babies may lose attention and interest when bored or tired; it is preferable to end an activity before that point. Suggestions for keeping the baby's attention and interest include the following:

- Initially conduct activities while a baby is seated on a parent's lap. This may offer help to a professional trying to engage a timid baby.

- Sing to the baby periodically while working with him or her. Using a familiar tune, such as *If You're Happy and You Know It* or *You Are my Sunshine,* improvise lyrics relevant to the teaching topic. Include the baby's name in the song.

- Determine the particular people, items, and activities that seem especially motivating for the baby. Try to include these into each activity when possible, either by saying the name or showing a photo of the person or object, or by having that person jointly participate in the intervention.

- Try to transition as seamlessly as possible from one motivating activity to another to avoid distracting interruptions. For example, if the next activity after playing with the shoe includes the use of a light box, then create a way to use the shoe to transition to the light box. For example, you could help the baby *walk* the shoe to the nearby light box. Put the shoe on the light box together as you reposition the baby. Stress the words shoe, lightbox, and on—maybe perhaps in a song. Gradually introduce another item to the light box to begin your next planned activity. Be sure to say "bye bye" to the shoe!

- Continue to change the objects or sounds used in in a particular activity if a baby seems to become bored. Sometimes making an unusual sound, such as a buzzing or a tongue clicking, while working with a baby and a particular toy can extend a baby's interest in that toy.

- Start activities using something that is known, such as a familiar object or routine, before adjusting an activity to include items that are unfamiliar to the baby, or actions that are slightly more challenging to perform.

- Shift the baby's physical position periodically.

- Be a little playful during the activity, if appropriate. Babies seem to love a little silliness!

The Activity Is Planned to Systematically Expand the Baby's Visual Skills

When combined, developmental profiles, interviews, checklists, the functional vision assessment, and the Early Visual Development Guide (see **Chapter 6**) all help identify progressive visual steps for babies with CVI. They can also help pinpoint which visual and developmental goals a baby has achieved, and which goals still need to be addressed by a planned activity or specific intervention. Introduction of the Early Visual Development Guide and suggestions for expanding a baby's visual skills is covered in **Chapter 6**.

The Activity Part of a Framework with Beginning, Middle, and End Cues

Unlike a baby with normal vision, a baby with CVI cannot use incidental looking to determine when an intervention session starts and stops. Therefore, nonvisual cues such as a specific phrase, song, or touch must provide that information. In a framed intervention session, each activity should start with an introductory cue, continue by presenting the actual activity, and then end with a concluding event, such as having the baby help put a toy away into the teacher's carry bag. In the absence of visual cues, this structure allows the baby to understand when an activity or intervention session starts and stops. Suggestions for creating a framework for a session include the following:

- Consistently begin an activity after a regular part of the baby's daily routine. By doing so, the baby can then anticipate an activity he or she expects to occur after another event. For example, if a baby consistently has a session using a light box after naptime, he or she will start to associate the two.

- Script specific words and actions into daily home routines and activities. The repetition of these exact words with the same actions will reinforce the connection between vocabulary and the concepts for which each word stands. Although this may seem especially artificial, it really works!

CREATING SUCCESSFUL INTERVENTIONS

When creating interventions to help a baby with CVI improve visual skills, each component of the intervention plays a role in its success. However, simply including a component within an intervention is not sufficient; the way in which each component of an intervention is presented is critical for a successful outcome.

Components of Successful Interventions

Many factors contribute to successful interventions. The following text focuses on several that are widely recognized as especially effective.

Direct Experience

Babies with CVI do not initially use distance vision well, nor do they have the ability to discriminate details. They cannot learn through listening or watching without also having direct, hands-on experience. These babies need to *directly interact* with objects, people, and activities in order to understand fully what is being presented. For example, when a parent is admiring flowers at a florist or in the garden, it is important for the baby who has CVI to actually touch and smell the flowers to get a concept of *flower*. Providing direct experience can be especially challenging when a baby who has CVI is part of a group of other children, such as during circle time. It is important to be sure that the baby who has CVI is provided with hands on experience and a demonstration even within the group. During story reading time, a baby with CVI needs a copy of the book being read, and ideally someone to help point out pictures or words.

Sound and Music

Sounds enhance a baby's interest in and memory of an activity or intervention. Babies can attend and learn by listening to the sounds around them once they know how to associate each sound with a real-life experience with which they are directly familiar. For example, it may be beneficial to make an audio recording of a particular intervention, and then play this recording for the baby periodically before revisiting the activity again. Melodic and rhythmic sound can also increase a baby's attention and interest, and also serve as transitions between different activities. For example, as mentioned previously, a teacher might recite a rhyme or sing a song with words that describe what activity will occur next. It is very important to connect sounds and words with direct experience for a baby who has CVI.

Language

An intervention should include planned words and concepts. For example, bathing can serve as a time to emphasize key words appropriate to the baby's level of language development. The word *water* can be emphasized for a baby with beginning language skills, while the word *splash* can be emphasized for a baby who is able to understand more receptive language. Verbal language specific to an activity can also be enhanced by adding signs, gestures, or cues, such as a tap on the hand, or by a connection with an item, such as water from the bath.

Scent

The sense of smell can enhance a baby's understanding and orientation within the environment. For example, the smell of bath oil can orient a baby to bath time just as the smell of food cooking can orient a baby to mealtime. Smell can also help calm a baby and stimulate his or her desire to explore (Anthony, Bleier, Fazzi, Kish, & Pogrund, 2002).

Touch

Babies with CVI along with other sensory issues, as mentioned previously, may be reluctant to experience touch. As a result, their early touch exploration may need to be guided as they are first learning to tolerate touch from others, and then as they start to tactually explore the environment themselves. Tactile exploration needs to be encouraged gradually—forcing a baby's hands to touch anything is <u>never</u> appropriate.

Motor Learning

Motor learning results from physically experiencing an action, object, or motion. It is learning that combines both movement and sensory experience. Motor learning is an essential intervention technique for babies with CVI to learn about their world because, at least initially, they cannot learn through observation. For example, like many children, babies who have CVI may spend time in their strollers each day. Without vision, their experience of the stroller may be limited to only what they touch: the seat, the backrest, and perhaps the guardrail. The addition of motor learning can help a baby who has CVI learn even more about his or her stroller. When not in the stroller, move his or her hands around the various parts of the stroller while a parent or teacher of children with visual impairments helps position the stroller for easy exploration and names parts aloud as they are encountered. The baby will eventually grasp the whole concept of *stroller*.

Equipment and Targets

Toys and other objects used in interventions can influence a baby's visual interest and engagement. In particular, it is important to use visually-motivating targets that are bright in color, have distinct designs such as geometric patterns, or produce sounds or movement that engage the baby. See **Object Visibility** in

Visually motivating targets like those seen in this photo are colorful, have distinct designs, and produce sound or movement. These characteristics added to toys or objects enhance a baby's visual interest.

Appendix A for ways to increase visual characteristics of an object. As always, increasing a baby's interest in an intervention helps ensure it will be successful.

Age and Developmental Level

When designing interventions, any activity selected should build on a baby's current skills and interests. It should also be age appropriate. A very young baby benefits from engaging in basic experiences. For example, if a baby is not yet responding to visual targets, experiences that encourage visual alerting are a foundation skill for learning more advanced vision skills. In contrast, an older baby benefits from experiences that build upon this foundation and engages their particular level of visual use. Older babies can practice visually locating a favorite toy before playing with it.

Child Oriented

Making sure that interventions consider and incorporate a baby's interests promotes effective teaching. Babies who have CVI are most interested and comfortable with actions or objects with which they are already a little bit familiar. For example, if a baby likes bouncing their feet up and down, a teacher of children with visual impairments can introduce the concept of cause and effect and incorporate the concepts of listening and curiosity into this activity by sliding a partially deflated Mylar balloon or a piece of bubble wrap material under the baby's feet. The unexpected responses caused by interacting with the material will help gain the baby's attention. When the baby bounces their feet up and down, they will feel and hear something unexpected when striking the balloon or bubble wrap. Because of these intriguing new sounds, they may be motivated to experiment. For example, the baby may bounce their feet against the balloon and bubble in order to recreate the sounds, or perhaps change the way in which they move their legs in order to create different sounds. This activity can help a baby understand and practice the concept of cause and effect: the idea that *I do something and something happens!* Once the baby's attention is gained, the teacher can slowly slide the balloon or bubble wrap along the baby's body and

A balloon, partially deflated like the one in this photo, can be used in an activity to teach cause and effect.

into their field of vision, offering an opportunity to view and handle the item.

Playful

Babies learn through play, and any intervention can be made playful. For example, adding a buzzing sound to an activity, or changing the volume on a sound-generating toy can pique a baby's interest. Strive to create or select activities that address targeted goals but are also fun and promote play. Using different sounds, incorporating language play such as rhymes, and moving in different ways are all ways to make activities fun and effective. These draw the baby's attention, helping to promote learning.

Functional

Functionally-based interventions incorporate the use of everyday objects in order to complete a task. More than simply presenting the baby with an activity to complete, functional interventions serve a larger purpose. In order to be considered a *functional* intervention, a task must have a clear purpose. For example, young children are commonly asked to insert pegs into the correct-shaped openings in a board but are usually not shown what purpose this task serves. As an alternative, instead of pegs, have a baby return an item such as a toothbrush or a marker to its proper holder. While the peg activity builds the same physical skills and concepts, this activity has the advantage of familiarizing babies with the purposes of everyday objects and where they are kept. Once a child practices a functional intervention like this one, the skills learned will become part of his or her daily routine.

Adjustable

A baby's ability to focus on a single activity for a long period of time is limited. A teacher can extend a baby's interest in an activity by slightly *adjusting,* or embellishing, the action, target,

A baby can be encouraged to maintain a position for an extend time while working on an activity if an interesting object is part of the activity. In this photo, the baby is holding a tummy position with head-up to watch the bell his dad is gently shaking.

or environment by adding a sound, by changing objects used, or moving to a different work area. For example, being placed into a prone position helps build trunk and neck muscles, but being left on his or her stomach can become stressful for a baby. However, if the baby is presented with interesting items that vary in size, shape, color, or movement, the baby's attention may be renewed, and they may be able to tolerate more time in a position that has a positive effect on their physical development.

Scaffolding

Once a baby with CVI learns a new skill, that skill becomes the foundation for learning other related but more complicated skills. Any activity or intervention that addresses one skill can gradually be expanded to include aspects of another more advanced skill. The instructional term for this is *scaffolding*. When employing scaffolding, a teacher of children with visual impairments systematically builds on a baby's existing skills. Each new skill, like a level in a physical scaffold, supports the learning of a more complicated skill, which, in turn, supports acquiring an even more complex skill.

For example, if a baby is gazing at a visually motivating target nearby, the teacher can encourage the baby to shift their gaze by moving the target just slightly to the baby's left or right. Alternatively, the teacher can encourage the baby to use hand-over-hand movement to reach and try to touch the target. Once the skill of gazing at a visually motivating target is learned, this skill plays a role in a more complicated task such as reaching for an object or being able to shift his or her gaze.

Design

Babies with CVI learn new skills if the teacher presents them in small increments of increasing difficulty. Suppose, for example, a baby is beginning to crawl toward a desired object or person. That baby is more likely to continue trying to move toward something if, at first, the target is very easy to reach, but then only gradually is moved farther and farther away. An additional skill of crawling over something very small, such as a blanket roll, can be added to the base skill of crawling. When an activity is *designed* in this way, it helps a baby achieve success by slowly adding to a single task's difficulty or complexity.

Teaching Strategies

Sound teaching strategies help ensure babies with CVI engage during interventions with their teachers as well as their parents. These strategies will also increase their ability to stay focused on an intervention. The following teaching strategies are essential tools when working with a baby with CVI.

Introducing the Intervention

Babies with CVI can be intimidated by sudden or unexpected movements. However, a baby may be more accepting of an intervention if the teacher first approaches the baby with an introductory sound-based activity, such as singing a special greeting song, or reciting a particular rhyme. After the starting sound activity, the teacher can then gradually introduce the actual intervention to be addressed that day.

Changes and Cues

Transitioning from one activity to another, or from one physical position to a different one, can cause a baby with CVI to become distracted, or perhaps even distraught. Cues are an effective way to help a baby more easily make this transition. Some examples of cues are tapping the baby lightly on his or her side, saying the word "turn" to indicate rolling over, or gently raising a baby's arms upward and saying "up" to prepare the baby to be held by an adult. At first, such cues can help a baby learn to adjust to position changes. However, eventually these cues may even motivate interest in the movement and help the baby learn to communicate wants such as being held by a caregiver.

Motivation

Motivators are an important part of effective interventions. Motivators should be specific to the baby, appropriate to the

The feeling of success after accomplishing a task or skill is a great motivator for learning as evidenced in this photo by the baby's wonderful, gleeful smile.

situation, and appropriate to the intervention. Babies, like adults, have specific motivators that can encourage them to initiate actions and stay engaged in an activity. For example, if a baby is motivated to look for and press a button on a favorite sound-producing toy, interest in the sound itself may be sufficient to lead the baby to want to press the button at another time just to recreate the pleasing result. The feeling of success that follows accomplishing a task can be especially motivating for older babies and children.

Teachers of children with visual impairments can determine what motivates a baby using their own observations as well as by reviewing parent questionnaires and interview notes. Some common motivators include the presence of one of the parents, parental attention, a bottle, pacifier, blanket, or a favorite toy. These motivators can be included as part of an intervention, such as an activity in which a baby looks for and then reaches out to grasp a favorite toy or pacifier. These motivators can also prolong a baby's interest in an activity. For example, while helping a baby learn how to roll over, having a parent positioned a foot or two away may encourage the baby to roll over simply to get closer to the parent—and maybe even get an extra snuggle, too.

Detractors, in contrast to motivators, are items, people, or events that inhibit a baby's interest or enthusiasm in an activity or intervention. Detractors can actually be used in positive ways during some activities, such as when encouraging a baby to use visual skills to select a more visually motivating target. For example, if an activity involves a baby learning to choose an item that the teacher names, use an item the baby is familiar with and drawn to, such as a favorite ball. Then, place the ball on a tray or light box along with another item that the baby is not familiar with, is not visually exciting, or which he or she does not like. When asked to find or pick up the ball, the baby will usually choose the favorite or more visually appealing item. Never use a detractor that can upset a baby. Verbal praise is another common motivator. Phrases such as "you pushed it" or "yes, you crawled to me" add to a baby's sense of accomplishment. Try to limit the use of the phrases "good boy" or "good girl." Not only are these phrases overused, they motivate a baby by having him or her please an adult instead of feeling well-deserved pride in his or her own successes.

Repetition

Babies typically enjoy repetition, and *creative repetition* can help babies learn a skill or concept. By repeating an intervention a set number of times and at specific times each day, a baby has increased opportunities to practice a skill. Even though babies typically enjoy repetition, they stay engaged even longer if the repeated action varies just slightly each time. For example, if a baby is learning to hit pieces of cereal with a toy hammer, the activity could be modified by giving the baby a big wooden spoon to use as a tool instead, or by changing the color of the cereal to be smashed. Eventually the task can be made more challenging by reducing the amount of cereal—this way the baby needs to look for the target *before* using the tool. In this intervention, a good motivator might be allowing the baby to eat pieces of the cereal.

Some babies who are visually impaired can develop *perseverative behavior:* the seemingly incessant repetition of a movement that does not appear to improve learning. For example, a child who is blind may repeatedly open the same kitchen cabinet door and then slam it closed again and again. While the sound produced by this action may provide auditory motivation for the baby, it quickly ceases to offer new learning opportunities. However, with some creative alternation, teachers can use such preservative behavior to create a learning opportunity. For example, if interesting objects and toys are attached to the inside of the cabinet door, and the baby is shown how to explore them, the repetitive opening of a cabinet door can instead be transformed into a learning opportunity.

Task Analysis

When employing *task analysis,* a teacher of children with visual impairments breaks down a complex task into its component parts, and then sequentially teaches the baby each part of it from the beginning to the end, one step at a time. Once the baby is able to perform all of these tasks consecutively, he or she has now learned how to complete a complex activity. **Sidebar 5.5** provides some examples of task analyses.

Backward Chaining

Similar to task analysis, *backward chaining* introduces the sequential steps in a task, one at a time. However, as the term implies, the difference is that the baby learns to perform a complex task in *reverse.* For example, the teacher first guides the baby through all of the steps of a complex task, such as grasping a wooden spoon and using it to strike a cooking pot it in order to make a sound. The baby works backwards with less help from the teacher in order to master the last step of the task. The last step (banging on the pot with a wooden spoon), is mastered first, while

Sidebar 5.5

Task Analysis

Task analysis involves breaking down the parts of a complex task into smaller, sequential steps, and then teaching each step one at a time (Pogrund, 2002a). In order to determine how to divide a task into its component parts, teachers and parents should perform the task themselves and take note of the steps involved. They can then teach the steps to the baby individually. Once a step is mastered, another is added, until the baby can perform all of the steps needed to complete the entire task.

Examples

A sample task for an infant can be to replace his or her pacifier. The task can be broken down as follows:

1. Locate the pacifier by touch. (It can be helpful to attach the pacifier to the baby's shirt with a pacifier clip or holder.)
2. Grasp the pacifier.
3. Bring the pacifier to the mouth.
4. Move the pacifier to fit between the lips correctly.

A sample task for toddlers might be hand washing. The task can be broken down as follows:

1. Find the sink.
2. Turn on the nozzle.
3. Wet the hands.
4. Find the soap.
5. Rotate the soap in the hands.
6. Return the soap to its holder.
7. Rinse the hands.
8. Turn off the nozzle.

(continued)

Sidebar 5.5 (continued)

9. Find a towel.

10. Dry the hands.

11. Return the towel.

the first step (reaching to find and grasp a spoon) is mastered last. Backward chaining can motivate a baby to complete all the steps of a complex activity with minimal assistance before they are able to complete it independently. Backward chaining allows the baby to experience the success of completing a task first, but still learning to master all of its steps.

Backward chaining is an effective strategy in teaching an older baby how to pull up his or her pants. First, the teacher or parent physically helps the child while he or she reaches for the pants. The child then grasps the pants that are already on his or her ankle and then jointly pulls the pants to the waist. The next step in backward chaining consists of the adult and child repeating the steps involved in pulling on the pants, but this time encouraging the child to pull the pants up to the waist independently without an adult's help. After successive sessions, the child eventually pulls on his or her pants independently.

Physical Guidance

Physically guiding a baby's hands can be a useful technique when performing an activity or exploring new objects. The two guiding techniques are hand-under-hand guidance and hand-over-hand guidance. When employing *hand-under-hand* guidance, the child places his or her hands on top of the teacher's hands, and then the adult's and child's hands move together to complete the task. In contrast, in *hand-over-hand* guidance, the teacher places his or her hands on top of the child's while directing the completion of a task (Holbrook & Rosenblum, 2017).

Hand-under-hand guidance is usually preferred with older children because it is less intrusive and allows the child to have more control (Chen, 2014b; Holbrook & Rosenblum, 2017). However, with babies, hand-over-hand is more effective because they need an adult to provide more physical guidance. Before guiding a baby's hands, a verbal cue should be provided to the baby. As already stated, you should <u>never</u> force a baby's hands.

Real Objects

The use of real objects was discussed in this chapter's section **Components of Successful Interventions**. *Real objects* play a major role in teaching a functional and useful lesson. Real objects are common everyday items such as spoons, mirrors, balls, toys, jewelry, or books. These objects can be effective when used in interventions because the baby is likely already familiar with them, and may even know these objects' names. A benefit of using real objects is that they likely continue to be a consistent part of the baby's daily experiences. Of course, familiar objects have another benefit in that they are readily accessible to most families. Another alternative to the classic pegboard activity is to have the child sort forks or spoons into their defined slots in a utensil tray.

Planned Visual Targets

Successful interventions typically employ visually motivating targets that a baby has already demonstrated the ability to see and in which the baby has already shown interest. As a visual skill becomes easier for a baby to accomplish, by adding planned visual targets, the intervention can be modified to make the task even more visually challenging. For example, a task that requires visually finding an object among a complex set of many can begin by having a target object be visually enhanced or placed with other items that are each differently colored than the object the baby is expected to find. However, that same task can be made more challenging by removing visual enhancements from the object in question or placing the object with items that are the same color.

CONCLUSION

Effective interventions include exercises, activities, planned daily routines, controlled learning environments, and life experiences designed to increase a baby's visual abilities and general development. When well planned, and carefully designed, an intervention can significantly impact a baby's developmental success in achieving goals.

When planning interventions, a teacher of students with visual impairments must take into consideration the parents' and baby's readiness to perform the intervention. The teacher of students with visual impairments must also take into account the characteristics of the environment in which an intervention is to take place, what objects or people seem to especially motivate the baby, and the strategies that are best suited to create a positive outcome. Be flexible—different types of interventions may be more effective at different times and in places. And have fun!

CHAPTER 6

Early Visual Development Guide

The Early Visual Development Guide is a planning tool designed to help parents and professionals provide interventions for a baby with cerebral visual impairment (CVI). The aspects of visual development addressed by this guide are ones that babies with typical vision achieve naturally in the first several months of life. Babies with CVI, on the other hand, may take longer to develop visual skills and benefit from early interventions specifically designed to address these first steps of visual development (Topor, 2014).

The guide presents initial skills a baby with CVI needs to acquire in order to begin early visual development (see **Figure 6.1**). It is intended to be a flexible tool; therefore, skills can be added or deleted as needed to address a baby's individual learning situation. The guide is not an assessment tool, and skills are not presented in a sequential order. The general principles behind the interventions suggested in the guide are simply stated: encourage the baby with CVI to use vision by providing them with an object or person they are likely to be interested in. Once the baby visually recognizes that object or person, make that object or person gradually more challenging to locate. Reinforce the *social* component of vision by allowing the baby to have access to whatever her or she is looking at.

EARLY VISUAL DEVELOPMENT GUIDE

Rationale for the Guide

Babies who have CVI have a unique visual disability that is unlike that of babies with ocular impairments. However, what makes CVI different can also be an advantage. The visual pathways in the brain of babies with CVI can often rewire and reorganize. New neural pathways can take over the processing of

Figure 6.1
Early Visual Development Guide

Child's Name: _____ DOB: _____

Visual Alerting

_____ Keeps eyes open when awake

_____ Tolerates visual stimulation

_____ Alerts to light

- _____ Briefly alerts to light at near in a dark room
- _____ Briefly alerts to light at near in low light room
- _____ Alerts to light at near in a room with normal light
- _____ Alerts to a shiny or illuminated target at near

_____ Alerts to movement at near and midrange

_____ Shows preference for specific colors (Note the colors)

_____ Alerts to visually motivating targets at near

_____ Alerts to visually motivating targets at midrange and beyond

Visual Engagement

_____ Holds brief fixation on stationary, favorite, lighted objects at near

_____ Holds brief eye contact or regards face of familiar person

_____ Fixates on an increasing number of visually motivating targets at near and midrange

_____ Locates visually motivating targets that are at near and at eye level

_____ Adjusts fixation when desired target is slightly moved from view

_____ Shifts gaze between two visually motivating targets at near or midrange

Figure 6.1 (continued)

_____ Spontaneously fixates on many visually motivating targets at near or midrange

_____ Fixates with less visual delay on visually motivating targets at near and midrange

_____ Gazes toward and maintains attention on targets at midrange and at far

_____ Fixates to indicate intention or a desired target

_____ Looks toward a named target or person at near or midrange

_____ Looks toward dropped visually motivating targets

_____ Fixates on a desired visually motivating target out of many at near

_____ Fixates on named photo or picture of a known object or familiar person

Visual Integration

_____ Moves position to improve fixation or view of target

_____ Maintains fixation while reaching toward a visually motivating target

_____ Visually locates and moves to desired or named target at midrange or far

_____ Imitates or responds to gestures, signs, or smiles viewed from increasing distances

_____ Uses visual interest during therapy sessions

Approximate distances:

Near: up to 12 inches; _Mid:_ 12 inches to 3 feet; _Far:_ approximately 3 to 6 feet.

visual data that normally are processed by damaged areas of the brain. This ability of the brain to rewire and reorganize means it is possible to help babies with CVI learn to increasingly use visual skills more effectively.

As has been stressed throughout this book, a crucial factor that can influence and enhance a baby's ability to develop visual skills is the *strategic* and *early* introduction of specific interventions. Any delay in introducing interventions does not take advantage of the critical period of brain plasticity (see **Chapter 3**) when a baby's brain is especially plastic. It is essential that both professionals and parents understand delaying early interventions could affect the baby's future visual abilities. The Early Visual Development Guide is designed to help professionals and parents identify the appropriate visual skills and interventions on which to focus in order to best enhance a baby's visual development.

Organization of the Guide

This guide divides the behaviors or visual skills a baby must learn into three areas: *visual alerting*, *visual engagement,* and *visual integration with other developmental skills.* Each area has its own section that describes behaviors related to that one particular visual skill.

Although a child's visual skills may progress sequentially, the behaviors related to each skill may be achieved in any order, while some may never be achieved at all. Once a skill has been acquired, it can be marked as completed, while skills that a baby is still learning are left without any notation. Although some of the suggested skills outlined within one topic may sometimes seem similar to those already described earlier in another area, read the text carefully because the latter skills may include the addition of subtle adjustments that require a slightly more complex visual skill. For example, a baby might *adjust fixation* when a target is slightly moved in visual engagement. However, in visual integration, a child may *move his or her physical position to improve fixation*, which is a more complex process. Any skills a baby is still trying to master can help identify goals and objectives to be included in the home action plan. (Activities to support skill development can be found in **Appendix A.**) Please note in the text that follows, visual distances are categorized as being near, mid, or far. Each has a specific meaning.

- **Near distances** are those up to 12 inches.
- **Mid distances** are those from 12 inches to 3 feet.
- **Far distances** are those 3 feet and beyond.

Visual Alerting

Visual alerting refers to subtle changes in a baby's behavior that indicate he or she has perceived a visual target. Although a baby with CVI may initially appear not to see a visual target, visual alerting behaviors indicate the brain is actually *neurologically* responding to visual stimuli. The signs that a baby is responding to visual stimuli can be subtle, including slight changes in facial muscles, eye movements, and breathing patterns. In addition, the baby who is responding to a visual stimulus may also become fussier, close his or her eyes, or turn away from an object shown. The visual alerting behaviors described below likely indicate a baby's earliest subconscious awareness of visual stimuli.

Keeps Eyes Open When Awake

Some babies with CVI do not keep their eyes open when they are awake. In some cases, these babies may have a condition unrelated to CVI called *ptosis* in which neurological disorders that affect the nerves or muscles of the upper eyelids cause the eyelids to fall or droop. In contrast, other babies with CVI may be hypersensitive to sensory stimulation. As a result, they may not be able to tolerate visual stimuli of any kind, and may close their eyes whenever they are presented with a visual stimulus. Suggestions for helping a baby gradually begin to open the eyes include the following:

- Refer a baby with ptosis to a pediatric ophthalmologist. They can determine whether the condition can be corrected surgically.

- Manually open a baby's eyelids gently and briefly during massage time in order to enable the baby to briefly see a visually motivating target such as a filtered penlight beam or a shiny pinwheel.

- Provide low light and soft sounds in the environment whenever a baby is quietly alert.

- Offer many repeated opportunities at regular intervals throughout the day for the baby to respond to either lights or movement.

- Use a regular cue at the end of an intervention. For example, a baby with CVI may attempt to control his or her discomfort to sensory stimulus by acting as if her or she is sleeping. By keeping the eyelids shut as if asleep, he or she can avoid experiences or sensations that are unfamiliar or unsettling until the baby becomes accustomed to them. Using a cue such as singing a "goodbye" song, hand-clapping a short rhythmic pattern, or tapping the baby's hand rhythmically may encourage the baby to anticipate the session's conclusion and inspire him or her to open his or her eyes, thereby extending the session a little longer.

- Introduce touch interventions and massage. For example, developmental, occupational, and physical therapists may introduce specific stimulation patterns using a soft brush in a touch intervention called *brushing,* which can help the baby become more accustomed to physical stimulation (Caulfield, 2000; Harris & Tada, 1983). The benefits of massaging infants has been affirmed by medical and therapeutic groups such as the International Association of Infant Massage Instructors, and in medical journals such as the Mayo Clinic Healthy Lifestyles online newsletter. In the author's experience, massage can often lower anxiety and reduce stress hormones, which can help ease a hypersensitive baby into tolerating sensory interventions (Field, 1995).

Tolerates Visual Stimulation

Damage to the brain in babies with CVI may result in *sensory processing disorders.* Sensory processing disorders may include hypersensitivity to touch, sound, and visual stimuli, making visual interventions difficult. Babies with CVI require help in order to learn to cope with the complexities of the sensory environment. Suggestions for increasing tolerance for visual stimuli include the following:

- Present sensory inputs to a baby one at a time rather than presenting several simultaneously (Roman-Lantzy, 2018). For example, when introducing an object that is especially visually stimulating such as a toy that features a happy face design, be sure that any distracting sounds in the background are diminished and the play area is not cluttered.

Babies with CVI require help in order to learn to cope with the complexities of the sensory environment. In this photo, the teacher of children with CVI presents some beads to a child. Sensory inputs should be presented one at a time rather than several simultaneously.

- Begin interventions in low light settings, and then gradually increase the amount of light over the course of the intervention. When working with a baby during a time that is not visually demanding, such as during a massage session, start with just one low wattage light source to illuminate the area. Gradually, once the baby demonstrates increased tolerance by keeping his or her eyes open wider and for longer, then add more lights or increase a particular lamp's wattage.

- Have the baby wear a visor, cap, or tinted lenses. As the baby keeps his or her eyes open wider or longer, indicating increased visual tolerance, gradually reduce reliance on these tools over time.

Alerts to Light

Visual alerting to light includes four different behaviors. Each of these behaviors describes a baby's ability to alert to a light source or to a nearby illuminated target under lighting of varying intensity.

- Briefly alerts to a small light source such as a penlight at near (about 2–5 inches away) in a *dark* room

- Briefly alerts to a small light source at near in a *low-light* (about 15 watts) room

- Alerts to light at near in a *normally-lighted* (roughly a 60-watt light source) room

- Alerts to a shiny or illuminated target at near in *any normally-lighted* room

Gradually introduce new targets that demand greater visual alertness. For example, instead of having a baby focus on a flashlight itself, have him or her attempt to focus on a target illuminated by a flashlight. These four different behaviors also indicate a baby's visual responses may change from briefly alerting to fully alerting, which may indicate his or her behaviors are more intentional. While these levels of visual alerting to light are generally sequential, it is important to remember that the visual responsiveness of babies with CVI fluctuates depending on various factors, such as their physical well-being or level of comfort within a particular area. In addition, as discussed in the section on physical readiness in **Chapter 5**, a baby may be better able to visually alert when his or her body is properly supported during visual activities. Suggestions for addressing and stimulating alerting behaviors include the following:

- Present a small penlight within a few inches of the baby's eyes in a dark area, with repetition at scheduled times. Note that this is a more aggressive exercise that may challenge a baby's level of visual comfort: conduct it cautiously, and limit to situations in which activating initial visual alerting is the goal. Although it may seem more aggressive than other techniques, in the author's experience, it has proven to be an effective means for initiating visual alerting for a baby who has previously demonstrated none or only minimal visual response. The teacher of children with visual impairments can also move the light to different locations in relation to the baby in order to determine the most responsive areas of the baby's visual field in which to introduce visual targets for stimulation and learning. Shining the light through a red or yellow filter, two colors that often visually stimulate a baby with CVI, may make it easier to stimulate visual alerting.

- If the baby does not respond to a penlight, briefly use a more intense light, such as a red flashlight directed through a red filter. Never use strobe lights to stimulate visual alerting since they can trigger seizures in some babies.

- If the baby consistently alerts to a light presented within a dimly-lit environment, slowly increase the environmental lighting until the baby can alert to a lighted target under normal lighting conditions.

- Follow a baby's daily routines with a visual activity. A baby may be more prepared to use vision if a visual activity consistently follows another activity such as diapering, massage, or eating.

- Reinforce the baby's visual experience. When the baby visually alerts to a light or target, the teacher or parent should offer verbal reinforcement such as saying, "You see that!" or, "You were looking at the light!" While the teacher or parent should speak enthusiastically, be mindful not to speak in a way that distracts the baby from the act of looking.

Alerts to Movement at Near and Midrange

Since they are more visually motivating, a baby with CVI is more likely to respond to shiny or reflective objects that give the impression of movement. Similarly, a baby who is in motion because he or she is being carried by a caregiver or is sitting in a moving swing or rocking chair may be more visually stimulated by nearby stationary objects. Suggestions for providing targets with movement properties include the following:

- Employ mirrors, Mylar pom-poms, or other shiny objects. Reflective objects can give the appearance of movement.

Shiny or reflective objects give the impression of movement which is very visually stimulating. This photo shows several examples of reflective and shiny objects to use to stimulate a baby's visual awareness.

- Place the baby in a room that has a ceiling fan. Sometimes the moving fan blades can encourage looking.

- Gently shake or wave visual targets in front of the baby.

- Use toys that move, such as a Slinky, pinwheel, or party spinner. Shining a flashlight through a Slinky may increase the baby's motivation to look.

- Provide objects around the baby that produce sound in addition to light and movement. Sound-producing objects enhance sensory stimulation, which includes vision.

Shows Preference for Specific Colors

Babies with CVI often react to certain colors more than others (Roman-Lantzy, 2018). In the author's experience, the colors that appear to stimulate the most visual attention from babies with CVI are red and yellow. Neon, vibrant, or highly-saturated colors can also elicit positive responses. Suggestions for enhancing the use of preferred colors include the following:

- Once a baby's preferred colors have been identified, add them to other targets by using stickers or ribbons.

- Use colored tape to highlight objects or decor in the baby's room, or use it to mark the outlines of a complex visual target such as a geometric pattern.

- Provide the baby with a variety of objects such as toys, utensils, or cups, in his or her preferred colors.

Alerts to Visually Motivating Targets at Near

Babies with CVI have difficulty with distance viewing and focusing on targets that are far away. As a result, they are more likely to attend and alert to objects presented close by. If the teacher of children with visual impairments eliminates any visual distractions that appear in the background, a baby has an easier time concentrating on target objects presented at near. Suggestions for providing visual targets at near include the following:

- Use objects that are familiar to the baby, but appear in visually motivating colors or designs.

Babies with CVI are visually attracted to many visually motivating objects. The bright pom pom in this photo incorporates many of those visually motivating characteristics such as color, reflective surfaces, and movement.

- Before beginning a daily routine, hold an object used as part of that routine near the baby. For example, presenting a bottle before feeding time may motivate the baby to start looking toward the bottle during subsequent feedings.

Alerts to Visually Motivating Targets at Midrange and Beyond

Once a baby visually alerts to motivating targets nearby, the distance at which those targets are presented can be gradually increased in order to encourage the baby to visually alert to targets that are farther away. Suggestions for providing targets at midrange (12 inches to 3 feet) and beyond include the following:

- Use lights in the baby's preferred color. At first, hold the lights close to the baby, but then gradually move them farther and farther away. Increasing the distance just an inch or two in each subsequent session is a good rule of thumb.

- Practice a reciprocal activity such as waving or smiling, gradually increasing the distance from the baby.
- Begin to talk to the baby when entering the room instead of waiting until entering the baby's line of vision.

Visual Engagement

Visual engagement is *interest* in visual targets. It can be observed in a behavior such as spontaneous direct visual fixation. Visual engagement differs from visual alerting because it includes *intention.* When a baby is visually engaged, he or she exhibits increased visual attention, interest in, and preference for certain visual targets. The baby is receptive and is prepared to learn to use vision to acquire information, relate to others visually, or look at objects that pique his or her curiosity. These and other behaviors that indicate visual engagement develop once a baby is able to alert spontaneously toward a variety of different targets.

Holds Brief Fixation on Stationary, Favorite, and Lighted Targets at Near

A baby looks at a visually motivating target when it is something with which he or she is already familiar and already enjoys. If an object is familiar and enjoyable, a baby will gaze intentionally. He or she will also hold his or her gaze for a longer time than when first alerting to the target. Suggestions for helping a baby to fixate gaze on targets at near include the following:

- Employ visual targets that include lights, or illuminate targets by shining a light on them, since babies with CVI can see bright objects more easily.
- Whenever presenting a visual target, be sure to allow sufficient time for the baby to respond to it. A baby with CVI needs more visual processing time to find and fixate on targets than a baby with normal vision does.
- Choose targets that a baby may find especially motivating. For example, a baby may feel more inclined to look at a pacifier if he or she knows a caregiver places it in his or her mouth after

Babies with CVI need extra time to find, fixate, and process visual targets. The baby in this photo is looking intently at a lighted toy. His visual interest may even increase as he looks at the toy.

he or she looks at it. Similarly, a baby may feel encouraged to look at his or her favorite blanket if he or she knows he or she is going to be snuggled in it whenever he or she does so.

Holds Brief Eye Contact or Regards Faces of Familiar People

Showing visual regard for faces and establishing eye contact with others can be more or less difficult for babies with CVI depending on the location of their brain damage (Fazzi, Molinari, & Hartmann, 2015). Babies with CVI may find the complexity of human faces challenging to see (Roman-Lantzy, 2018). As a result, instead of looking at a person's face or eyes, a baby may instead look away from or look at the person's hairline. However, learning how to establish eye contact is an important visual and social skill to learn in order to bond and communicate socially with others. Teachers and parents can help babies with

CVI learn to establish eye contact and visually regard faces in the following ways:

- Place objects featuring face motifs around the baby's crib in order to help the baby become familiar with facial details and patterns. Party plates decorated with happy faces are easy to obtain or create and place on the sides of a crib.

- When working with a baby, teachers and parents can provide verbal reminders for the baby to look at their face at appropriate times. For example, teachers and parents can say, "look at me," to remind a baby to gaze at their face when greeting him or her.

- Wear eyeglasses featuring dark rims. These can accentuate the eyes, making it easier for a baby with CVI to look toward them. (This might seem silly, but it works!)

Learning to establish eye contact for a baby with CVI is very important to building visual and social skills which help him or her bond and communicate socially with others. In this photo, the baby is practicing making eye contact and is intently looking at the adult's mouth with interest.

- Attract attention to the face by accentuating its features. For example, applying makeup around the eyes and bright lipstick, or simply wearing a large fake mustache can draw the baby's attention toward the face.

Fixates on an Increasing Number of Visually Motivating Targets at Near and Midrange

As a baby's inventory of visual targets grows, and he or she is able to regard targets presented in the central and preferred visual fields, the baby is able to begin to fixate on an even larger number of targets. When a baby can fixate on a target at near or midrange, he or she can now fixate a little faster. The baby may even start to fixate on targets that are not particularly bright or specifically colored or designed. Suggestions for helping to increase a baby's ability to fixate on a greater number of targets include the following:

- Gradually add new visually motivating items to the repertoire of familiar objects used during playtime.
- Try to introduce new toys or items that feature more subtle visual characteristics. For example, instead of using a shiny toy in a baby's preferred color, try using one decorated in pastel colors.

Locates Visually Motivating Targets That Are at Near and at Eye Level

If a baby finds an object interesting during a session, he or she may begin to spontaneously seek it in subsequent interactions. When a baby spontaneously seeks a particular toy or object, it is a sign that a baby's visual interest and memory are increasing for nearby targets and that the baby is starting to visually engage with them more often. Note that nearby targets located at a baby's eye level are more likely to be seen first. Suggestions for increasing ability to locate targets at near include the following:

- Place some of a baby's favorite items around his or her crib. Doing so may encourage looking at them before and after sleeping.

- Place a wrist rattle, hair scrunchie, or toy watch on the baby's wrist. Each of these encourage a baby's visual attention.

Adjusts Fixation When Desired Target Is Slightly Moved

If a baby is looking at an interesting visual target and it is moved slightly outside of the baby's direct fixation, the baby adjusts fixation by adjusting his or her gaze, or by slightly turning his or her head toward the target. Suggestions for helping a baby with CVI adjust fixation when a target is moved include the following:

- Present targets to the left or right of the baby's midline instead of directly in front of him or her. Targets presented to the left or right may be easier for the baby to see because the visual field loss associated with CVI can interfere with midline fixation. Once the baby has fixated on an object, shift the position of the target very slightly, and then wait for the baby to re-fixate.

- Move a colorful puppet, an object decorated with a happy face design, a visually motivating, or favorite target slightly away from a baby's direct line of sight. This encourages the baby to actively look after the object has been moved.

Shifts Gaze Between Two Visually Motivating Targets at Near or Midrange

When a baby shifts gaze, he or she redirects fixation from one target to another. Shifting gaze indicates that a baby is simultaneously aware of more than one object and is also able to purposefully re-fixate from one object to another. Suggestions to help a baby learn to shift gaze include the following:

- Provide two favorite targets, holding them a few inches apart either laterally or diagonally from the baby. Activate each target one at a time, either by gently moving or jiggling it, or by having it produce a sound. First activate one target, and then wait for the baby to look at it. Next, activate the second target, and once again, wait for the baby to look. Repeat the activity.

- Offer verbal reinforcements, such as "you saw the toy" or "you looked at the ball." Doing so helps the baby connect the verbs *see* or *look* with the object's name as well as with the physical act of looking. Note, however, that this activity is intended to encourage the baby to use vision, and not merely respond to your voice or commands.

Spontaneously Fixates on Many Visually Motivating Targets at Near or Midrange

Once a baby is developmentally ready to start looking spontaneously, he or she may now look about the environment without any adult intervention or encouragement in order to locate favorite objects. Providing a controlled learning environment (as explained in **Chapter 5**) may also encourage the baby to spontaneously look around. Suggestions to encourage spontaneous looking include the following:

- Ensure the environment is relatively quiet, and the baby is alert and feels physically comfortable. During these quiet alert times, it is important to place favorite objects nearby to engage the baby.

- Affix objects to areas in the environment that the baby notices when he or she is looking around. For example, hang a red bell or stuffed Elmo toy on a high chair tray to encourage looking during mealtime.

- If a baby is seated, make sure his or her body is fully supported. As an alternative, place the baby on his or her back in order to prevent distractions resulting from bodily discomfort.

Fixates with Less Visual Delay on Visually Motivating Targets at Near and Midrange

Babies with CVI frequently exhibit *visual latency*, or a lag time between when a target is presented for observation and when they actually fixate on it. The length of this delay is reduced after babies have multiple visual experiences and continued practice in looking. Suggestions to reduce visual latency include the following:

- Present visually motivating targets, such as lights or shiny objects, or items that move or make noise during a play session.

- Repeat familiar visual activities within different daily routines to help the baby learn to fixate more rapidly. For example, regularly show the baby a spoon before actually using it to bring food to the mouth, or consistently show the baby his or her diaper before beginning a diaper change.

Gazes Toward and Maintains Attention on Targets at Midrange and at Far

Babies with CVI have difficulty with distance viewing—many may behave as if they are nearsighted (Roman-Lantzy, 2018). Experience, motivation, and practice may help a baby start to use distance vision more often. Suggestions for encouraging distance vision include the following:

- Say the names of familiar objects when the baby is interacting with them. Eventually, the baby knows what object to look for in the distance whenever the name of the target is spoken.

- Point out visually interesting objects at a distance such as brightly colored cars, trucks, and signs when traveling with the baby.

Fixates to Indicate Intent or a Desired Target

A baby may spontaneously use vision to indicate intent or desire. For example, he or she may fixate directly on a target he or she wants to play with or may look at a person by whom he or she wants to be picked up. Suggestions for encouraging use of vision to indicate *intent* include the following:

- Teach the baby that using vision can produce actions. For example, if the baby looks at a chime toy, move it closer to him or her so he or she can touch it or manipulate it to produce a noise. As a result, he or she may start to connect looking at a toy with being given it.

A baby can learn to use vision to indicate intent or desire. The little girl in this photo is using eye contact to show interest in the activity with her mother.

- Remind the baby verbally or with a gesture to look at a familiar or favorite person before being picked up. Eventually, the baby will be encouraged to use eye contact to indicate whenever he or she wants to be held by a caregiver.

Looks Toward a Named Target or Person at Near or Midrange

A baby visually locates a favorite object or person, even at a distance, when he or she is specifically asked to look at or find that specific person or target. This skill involves both searching and fixating within a baby's near and midrange field in response to a verbal request. Suggestions for encouraging looking include the following:

- Play a "people finding" game. For example, ask the baby to look for a parent who is nearby in order to practice differentiating one adult from another. A reward for using vision in this way may be to be picked up and played with by whichever person was named.

- Place a large piece of furniture such as a highchair in a different location about six feet from the baby, and then ask whether he or she is able to find it.

Looks Toward Dropped Visually Motivating Targets

A baby may look for items that have moved away suddenly. This behavior indicates the development of visual curiosity as well as an understanding of the concept of object permanence. Suggestions for encouraging visual curiosity and understanding object permanence include the following:

- Play "peek-a-boo" games. Have an adult partially hide and then quickly appear in order to help build the concept of object permanence.

- Drop visually motivating and lighted targets and toys. When a target is visually stimulating, it will be easier to locate. In addition, if a baby is interested in an object, he or she is more likely to want to search for it. For example, when the baby is in his or her infant seat on the floor, sit close by and engage the baby with a favorite toy such a yellow squeaky rubber duck. While the baby is looking toward the duck, let it fall to the ground. If the baby does not look toward the fallen duck right away, squeeze it so it squeaks, or jiggle it until the baby looks at it. After repeating this activity several times with one object, switch to a different favorite toy or item. As the baby's skill in locating dropped items improves, drop items at greater distances from the baby.

- Play the drop and find game just described, but instead use a target that makes a continuous sound, such as a kitchen timer or a music box. If a dropped object makes sounds without interruption, the sound may help the baby locate it.

Fixates on a Desired Visually Motivating Target Out of Many at Near

A baby can now begin to look at several objects and visually distinguish a desired item among several. This indicates the baby is now able to search and choose. Suggestions to encourage discerning a motivating target from amongst others include the following:

- Provide the baby three items to look at. One should be a desired favorite target, while the other two should be items in which the baby is not particularly interested. If an adult says the name of the favored target, a baby may be more inclined to look at that one before looking at the two others. Repeating this activity with the same three objects will help ensure the baby learns to identify the specifically named and desired item when placed among all three.

- Present multiple objects on a display board, cookie sheet, or light box. Each of these surfaces provides an uncluttered background, which makes it easier for the baby to see and distinguish among visual targets arranged in a group.

- When playing the *select the named item* game described above, reward the baby by providing the named target once the baby has fixated on it.

Fixates on a Named Photograph or Picture of Known Object or Familiar Person

Once a baby begins to recognize certain objects and people by their appearances and names, he or she may next be able to visually associate actual people or objects with photographs of them. A baby should be able to make this association because he or she both knows the name of the item or person and has an interest in them. Eventually, a baby with CVI may even associate a photo of an object with a stylized illustration that bears a close likeness to the object. Suggestions for encouraging understanding of symbolic representations of familiar objects and people include the following:

- First, show the baby two actual targets or toys—one favorite and one neutral. Then, show photographs of these two targets while repeating their names aloud and simultaneously holding both the named item and the photograph of it. After this demonstration is repeated several times, show the baby only the photograph of the favorite target or toy and then ask the baby to look at or select the actual object on a tray placed in front of him or her.

- After the baby can associate actual toys or objects with photographs of those objects, he or she can begin to learn to associate them with realistic illustrations that clearly resemble the real thing. Using the same procedure described above, the baby begins to associate objects shown with illustrations of those same objects.

- Show the baby three photographs of three different objects, but without the actual items present. Then ask the baby which item depicted in a photograph he or she most wants to hold. Once the baby is able to indicate the photo of the item he or she wants—either by looking, reaching, or verbalizing—the baby should be given the actual item to play with. Eventually, this activity can be repeated with illustrations of the three objects.

- Place photographs of toys found within the baby's sleeping area in his or her crib, promoting time for quiet review. If the baby has a favorite stuffed bear in the crib, secure a photograph of that bear on the side rails of the crib. Eventually, repeat this process using an illustration of a stuffed bear.

- Keep photographs and stylized pictures in an album that can be used when telling a bedtime story. Parents might sit with the baby before bed and encourage them to leaf through the book with help as needed. If the baby turns to a page that includes his or her own photograph, the parents might tell a short story about them. Photographs of objects could also provide the parent an opportunity to describe how the baby interacted or played with that object recently. Imagination and enthusiasm when looking at this book is key to its effectiveness.

Visually Locates Desired Visually Motivating Target within a Group or Cluster of Items

Once a baby is able to use vision more selectively, the baby can then begin to visually identify a target presented against a more visually complex background. For example, the baby may be able to locate a particular favorite toy among others stored in a box or on a shelf, or on a more complex visual field like a patterned tablecloth or bedspread. Suggestions to enhance the ability to locate targets against complex backgrounds include the following:

- Initially space a few objects three or four inches apart from each other, then gradually add additional items to increase visual complexity. First, have a baby find a toy in a box that contains only two or three items. Over time and after repeating this activity, add additional objects to the box to make finding the toy increasingly more visually challenging.

- Line up items and toys on a bookshelf that is at the baby's eye level when he or she is seated. On several occasions, sit with the baby and name the items on the shelf. Occasionally pick up one of the items while naming it and let the baby play with it. Return the item to the shelf, repeating its name several times while doing so. After several repetitions, ask the baby to find a toy by name: "Can you get Dad the polka dot elephant toy we like?" Help the baby find the named toy if he or she seems confused. Repeat this game often.

Visual Integration

Visual integration is the simultaneous use of vision along with other actions, such as listening, moving, or speaking. Once a baby is better able to spontaneously use his or her visual abilities, the baby can then begin to use vision while simultaneously using other developmental skills. For example, a baby may be able to maintain visual fixation on a favorite toy while also reaching for it or looking closely at it while rotating the toy in order to examine it better. Similarly, he or she can look toward a desired person while simultaneously moving toward that person.

Moves Position to Improve Fixation or View of Target

As a baby begins to maintain fixation on targets that are visually interesting, the baby can then move his or her head, or try to move the body's trunk to regain fixation on a target that has been relocated. Suggestions to encourage movement and fixation include the following:

- After the baby has fixated on a favorite target, move the target slightly to the side, giving the baby another opportunity to practice locating it.

- As the baby learns to move his or her head to adjust fixation, continue to move targets farther and farther away from the original fixation point. Encourage the baby to either look for or move toward the object.

- Once the baby can more readily locate moved targets, try playing a hideand seek game with them. Place the target or toy partially behind a nearby piece of furniture or blanket, and then encourage the baby to look for it.

Maintains Fixation While Reaching Toward a Visually Motivating Target

Babies with CVI have difficulty combining visual fixation with other developmental skills such as movement. A baby may start to attempt to reach for a previously viewed target because of growing interest and engagement. However, he or she may not be able to maintain his or her gaze while simultaneously reaching for the target. Suggestions for encouraging looking and reaching in tandem include the following:

- Make sure the baby's body is properly supported, using prescribed braces or body supports as necessary.

- Gently guide the baby through the process of reaching for a target using hand-over-hand guidance, gradually reducing support until the baby can start to reach independently. Remind the baby to look at the toy and reach for it together.

- Allow sufficient waiting time to allow the baby to generate visual motor activity.

- Move a desired target slightly so the baby cannot physically connect with it from visual memory. The baby needs to redirect his or her gaze to find the object, gradually learning the need to maintain fixation and reach simultaneously in order to obtain the target.

- Offer multiple opportunities to practice combining vision with movement.

- Practice engaging visually while listening to a parent or teacher reading a book. If a page on a book contains one or two images, tell a short story about the images. This can help a baby learn to look and listen simultaneously.

Babies with CVI can have difficulty combining visual fixation with other developmental skills such as movement. The highly visually motivating toy in this photo has drawn the baby's visual attention and inspired visually integrated reaching.

Visually Locates and Moves to Desired or Named Target at Midrange or Far

As a baby develops visual curiosity, placing targets at increasing distances can entice a baby with CVI to physically move farther into his or her environment. Once a baby starts to move—either by rolling over, belly crawling, or crawling on all fours—help the baby locate and move to reach the desired target. Doing so motivates the use of vision to find other targets located farther away from the baby. A baby's first efforts may result in him or her covering only a very small distance, so it is important not to place targets too far away before the baby is ready to reach them. If an object is placed too far away, a baby may not see it at all, or may simply become discouraged and stop attempting to move toward it. Suggestions for encouraging movement include the following:

- Play games that combine the activities of visually finding targets and then moving toward them.

- Use favorite toys, lighted objects, or visually motivating targets in the baby's favorite color, placed at midrange, so that the targets are easier for the baby to see.

- Place oversized, familiar targets at midrange, giving the baby practice to locate them and then move to obtain them.

Imitates or Responds to Gestures, Smiles, or Objects Viewed from Increasing Distances

Using reciprocal gestures can encourage distance vision. Suggestions for encouraging reciprocal gestures include the following:

- Once the baby has practiced smiling at or waving back to adults positioned nearby, repeat this activity, placing adults at gradually increasing distances from the baby and at varying locations.

- Have adults speak to the baby while they also gradually move farther away from him or her.

- Engage the baby's interest when positioned at a slight distance by talking animatedly about something while hold it, such as a family pet.

Uses Visual Interest During Therapy Sessions

A baby's visual curiosity can prove to be a positive distraction when it is integrated into movement and exercises that address general development. A baby may need to engage in many therapy sessions in order to address difficulties related to CVI or other physical disabilities. As such, a baby may participate more successfully when visually interesting targets are provided. Both the baby's parents and teacher of children with visual impairments can demonstrate to therapists and other specialists how to use visual interest to increase attention during therapy sessions. Suggestions to enhance visual interest include the following:

- During activities such as tummy time—assuming the baby has sufficient core, head, and neck strength—present interesting targets and toys in front of him or her, or backlit by a light box or placed in front of a trifold screen. This can help hold the baby's attention while working on building trunk and neck strength.

- When using adaptive equipment such as a standing table, place a visually interesting target or toy on it with which the baby can interact. Be sure the target or toy is secured, so it does not slide away from the baby's reach, and clear all clutter from the table.

- Guide the baby in repeatedly swatting at a suspended toy or ball with his or her hand in order to increase arm strength and eye-hand coordination. Start with the target lowered, so it is close to the baby's hand. Then, gradually raise it higher once he or she can successfully hit the target.

Next Steps

A baby with CVI who has learned the skills presented in this guide is aware of visual stimulations. The baby is looking intentionally, spontaneously, and with increasing interest. The baby uses vision to respond to questions, generate an action, or select a desired or named target. He or she is also using visual abilities simultaneously with other developmental skills and is motivated by visual interest and curiosity.

After a baby with CVI has progressed through the three topic areas of visual skills presented in the guide, he or she is now ready to start using more advanced visual-motor and visual perceptual skills. The baby is ready to learn to play by imitating others, and to begin early literacy skills. Other resources such as Dr. Roman's scale (Roman-Lantzy, 2007), Dr. Dutton's interview (Dutton, 2015a), and information from current texts about children with cortical visual impairment (some of which are noted in this book's resources) provide information about these and more advanced visual skills to include in goal planning and developmental interventions.

FINAL WORDS

Babies with CVI can learn visual skills even though they appear to have little or no vision in the early months of life; this is a fact emphasized repeatedly throughout this book. It is especially important that both parents and professionals understand that although the human brain remains plastic throughout a person's life, the particular plasticity of a baby's brain makes learning to use vision more successful early in life. *Time is of the essence.* Incorporate early visual interventions into daily events while attending to a baby's many other needs. To postpone early visual interventions because of other needs may affect positive visual learning. Interventions that help babies resolve the visual challenges presented by CVI are key to this early learning. Step-by-step interventions designed to help develop early visual learning are identified in the *Intervention Readiness Guide* and the *Early Visual Development Guide.*

It is also important that professionals working with babies with CVI understand parents of these babies are not just clients, but also partners. Parents are the ones who continue to help their children beyond infancy, helping them learn and develop skills into childhood and adulthood. It is also important for professionals

This photo of happiness between the adult and baby suggests that parents of babies with CVI can see how the energy, time and persistence they put into implementing the early visual and developmental interventions can help their children lead successful, productive, and meaningful lives.

and parents alike to understand that the parents' journey from grief and confusion to eventual acceptance and understanding has an impact on their baby's development and influences the parents' ability to consistently follow through with recommended interventions.

Professionals need to realize while the needs and intervention approaches for babies who have an ocular visual diagnosis often overlap those with CVI, there are nonetheless important differences. These differences must be taken into account when determining goals, planning interventions, and attending to a baby's needs.

Parents of babies with CVI may understandably feel discouraged and have little idea how the hopes and dreams they have for their baby and family will be achieved. However, it is important for parents to understand that although they may currently feel both confused and overwhelmed, there will come a time when these emotions will be replaced by pride and happiness about their baby's successes!

I know *positively* that success awaits babies, children, and adults with CVI at every juncture of their lives. Stories from my experience have validated this.

There is Cindy: she has multiple disabilities along with CVI. She lives in a group home and works at a fast-food restaurant. She and her mother remain close friends.

There is Caleb: he has both cerebral palsy and CVI but is currently working his way through college. He wants to enter the clergy and loves to drive a tractor on his family's farm.

There is Ally: she has significant health difficulties along with CVI. She is an artist who makes jewelry. Her creations are in high demand by her customers.

There are other artists, as well. Lisa has CVI and is a marvelous singer, while Melinda, who has CVI along with sensory defensiveness and cerebral palsy, is a photographer. Following behind them is seven-year-old Maia. She attends school in a regular classroom with the support of vision professionals. She loves dance and art and likes to read chapter books. She has an incredible sense of humor!

There is no denying the fact that parents of babies with CVI face challenges that parents of children with normal vision never face. However, it is also likely that parents of babies with CVI may feel an extra feeling of excitement with their child's successes and accomplishments. They can see for themselves how the energy, time, and persistence they put into implementing the early visual interventions recommended by their teacher of children with visual impairments can help their children lead successful, productive, and meaningful lives.

APPENDIX A

Bottle Decorations

Purpose:

- To help babies with CVI visually alert to their bottle and learn to hold it independently.

Description:

Visually motivating items added to a bottle can help a baby pay visual attention to the bottle.

Materials:

Some items that can be added to the bottle for visual interest include the following:

- Scrunchies and wristbands
- Tin foil bunches
- Black or colored electrical tape placed as horizontal stripes
- Socks with visually interesting designs
- Hair beads, elastics, and ribbons
- Happy face motifs
- Bells

Directions: In a box or drawer gather items that can easily be added to a baby's bottle (and to other objects) that will increase its visual appeal. Decorate the outside of the bottle with several of the visually motivating items. Consider putting a terry wristband near the middle of the bottle for the baby to grasp while learning to hold the bottle. Suggestions:

- Be sure to consider safety when decorating the bottle.
- Help the baby start to hold the bottle by placing the baby's hands on it and then covering them with yours. This additional support can gradually be removed.

Carriers and Slings

Purpose:

- To allow a baby to remain close to the parent's body
- To enable the baby to hear communication and a variety of environmental sounds from the parent's chest
- To stimulate the baby with movement

Description:

Babies with CVI benefit from movement stimulation. While these babies cannot observe others engaging in movement, they can learn about movement through experience. Holding a baby close in a carrier increases intimacy with the baby, enhances bonding, and stimulates the baby through touch and movement. Movement stimulates the vestibular system, which, in turn, stimulates other areas of the brain (Steendam, 1989).

Materials:

Baby front carrier that supports the head, a side sling, or sheet wrap

Directions: Carefully place the baby in the carrier or sling when he or she is relaxed and comfortable. Gently move the baby and the carrier or sling to the adult's body. Practice moving together with the baby in the carrier in a familiar environment for a short time. If using a sheet wrap consider having a second person available to help hold the baby while the sheet is being positioned. Directions for making a baby wrap are available on the internet.

Suggestions:

- Movement times, such as walking, are recommended while the baby is in a carrier.
- Encourage other adults who play with the baby to use the carrier.

- Start using a carrier first. It is a little easier to use. Once parents feel comfortable with the carrier, they can begin to use the sling or the baby wrap.

Chest Play

Purpose:

- To increase bonding through physical contact
- To increase head and neck strength
- To have fun

Description:

Parents can play and bond with their baby while also helping to build core strength, including head and neck strength. Babies with CVI may not be exercising their neck and head control by looking around as sighted babies do and can benefit from activities that will help build these muscles. Weak head and neck muscles can also weaken trunk strength and slow down motor development.

Directions:

- Place the baby on the parent's chest.
- Massage back and tickle baby under chin while talking and singing.

Eyeglasses

Purpose:

To help a child adjust to wearing eyeglasses

Description:

Eyeglasses can feel heavy and unfamiliar, and babies may not feel comfortable with things with which they are not accustomed. For example, babies who have tactile sensitivity are frequently upset when something touches their face. Therefore, it helps to introduce eyeglasses gradually. Pairing the wearing of glasses with an enjoyable activity can distract the baby from the strange feel of the eyeglasses.

Directions:

- Keep the eyeglasses clean.
- Ensure the eyeglasses are as comfortable as possible. Check that they do not pinch, leave marks, or slide down the nose.
- Take the eyeglasses on and off the baby gently so that the frames or strap do not pull his or her hair.

Suggestions:

- It can be helpful for babies to realize that parents and siblings are wearing eyeglasses too, even if they may only be wearing play glasses.
- Find key times to introduce the eyeglasses. For example, when the baby is engaged in happy activities, such as bottle time, cuddle time, music time, or TV time.
- Have the baby wear the eyeglasses for a short time during one or two favorite activities. Gradually increase the amount of time the baby wears the eyeglasses.
- After the baby gets used to wearing the eyeglasses during these activities, add eyeglasses to other favorite activities. Keep adding activities and increasing the time eyeglasses are worn until the baby is accustomed to them.

Gentle Roughhouse Play

Purpose:

- To increase bonding
- To promote fun through physical play
- To provide movement stimulation

Description:

Parents may be timid about playing physically with their child who has CVI. Some parents may be afraid that their baby will get hurt, but physical play can be gentle as well. This type of play can build bonding through fun and stimulating exercise.

Materials:

Music can be used.

Directions:

- Have parents put the baby on their knees, holding the child firmly at the core.
- The parent's knees can be rocked to the left and right slowly to allow the baby to regain balance, or jiggled, bouncing the baby rhythmically in time to an upbeat song.
- Have parents hold the baby under his or her arms and move up and down quickly; for adventurous children, toss them in the air briefly.

Suggestions:

- Watch the baby's reactions: exhilaration is good, but fear is not.

Massage

Purpose:

- To draw a baby's attention to his or her own body
- To accustom a baby to being touched by others
- To teach the names of body parts
- To stimulate the tactile system

Description:

The sense of touch is critically important to all children, especially in their earliest years of life. Deep massage and touch can stimulate brain areas that enhance vision and language. Touch and massage can also help children with CVI learn about their own bodies. Massage is a wonderful way for parents to be close to their baby and help their child develop. During massage, parents can help their baby develop awareness about the body by naming its part. It is important to provide massage to the baby every day.

Directions:

- Undress the baby as much as possible before starting the massage.
- Help the child lie on his or her back.
- Start on one side of the body and deeply massage from trunk to end of arm.
- Massage hands thoroughly, especially the fingers.
- Pat the trunk but do not concentrate on it.
- Massage from the hip down along the leg to the feet and toes; bend and straighten the leg.
- Move to the other side of the body, following the same steps for the arms and legs.
- Gently stretch both arms out wide and then into the middle.
- Remember not to use force.
- Sing. ("Pat-a-Cake" works well.)
- Play "Pat-a-Cake" with the hands and feet; play with one hand and its opposite foot, then with the other hand and its opposite foot.
- Have fun.

Suggestions:

- Have parents use a firm touch and hard, slightly rough textures when providing the massage. Vary the textures during some of the massages.

- Have parents incorporate massage into the bath or dressing routine.
- Have parents name body parts during the massage.
- Watch for the child's reaction. A baby may need time to become comfortable with tactile sensation and may not at first appear to enjoy beginning massage sessions. For touch-sensitive children, do something else pleasurable during the tactile experiences, such as singing or moving.

NOTE: Consult with a physical or occupational therapist about massage approaches and techniques.

Object Boards

Purpose:

- To encourage a baby to explore objects and build object concepts by providing a place where familiar objects are predictably available

Description:

Babies can be discouraged from tactile exploration if the objects they are engaging with suddenly disappear. Because objects on an object board are stable and predictable, a child with CVI can explore the objects without frustration and with adequate time.

Materials:

- Peg board cut to the size that is appropriate for the location where it will be used
- A variety of engaging objects to put on the board (e.g., bells, measuring spoons, baby bottle, pacifier, little book)
- Short pieces of elastic for hanging items (The elastic should be long enough to stretch when the baby is handling objects, but short enough for safety, approximately 3–5 inches).

Directions:

- Hang objects on the board at well-spaced intervals.
- Group the objects in twos and threes.
- Include a sound producing object in each group so that noise can result from exploration.
- Attach the object board to the wall or a leg of furniture, or place it flat on the floor.

Suggestions:

- To prevent sharp edges that can hurt a baby, consider making the corners of the object board round.
- Supervise the baby when he or she is playing with the object board.
- Do not leave the object board around where it can be disturbed by other children.
- Object boards can be thematic or used as storyboards, or they can be specific to each room (for example, a board for the kitchen, the bathroom, or the sandbox area).

Object Hangers

Purpose:

- To encourage a baby to look and reach

Description:

An object hanger is a controlled learning environment that is used to present visually motivating, cause-and-effect objects near a baby to which the baby can visually alert. Eventually the baby should be able to find objects independently and start to use vision to find favorites.

Box Hanger Directions:

- The box should be approximately 2.5 by 3 feet (e.g., a shipping box).
- Place the box on its side with the opening facing out.
- Create 8 holes on the upper side of the box, from which you will suspend objects.
- Collect 6-8 objects (e.g., cups, plates, bells) that are visually motivating and can be suspended from elastic in the box.
- Cut elastic into thin strips long enough to attach to the object and secure at the top of the box.
- Place each strip of elastic in fish tubing to prevent the baby's hand from getting caught.
- Place the elastic strips through each of the holes.
- Secure the elastic with a ring, bolt, or paper clip on top of the box.

Toy Hanger Directions:

- The hanger should be a thick material; it can be made from a PVC pipe or bought commercially.
- Collect 6 to 8 objects (e.g., cups, plates, bells) that are visually motivating and can be suspended with elastic or yarn from the hanger.
- Cut elastic into thin strips long enough to attach to the object and secure on the lower bar of the hanger and on the side pieces.
- Place each strip of elastic in fish tubing to prevent the baby's hand from getting caught.
- Tie the elastic strips around the lower bar.
- Secure the elastic with a ring, bolt, or paper clip if needed.

Suggestions:

- Objects need to be very close to the baby's face.
- Do not crowd objects hanging in the box.
- While the baby may be placed inside the box, there should be plenty of light and the baby should be comfortable.
- Observe the baby in the box or under the object hanger; the baby should *never* be alone when in the box or under the hanger.
- Try to resist talking to the baby or moving the baby's hands toward the objects. Let them discover independently as much as possible.

Object Visibility

Purpose:

- To make ordinary objects easier for a baby to see

Description:

Brightness, movement, and motivating patterns can make many objects easier for the baby to alert to visually. Adding visual excitement to a baby's favorite objects can motivate the baby to use vision to see them.

Materials:

An adaptation kit for making objects more visually motivating may include the following:

- Decorating scissors
- Tape (e.g., transparent, electrical, painters, masking, duct)
- Red and yellow decorations
- Mylar paper from old balloons
- Foil wrap
- Shiny holiday decorations
- Pipe cleaners
- Bubble wrap
- Beads and bells
- Shiny glittery decor
- Puff paint, regular paint, and markers
- Happy face stickers

Directions:

In a box or drawer gather items for the adaptation kit that can easily be added to other objects to increase the items' visual appeal. Decorate things like toys, pictures, the rails of the crib, the highchair tray, the car seat with several of the visually motivating items.

Note: Decorations that could be placed inside the mouth or that have parts that could flake into the eyes are not suitable for young babies.

Observing a Baby with CVI

Purpose:

- To observe the baby to understand his or her needs

Description:

Careful observation of a baby's actions helps parents and teachers get to know a baby better and understand the baby's needs. Observation provides information about how to communicate, play, work, and motivate the baby. These observations can help when planning activities.

Directions:

- Observe the baby when he or she is engaged in an activity
- Write down exactly what you observe: how the baby reacts and what happened to generate the reaction.
- Note what difficulties the baby may have had with the activity as well as what steps the baby easily performed.

Suggestions:

- Try not to talk or interact with the baby; just observe.
- Resist interpreting what you think the baby is thinking; simply watch.

Penlight Play

Purpose:

- To introduce a light source to a baby at consistent and routine times in an effort to increase awareness of vision.

Materials:

A penlight, which may be filtered

Description:

Babies who are not yet aware of vision may benefit from having a small, possibly filtered, light introduced toward the eyes. Having this activity repeated several times during daily routines is helpful.

Directions:

- At regular intervals throughout the day, such as during a diaper change, place the baby into a well-supported position.
- Use a light source like a pen light and possibly filter it with a red or yellow balloon that has been cut to fit the light.
- Introduce the light source first to the right eye and then the left eye.
- Hold the light 2–3 inches from each eye and show it to the baby for a few seconds for each eye.
- Look for a reaction to the light, such as a widening of the eyes, turning to the light, stopping other behaviors, or closing the eyes. When the reaction is observed, use words to reinforce the fixation on the light, such as, "You are looking at the light. You see the light." Repeat these words every time the baby uses vision in this activity.
- After the baby is aware of the light, move the light an additional inch or so from the center each time it is reintroduced.
- Encourage the baby to find the light, waiting for the baby to turn toward the light. Repeat on each side.
- Once the baby starts to readily turn toward the light, begin to help the baby reach to touch the light.
- If at any point the baby seems bothered by the light, stop the activity.

Suggestions:

- Think of ways that the light can be connected to something meaningful to the baby. For example, a small light can be attached to the baby's bottle or held simultaneously while feeding with a spoon.

- Use the light to illuminate a pacifier, a bottle, or a spoon so that the baby can more easily find it during mealtime.

Swaddling a Baby

Purpose:

- To soothe and calm a baby by wrapping him or her snugly in an infant blanket

Description:

Babies with CVI benefit from swaddling which reduces extraneous movements that can cause an unsettling startle response and limits tactile sensations. Being swaddled may feel like being in the comfort of the womb.

Directions:

- Lay a receiving blanket on a flat surface and fold down the top corner about 6 inches to form a straight edge.
- Place the baby on his or her back so that the baby's shoulders are just below the edge of the blanket.
- Bring the baby's left arm down to its side, leaving the arm slightly bent.
- Pull the corner of the blanket near the left arm over the baby's left arm and chest, and tuck the leading edge snugly under the baby's back on the right side.
- Pull the bottom of the blanket up and over the baby's feet.
- Bring the baby's right arm down to its side, leaving the arm slightly bent.
- Pull the corner of the blanket near the right arm over the baby's right arm and chest, and tuck the edge under the baby's left side.
- Refer to directions on the internet when necessary.

Warm-Up Movements

Purpose:

- To help a baby prepare for interventions

Description:

It is important that babies with CVI have time to warm up their sensory systems before beginning visual learning activities. After babies experience movement, they become more alert and frequently are more able to fixate on targets (Steendam, 1989).

Directions:

- Swing the baby in a blanket or hammock while singing.
- Dance with the baby for fun and as a warm-up for everyone.
- Gentle roughhouse play may help a baby alert.
- Bouncing on a ball or in a baby bouncer may be stimulating to the baby.
- Swishing in a bathtub can be a fun movement for a baby.

Suggestions:

- Movement and touch activities are often tolerated better with singing and play.
- Remember to move to the left and right, as well as up and down.

APPENDIX B

Locating Programs for Families of a Baby with CVI

Finding information to locate an appropriate program for a child with visual impairments and cerebral visual impairment can be a little daunting. In addition to the following list, which can be changeable, parents can also serve as a resource for information about programs from other parents.

- State Part C programs refers to the IDEA **Part C** formula grant **programs**, which assist **states** in providing early intervention services for infants and toddlers (from birth through age two), and their families. Part C programs for each state can be located through Early Childhood Technical Assistance Center (https://ectacenter.org/contact/ptccoord.asp)

- Services for children with special needs are provided for and defined in IDEA, the Individuals with Disabilities Education Act, part C (https://sites.ed.gov/idea/regs/c), which specifies information about services for babies and toddlers.

- The Texas School for the Blind lists the schools and other entities supporting visual impairment in the United States (https://www.tsbvi.edu/instructional-resources/2785-schools-for -the-blind-in-the-united-states).

- Special education departments in some school districts also provide early intervention services. These departments often are aware of vision service providers. Each state is different. Contact a child's local school district to find where in the state to inquire about programs.

- www.FamilyConnect.org is a family site operated by American Printing House for the Blind and offers information and connections.

- American Printing House for the Blind (www.aph.org) is a site which offers a wide variety of information about visual impairments and blindness and has a CVI information website.

Supportive Websites for Parents of a Baby With Cerebral Visual Impairments (CVI)

Occasionally parents of a baby newly diagnosed with CVI will discover websites that have information about cerebral visual impairment. It is not unusual for parents to get overwhelmed and even anxious while reading information about CVI they discover online or through communicating with other parents on blogs. Therefore, it is often helpful if a family lets a teacher of children with visual impairments guide them to reliable websites and then help them clarify the information they find online.

The following websites are helpful to parents whose baby has recently been diagnosed with CVI:

www.familyconnect.org: a family-oriented site from American Printing House for the Blind (APH), which offers parents of children with visual impairments, who are blind or have multiple disabilities including vision loss, a place to support each other, share stories and concerns, and link to local resources.

www.aph.org: from American Printing House for the Blind, the World's largest company devoted to researching, developing, and manufacturing products for people who are blind and visually impaired.

www.lilliworks.org: offers information and resources specific to the equipment and teaching theory of *Active Learning* by Lilli Nielsen. Active learning is a teaching strategy based on the fact that babies and children learn by doing. It includes specific materials and strategies.

www.wonderbaby.org: a site funded by Perkins School for the Blind offers advice, information, resources, and encouragement by parents to support parents of babies who are blind or have additional challenges. The site also lists applications for mobile devices such as an iPad that are especially helpful to children with CVI.

www.pathstoliteracy.org: a site which is a collaboration between Perkins School for the Blind and Texas School for the Blind and Visually Impaired with the goal of sharing strategies, resources, research, and ideas for using technology to enhance literacy for children who are blind or visually impaired.

www.tsbvi.edu: a site from Texas School for the Blind and Visually Impaired which offers information, ideas, articles, and suggestions.

www.Littlebearsees.org: a website by parents offering information and support for parents with a child with cerebral visual impairment. The site also lists applications for mobile devices such as an iPad that are especially helpful to children with CVI.

www.blindbabies.org: provides a fact sheet about cerebral visual impairment that is both informative and easily readable.

www.cvi.aphtech.org: a resource for research articles, books, websites, blogs, strategies, and support for parents, teachers.

www.cviconnect.co: CViConnect is a community of professionals and technology that offer hope and confidence in the form of personalized education, training and support for children with Cortical Visual Impairment.

APPENDIX C

A Different View: A Training Guide about Babies with Cerebral Visual Impairment

Babies with cerebral visual impairment typically are supported by several professionals including early intervention specialists, therapists, and daycare providers. Teachers of children with visual impairments frequently provide training and information to these professionals about the intervention needs of babies with vision loss and cerebral visual impairment. Experience has proven that providing these busy professionals with copious information about visual impairment and cerebral visual impairment can be overwhelming. While *A Different View* offers accurate information about CVI, this information is presented more concisely than elsewhere in the text, taking into account the time constraints faced by busy professionals. Teachers or parents can first leave this summary information for a specialist to read. Then, when time permits, a teacher or parent can expand on this information as necessary and appropriate so professionals can best help the baby they are serving. Readers are encouraged to reproduce the material in Appendix C to share with others who will be supporting their child.

About Babies with Cerebral Visual Impairment:

Babies with cerebral visual impairment (CVI) have vision difficulties that are the result of a brain-related injury that interrupts typical visual processing. Babies with CVI often experience limited and confusing visual information, and should be served by a vision professional, such as a teacher of children with visual impairments. Babies with CVI can often demonstrate improved visual ability after the application of strategic interventions.

Babies with typical sight learn information about their world by looking. They can see actions and items both nearby and far away. Babies with CVI live in a world that seems smaller since it is limited to their near environment that they can touch, hear, or smell. The sounds, smells, events, and objects in the world of a baby with CVI seem disconnected and confusing unless the baby can be helped to understand and connect these concepts. An important role of parents, caregivers, teachers, and therapists is to help a baby with CVI conceptualize a meaningful world, one part at a time, through the experience of touching, hearing, and doing.

Characteristics

Babies with CVI may show several of the following characteristics:

- They may not appear to be blind.
- They may have additional ocular impairments.
- They may be able to visually perceive some targets but not others.
- Their visual ability may vary depending on the environment, the target, and their interest level.
- They may have absent or atypical visual reflexes.
- They may be light sensitive (photophobic).
- They may appear to gaze at light.
- They may be attracted to light and reflective materials.
- They may have difficulty with unfamiliar objects.
- They may exhibit visual field preferences.
- They may have a delay in visual responses.
- They may have additional sensory processing disorders that can affect touch, hearing, or vision.
- They may have difficulty with visual crowding or clutter when too many objects are presented together.

Intervention Readiness Suggestions

Teachers and parents can help prepare a baby for interventions by doing the following:

- Help the baby feel comfortable, well supported, and calm.
- Plan an activity that is interesting to the baby.
- Include elements that are motivating for the baby.
- Assure that the baby has eyeglasses if needed.
- Alter the environment to decrease distractions.
- Adjust the environmental lighting.
- Provide movement and tactile stimulation, such as providing a brief massage before vision work.

Working with a Baby with CVI

- Talk to the baby in concrete terms (e.g., "The ball is on the table" rather than "The ball is here.").
- Provide the baby with verbal cues before objects are moved.
- Inform the baby when you approach or leave.
- Work on tasks or actions from behind the baby using hand-over-hand guidance so that the baby can feel the natural movements of the action, while never forcing a baby's hands.
- Provide a reason for the baby to move, such as a motivating visual object, so the baby is moving either *to* or *for* something when practicing movement interventions.
- Show the baby parts of any equipment that will be used during an activity.
- Be consistent, following a routine and schedule. Employ a beginning and end signal for activities.
- Incorporate the activity into other experiences as appropriate.
- Use real objects such as kitchen utensils or balls to make an activity meaningful.

- Work toward increased independence.
- Teach the individual steps of an activity first instead of the entire activity all at once.
- Encourage the baby to employ any usable vision he or she has during an activity.
- Avoid overstimulation, including distractions and competing sensory information.
- Change activities and positions every 15 minutes.
- Work in natural settings for meaningful results.
- Help the baby reinforce looking response with touch and verbal descriptions.
- Use adaptive devices to facilitate correct head and neck posture.
- Plan and use appropriate transitions between activities.
- Find an optimal position for stability and movement.
- Use repetition
- Create a controlled learning environment
- Create activities that enhance independence and promote communication.
- Encourage active learning through self-initiated discovery.

REFERENCES

American Association Pediatric Ophthalmology and Strabismus. (n.d.). *Retrieved from https://aapos.org/glossary/vision -therapy*

American Optometric Association. (n.d). Visual acuity: What is 20/20 vision? Retrieved from https://www.aoa.org/patients -and-public/eye-and-vision-problems/glossary-of-eye-and -vision-conditions/visual-acuity

Anderson, S., Boigon, S., Davis, K., & DeWaard, C. (2007). *The Oregon Project for Preschool Children Who Are Blind or Visually Impaired* (6th ed.). Medford: Southern Oregon Education Service District.

Anthony, T. L., Bleier, H., Fazzi, D. L., Kish, D., & Pogrund, R. L. (2002). Mobility focus: Developing early skills for orientation and mobility. In R. L. Pogrund & D. L. Fazzi (Eds.), *Early focus: Working with young children who are blind or visually impaired and their families* (2nd ed., pp. 326–404). New York, NY: AFB Press.

Barraga, N. C., & Erin, J. N. (1992). *Visual handicaps and learning* (3rd ed.). Austin, TX: Pro-ED.

Barraga, N. C., & Morris, J. E. (1980). *Program to develop efficiency in visual functioning.* Louisville, KY: American Printing House for the Blind.

Bishop, V. E. (2000). Early childhood. In A. J. Koenig & M. C. Holbrook (Eds.), *Foundations of education: Vol. II. Instructional strategies for teaching children and youths with visual impairments* (2nd ed., pp. 225–263). New York, NY: AFB Press.

Bishop, V. E. (2004). *Teaching visually impaired children* (3rd ed.). Springfield, IL: Charles C Thomas.

Brodsky, M. C., Fray, K. J., & Glasier, C. M. (2002). Perinatal cortical and subcortical visual loss: Mechanisms of injury and associated ophthalmologic signs. *Ophthalmology*, 109(1), 85–94.

Catteneo, Z., & Merabet, L. B. (2015). Brain plasticity and development. In A. H. Lueck & G. N. Dutton (Eds.), *Vision and the brain: Understanding cerebral visual impairment in children* (pp. 105–123). New York: AFB Press.

Caulfield, R. (2000). Beneficial effects of tactile stimulation on early development. *Early Childhood Education Journal*, 27(4), 255–257.

Chen, D. (2014a). Early intervention: Purpose and principles. In D. Chen (Ed.), *Essential elements in early intervention: Visual impairment and multiple disabilities* (2nd ed., pp. 3–33). New York, NY: AFB Press.

Chen, D. (2014b). Interactions between young children and caregivers: The context for early intervention. In D. Chen (Ed.), *Essential elements in early intervention: Visual impairment and multiple disabilities* (2nd ed., pp. 34–84). New York, NY: AFB Press.

Correa, V. I., Fazzi, D. L., & Pogrund, R. L. (2002). Team focus: Current trends, service delivery, and advocacy. In R. L. Pogrund & D. L. Fazzi (Eds.), *Early focus: Working with young children who are blind or visually impaired and their families* (2nd ed., pp. 405–441). New York, NY: AFB Press.

Croft, N. B., & Robinson, L. W. (1984). *Growing up: A developmental curriculum.* Austin, TX: Parent Consultants.

Dennison, E. (2003). *Eye conditions in infants and young children that result in visual impairment, and syndromes and other conditions that may accompany visual disorder.* Logan, UT: SKI-HI Institute.

Dennison, E., & Lueck, A. H. (Eds.). (2006). *Proceedings of the summit on cerebral/cortical visual impairment: Educational, family, and medical perspectives*, April 30, 2005. New York, NY: AFB Press.

Dockrell, J., & Messer, D. J. (1999). *Children's language and communication difficulties: Understanding, identification and intervention*. New York, NY: Cassell.

Duffy, M. A. (n.d.). *Low vision and legal blindness terms and descriptions*. Retrieved from http://www.visionaware.org /info/your-eye-condition/eye-health/low-vision/low-vision -terms-and-descriptions/1235

Dutton, G. N. (2015a). Assessment of functional vision: History taking for children with CVI. In A. H. Lueck & G. N. Dutton (Eds.), *Vision and the brain: Understanding cerebral visual impairment in children* (pp. 261–276). New York, NY: AFB Press.

Dutton, G. N. (2015b). The brain and vision. In A. H. Lueck & G. N. Dutton (Eds.), *Vision and the brain: Understanding cerebral visual impairment in children* (pp. 21–38). New York, NY: AFB Press.

Dutton, G. N. (2015c). Disorders of the brain and how they can affect vision. In A. H. Lueck & G. N. Dutton (Eds.), *Vision and the brain: Understanding cerebral visual impairment in children* (pp. 39–82). New York, NY: AFB Press.

Dutton, G. N., & Lueck, A. H. (2015). Impairment of vision due to damage to the brain. In A. H. Lueck & G. N. Dutton (Eds.), *Vision and the brain: Understanding cerebral visual impairment in children* (pp. 3–20). New York, NY: AFB Press.

Early Childhood Technical Assistance Center. (n.d.). *Early intervention services: Key principles and practices*. Retrieved from http://ectacenter.org/topics/natenv /keyprinckeyprac.asp

Education for All Handicapped Children Act, Pub. L. No. 94-142 (1975).

Erin, J. N. (2010). Developing the university curriculum to include CVI: A work in progress at the University of Arizona [Roundtable]. *Journal of Visual Impairment & Blindness*, 104(10), 656–658.

Erin, J. N., Fazzi, D. L., Gordon, R. L., Isenberg, S. J., & Paysse, E. A. (2002). Vision focus: Understanding the medical and functional implications of vision loss. In R. L. Pogrund & D. L. Fazzi (Eds.), *Early focus: Working with young children who are blind or visually impaired and their families* (2nd ed., pp. 52–106). New York, NY: AFB Press.

Fazzi, D. L., & Klein, M. D. (2002). Cognitive focus: Developing cognition, concepts, and language. In R. L. Pogrund & D. L. Fazzi (Eds.), *Early focus: Working with young children who are blind or visually impaired and their families* (2nd ed., pp. 107–153). New York, NY: AFB Press.

Fazzi, D. L., Klein, M. D., Pogrund, R. L., & Salcedo, P. S. (2002). Family focus: Working effectively with families. In R. L. Pogrund & D. L. Fazzi (Eds.), *Early focus: Working with young children who are blind or visually impaired and their families* (2nd ed., pp. 16–51). New York, NY: AFB Press.

Fazzi, E., Molinaro, A., & Hartmann, E. (2015). The potential impact of visual impairment and CVI on child development. In A. H. Lueck & G. N. Dutton (Eds.), *Vision and the Brain: Understanding cerebral visual impairment in children* (pp. 83–104). New York, NY: AFB Press.

Field, T. (1995). Massage Therapy for Infants and children. *Journal of Developmental & Behavioral Pediatrics*, 16, 105-111 .http://dx.doi.org/10.1097/00004703-199504000-00008

Fraiberg, S. (1977). *Insights from the blind*. New York, NY: Basic Books.

Good, W. V., Jan, J. E., Burden, S. K., Skoczenski, A., & Candy, R. (2001). Recent advances in cortical visual impairment. *Developmental Medicine & Child Neurology*, 43(1), 56–60.

Groenveld, M., Jan, J. E., & Leader, P. (1990). Observations on the habilitation of children with cortical visual impairment. *Journal of Visual Impairment & Blindness*, 84(1), 11–15.

Harrell, L. (1992). *Children's vision concerns: Look beyond the eyes*. Placerville, CA: L. Harrell Productions.

Harris, S. R., & Tada, W. L. (1983). Providing developmental therapy services. In S. G. Garwood & R. R. Fewell (Eds.), *Educating handicapped infants: Issues in development and intervention* (pp. 343–368). Rockville, MD: Aspen Systems Corp.

Hatton, D. D. (2001). Model registry of early childhood visual impairment: First-year results. *Journal of Visual Impairment & Blindness*, 95(7), 418–443.

Healey, W. (1996). Helping parents deal with the fact that their child has a disability. *CEC Today*, 3(5). Retrieved from http://www.ldonline.org/article/5937/

Holbrook, M. C., & Rosenblum, L. P. (2017). Supporting differentiated instruction and inclusion in general education. In M. C. Holbrook, C. Kamei-Hannan, & T. McCarthy (Eds.), *Foundations of education: Vol. II. Instructional strategies for teaching children and youths with visual impairments* (3rd ed., pp. 231–260). New York, NY: AFB Press.

Holbrook, M. C., Wright, D., & Presley, I. (2017). Specialized assessments. In M. C. Holbrook, C. Kamei-Hannan, & T. McCarthy (Eds.), *Foundations of education: Vol. II. Instructional strategies for teaching children and youths with visual impairments* (3rd ed., pp. 108–164). New York, NY: AFB Press.

Hoyt, C. (2003). Visual function in the brain-damaged child. *Eye,* 17, 371–386.

Hyvärinen, L. (2004). CVI lecture series, SKI-HI Institute. North Logan, UT: HOPE Publishing.

Hyvärinen, L. (n.d.). Lea-test. Retrieved from http://www.lea-test.fi

Individuals with Disabilities Education Improvement Act (IDEA), 20 U.S.C. § 1400 (2004).

Jan, J. E., Groenveld, M., Sykanda, A. M., & Hoyt, C. S. (1987). Behavioural characteristics of children with permanent cortical visual impairment. *Developmental Medicine & Child Neurology,* 29(5), 571–576.

Kran, B. S., & Mayer, D. L. (2015). Assessment of visual function and functional vision: Clinical assessment and suggested methods for educators. In A. H. Lueck & G. N. Dutton (Eds.), *Vision and the brain: Understanding cerebral visual impairment in children* (pp. 277–342). New York, NY: AFB Press.

Kübler-Ross, E., & Kessler, D. (2005). *On grief and grieving: Finding the meaning of grief through the five stages of loss.* New York, NY: Scribner.

Langley, M. B. (1998). *ISAVE: Individualized Systematic Assessment of Visual Efficiency.* Louisville, KY: American Printing House for the Blind.

Lappin, G., & Kretschmer, R. E. (2005). Applying infant massage practices: A qualitative study. *Journal of Visual Impairment & Blindness,* 99(6), 355–367.

Lueck, A. H., Chen, D., Kekelis, L., & Hartmann, E. (2008). *Developmental guidelines for infants with visual impairment: A guidebook for early intervention* (2nd ed.). Louisville, KY: American Printing House for the Blind.

Lueck, A. H., & Dutton, G. N. (2015a). Introduction. In A. H. Lueck & G. N. Dutton (Eds.), *Vision and the Brain: Understanding cerebral visual impairment in children* (pp. xvii–xxi). New York, NY: AFB Press.

Lueck, A. H., & Dutton, G. N. (Eds.). (2015b). *Vision and the Brain: Understanding cerebral visual impairment in children.* New York: AFB Press.

Metell, M. (2015). "A great moment . . . because of the music": An exploratory study on music therapy and early interaction with children with visual impairment and their sighted caregivers. *British Journal of Visual Impairment*, 33(2), 111–125.

McLeod, S. (2017). Maslow's heirarchy of needs. *Simply Psychology.* Retrieved from https://www.simplypsychology.org/maslow .html

Morgan, E., & Watkins, S. (1989). *INSITE developmental checklist: Assessment of developmental skills for young multihandicapped sensory impaired children.* North Logan, UT: Hope Publishing.

Moses, K. (1987, Spring). The impact of childhood disability: The parent's struggle. *Ways Magazine.*

National Association for the Education of Young Children (n.d.). Find child care and preschool. Retrieved from https:// families.naeyc.org/find-quality-child-care

Nielsen, L. (1992). *Space and self: Active learning by means of the Little Room.* Lake City, FL: Vision Associates.

Orel-Bixler, D. (2014). Clinical vision assessments for young children. In D. Chen (Ed.), *Essential elements in early intervention: Visual impairment and multiple disabilities* (2nd ed., pp. 135–213). New York, NY: AFB Press.

Pawletko, T., Chokron, S., & Dutton, G. N. (2015). Considerations in the behavioral diagnosis of CVI: Issues, causes, and potential outcomes. In A. H. Lueck & G. N. Dutton (Eds.), *Vision and the Brain: Understanding cerebral visual impairment in children* (pp. 145–173). New York, NY: AFB Press.

Pogrund, R. L. (2002a). Independence focus: Promoting independence in daily living and recreational skills. In R. L. Pogrund & D. L. Fazzi (Eds.), *Early focus: Working with young children who are blind or visually impaired and their families* (2nd ed., pp. 218–249). New York, NY: AFB Press.

Pogrund, R. L. (2002b). Refocus: Setting the stage for working with young children who are blind or visually impaired. In R. L. Pogrund & D. L. Fazzi (Eds.), *Early focus: Working with young children who are blind or visually impaired and their families* (2nd ed., pp. 1–15). New York, NY: AFB Press.

Pruett, K. M. (2002). Behavioral focus: Developing positive behavioral supports. In R. L. Pogrund & D. L. Fazzi (Eds.), *Early focus: Working with young children who are blind or visually impaired and their families* (2nd ed., pp. 250–286). New York, NY: AFB Press.

Roman, C., Baker-Nobles, L., Dutton, G. N., Luiselli, T. E., Flener, B. S., Jan, J. E., . . . Nielsen, A. S. (2010). Statement on cortical visual impairment [Comment]. *Journal of Visual Impairment & Blindness, 104*(2), 69–72.

Roman-Lantzy, C. (2007). *Cortical visual impairment: An approach to assessment and intervention* (1st ed.). New York, NY: AFB Press.

Roman-Lantzy, C. (2018). *Cortical visual impairment: An approach to assessment and intervention* (2nd ed.). New York, NY: AFB Press.

Russell-Eggitt, I., Harris, C.M., Kris, A. (2008). Delayed visual maturation: an update. *Development Medicine and Child Neurology*, 40(2),130-6.

Sacks, S. Z., & Page, B. (2017). Social skills. In M. C. Holbrook, C. Kamei-Hannan, & T. McCarthy (Eds.), *Foundations of Education: Vol. II. Instructional strategies for teaching children and youths with visual impairments* (3rd ed., pp. 753–803). New York, NY: AFB Press.

Saunders, K. J. (2015). Refractive errors, impaired focusing, and the need for eyeglasses in children with CVI. In A. H. Lueck & G. N. Dutton (Eds.), *Vision and the Brain: Understanding cerebral visual impairment in children* (pp. 189–204). New York, NY: AFB Press.

Sibling Support Project (n.d.). Sibshops. Retrieved from https://www.siblingsupport.org/sibshops

Steendam, M. (1989). *Cortical visual impairment in children: A handbook for parents and professionals.* Burwood, Australia: Royal Blind Society of New South Wales.

Steendam, M. (2015). Assessments linked to interventions: Observational assessment of young children and children with multiple disabilities. In A. H. Lueck & G. N. Dutton (Eds.), *Vision and the Brain: Understanding cerebral visual impairment in children* (pp. 391–410). New York, NY: AFB Press.

Strickling, C. A., & Pogrund, R. L. (2002). Motor focus: Promoting movement experiences and motor development. In R. L. Pogrund & D. L. Fazzi (Eds.), *Early focus: Working with young children who are blind or visually impaired and their families* (2nd ed., pp. 287–325). New York, NY: AFB Press.

Strickling, C. (1998). *Impact of vision loss on motor development: information for occupational and physical therapists working with students with visual impairments.* Texas School for the Blind and Visually Impaired.

Tallent, A., Tallent, A., & Bush, F. (2012). *Little bear sees: How children with cortical visual impairment can learn to see.* Deadwood, OR: Little Bear Sees Publishing/ Wyatt-MacKenzie.

Topor, I. (1999) Functional vision assessment & interventions. In D. Chen, Ed. *Strategies for Early Intervention with Infants Who Are Visually Impaired and Have Multiple Disabilities and Their Families.* NY: American Foundation for the Blind.

Topor, I. (2014). Functional vision assessment and early intervention practices. In D. Chen (Ed.), *Essential elements in early intervention: Visual impairment and multiple disabilities* (2nd ed., pp. 214–293). New York, NY: AFB Press.

Topor, I., Rosenblum, L. P., & Hatton, D. D. (2004). *Visual conditions and functional vision: Early intervention issues.* Chapel Hill: University of North Carolina at Chapel Hill, FPG Child Development Institute, Early Intervention Training Center for Infants and Toddlers with Visual Impairments.

Tychsen, L. (2001). Critical periods for development of visual acuity, depth perception and eye tracking. In D. B. Baily, J. T. Bruer, F. J. Symons, & J. W. Lichtman (Eds.), *Critical thinking about critical periods* (pp. 67–80). Baltimore, MD: Paul H. Brookes.

GLOSSARY

B

backward chaining: an instructional strategy used to teach sequential tasks by teaching one step at a time in reverse order, so the student begins with a completed task.

bilateral: affecting both sides.

binocularity: the ability to use both eyes to focus on a visual target and create a single stereoscopic image.

blindness: the lack of functional vision.

brain damage: any injury to the brain that impairs its functions, often permanently.

brain plasticity: the ability of the brain to change its activity in response to stimuli by reorganizing its functions, structure, or connections.

C

cataracts: an opacity of the crystalline lens of the eye that results in a loss of visual acuity.

cerebral palsy: a non-progressive disorder of voluntary movement and posture that is caused by damage to the brain before or during birth or within the first few years of life.

cerebral visual impairment: a neurological visual disorder, typically indicated when there is a normal or close to normal eye examination that does not explain visual performance, a medical history that typically includes neurological problems, and the presence of unique visual or behavioral characteristics. Cerebral visual impairment is generally considered to be broader in scope and encompasses cortical visual impairment. The definition of CVI continues to evolve as more is learned about the brain and sensory processing.

cognition: the activities of learning, remembering, thinking, and understanding.

cognitive impairment: an impairment that greatly limits someone's conscious intellectual activity to the point at which normal functioning within society is not possible without treatment or interventions.

concave lens: a lens that curves inward that spreads out, or diverges, light rays refracted through it; also called a *minus lens.*

convex lens: a lens that bends light rays inward and is used to correct hyperopia; also called a *plus lens.*

cornea: the transparent tissue at the front of the eye that is curved and provides approximately 66 percent of the eye's refracting power.

corneal opacity: a disorder which occurs when the cornea becomes scarred, limiting the amount of light that can reach the retina.

cortical: pertaining to the cerebral cortex.

cortical visual impairment: *see* cerebral visual impairment.

cytomegalic inclusion body disease: a condition caused by an infection with cytomegalovirus (CMV), a type of herpes virus; the most common cause of congenital abnormalities in the United States.

delayed visual maturation (DVM): a condition in which visual development is delayed so a child will seem to be visually impaired. Nystagmus may be present, and the delay may be related to abnormalities in the anterior visual pathway. Visual function generally develops at 6–24 months and continues to improve until age 2–3 years.

dorsal stream: occipital and posterior parietal lobes that map the surroundings and brings about visual guidance of movement. Sometimes known as the "where" pathway, it functions at a subconscious level.

Down syndrome: a condition caused by an extra chromosome 21 resulting in distinct physical characteristics: moderate to severe developmental delays, possible cardiac abnormalities, hearing impairment, and various visual impairments.

echolalia: repetition of phrases, words, parts of words, or vocal sounds. It can be immediate (occurring immediately or shortly after hearing a stimulus) or delayed.

encephalitis: inflammation of the brain that is typically caused by infection by a virus, or less commonly by bacterial or fungal infection or an autoimmune reaction.

eye: a nearly spherical, hollow organ with a photosensitive retina located in the skull that is the organ of sight.

fetal stroke: a stroke that occurs between 14 weeks of gestation through labor and delivery that can cause cerebral palsy, seizures, or learning disabilities.

fixation: the ability to keep the eyes steady on a target of interest.

functional magnetic resource imaging (fMRI): a technique for measuring brain activity that detects changes associated with the flow of blood.

functional vision assessment (FVA): an assessment of an individual's use of vision in a variety of tasks and settings, including measures of near and distance vision; visual fields; eye movements; and responses to specific environmental characteristics, such as light and color. The assessment report includes recommendations for instructional procedures, modifications or adaptations, and additional tests.

ganglion cell: a nerve cell that has its body outside the central nervous system

glaucoma: An ocular disease characterized by an increase in intraocular pressure. It may cause damage to the ocular tissues, including the optic nerve, and loss of visual field.

glucose: A simple sugar that is the source of energy for cell functioning that also plays a major role in regulating metabolism.

gross motor: Movement that involves the large muscles of the body such as those in the arms and legs (e.g., crawling, running, or jumping).

hearing impairment: an impairment in hearing, which can be either permanent or fluctuating, that adversely affects a child's educational performance but is not included under the definition of *deafness.*

hypertropia: the upward deviation of one eye.

hypotropia: the downward deviation of one eye.

hydrocephalus: a condition due to impaired circulation of cerebral spinal fluid (CSF), causing increased intracranial pressure, commonly with increased CSF volume expanding the water spaces in the brain (the ventricles).

Individuals with Disabilities Education Improvement Act (IDEA): the amendments to the Education for All Handicapped Children Act, the federal legislation that safeguards a free appropriate public education for all eligible children with disabilities in the United States, reauthorized in 1990, 1997, and 2004 (the last is referred to as the Individuals with Disabilities Education Improvement Act).

infant mortality: the rate of deaths occurring during the first year of life.

interventricular hemorrhage (IVH): bleeding either inside or around the ventricles in the brain which can put pressure on nerve cells and damage them.

joint attention: attention overtly focused by two or more people on the same object, person, or action at the same time, with each being aware of the other's interest in that visual target.

lateral geniculate bodies: small knee-shaped structures deep inside the brain that act as relay stations to convey visual information from the eyes through the brain.

learning disability: a disorder that affects a person's ability to understand or use spoken or written language, do mathematical calculations, coordinate movements, or direct attention.

legal blindness: visual acuity for distance vision of 20/200 or less in the better eye after best correction, or a visual field of no greater than 20 degrees in the better eye.

lens: the transparent biconvex structure within the eye that allows it to refract light rays, enabling the rays to focus on the retina; also called the crystalline lens. Also, any transparent material that can refract light in a predictable manner.

light perception (LP): the ability to discern the presence or absence of light, but not its source or direction.

low vision: visual impairment that is severe enough to impede a person's ability to learn or perform usual tasks of daily life but still allows some functionally useful visual discrimination. It covers a range from mild to severe visual impairment, but excludes total blindness.

magnetic resonance imaging (MRI): a neuroimaging procedure that shows the anatomical features of the brain in great detail and can be used to study brain structure following injury.

meningitis: a serious and often life-threatening disease marked by inflammation in the outer layer of the brain or spinal cord.

microcephaly: significantly smaller head than normal for age and gender based on standardized charts.

motor skills: skills related to fine and gross physical movement.

multiple disabilities: two or more concomitant disabilities (physical, cognitive, behavioral, or emotional) that have a direct effect on the ability to learn or interact with the environment.

myopia: a refractive error resulting from an eyeball that is longer than "typical"; corrected with a concave (minus) lens; also known as nearsightedness.

neurological visual impairment: a visual impairment that is caused by an injury to or disorder within the brain rather than the structure of the eye.

nystagmus: unintentional or involuntary to- and- fro movement of the eyes.

object permanence: the understanding that objects still exist when they cannot be seen, heard, touched, smelled, or sensed.

occipital lobe: the primary processing region of the brain for visual information.

ocular visual impairment: visual impairment caused by a disorder of the eye or optic nerve (but not the brain).

Office of Special Education Programs (OSEP): part of the United States Department of Education, OSEP provides leadership and support for professionals working with children with disabilities, as well as protecting the educational rights of children with disabilities from age 3 through 21.

optic ataxia: impaired accuracy of movement of the limbs and body through visual space because visual guidance of movement is impaired.

optic chiasm: the X- shaped structure formed by the joining up of the optic nerves, which cross and then become the optic tracts just below and leading into the brain.

optic nerve: the sensory nerve that carries electrical impulses from the eye to the brain.

optic nerve atrophy: the degeneration or malfunction of the optic nerve, characterized by a pale optic disk.

optic nerve hypoplasia: a congenitally small optic disc, usually surrounded by a light halo representing a regression in growth during the prenatal period; may result in reduced visual acuity.

optic radiations: a collection of nerve axons that carry information from the lateral geniculate bodies to the visual cortex in the occipital lobes.

optic tract: bundles of nerve fibers that emerge from the back of the optic chiasm on each side that carry visual information to the lateral geniculate bodies.

optotype: the letters, numbers, or symbols of different sizes employed in testing the acuity of vision.

parietal lobe: the part of the brain that processes information about temperature, taste, touch, and movement.

periventricular leukomalacia (PVL): a type of brain injury that affects primarily premature infants that involves the death of small areas of brain tissue around fluid-filled areas called ventricles.

preferential looking: a method of evaluating vision in which a patterned stimulus is presented in one of two possible locations and the fixation (looking behavior) of an infant or nonverbal child is assessed to determine whether the stimulus was detected.

prosopagnosia: the inability to recognize faces.

receptive language: the ability to understand information and words.

refractive error: a focusing inaccuracy within the eye such that light rays do not come into clear focus on the retina, resulting in a blurred image.

retina: the innermost layer of the eye, which receives the image formed by the lens, containing light-sensitive nerve cells and fibers connecting with the brain through the optic nerve.

retinopathy of prematurity: a series of retinal changes (formerly called retrolental fibroplasia), from mild to total retinal detachment, seen primarily in premature infants, that may be arrested at any stage. Functional vision can range from near normal to total blindness.

rubella: a common mild viral infection that, when contracted by women during the first trimester of pregnancy, has a likelihood of generating fetal abnormalities, such as mental retardation, heart disease, hearing defects, and eye disorders.

scaffolding: the provision of varying instructional supports to help students learn new concepts or engage in difficult tasks.

seizure disorder: a sudden, involuntary contraction that disrupts the functioning of the nervous system and may result in changes in awareness, motor activity, and general behavior that occur alone or in combinations. A partial seizure occurs in one area of the brain in one cerebral hemisphere; generalized seizures occur in both hemispheres or begin in one and travel to the other.

sensory integration disorder: a difficulty with organizing and responding to information received by the senses.

septo-optic dysplasia: a disorder in early brain development which includes under-development of the optic nerves, abnormal development of the structures that separate and connect the right and left halves of the brain, and under-development of the pituitary gland.

shaken baby syndrome: a group of symptoms that tend to occur in an infant which has been severely shaken or tossed, which can cause internal trauma primarily to the brain or death in some cases.

Snellen chart: the traditional eye chart, whose top line consists of the letter *E* and which is used to determine visual acuity in routine eye examinations.

spatial awareness: the ability to be aware of objects in space and the body's position in relation to them.

spina bifida: a birth defect that occurs when the spine does not develop completely before birth and does not completely cover the spinal cord

stereopsis: fine depth perception that results from the brain's interpretation of the slight difference between the disparate pictures of the same visual scene provided by the two eyes.

strabismus: an extrinsic muscle imbalance that causes misalignment of the eyes.

Teller Acuity Cards: a subjective method for measuring resolution (grating) acuity in infants, young children, and adults who cannot respond verbally to standard acuity measurements.

temporal lobes: the areas of the brain under the temples that analyze the input from the senses. They provide the memory banks that underpin knowledge and recognition.

total blindness: the complete lack of light and form perception; recorded as NLP (no light perception).

toxoplasmosis: a congenital infection in utero (caused by microorganisms in animal feces and raw meat) that may produce cataracts, blindness, jaundice, seizures, large lymph nodes, and pneumonia in infants; characterized by inflammation of the retina and choroid that causes scarring.

ventral stream: visual pathway between the occipital and temporal lobes, sometimes known as the "what" pathway, which supports the process of visual recognition. Dysfunction can cause impaired recognition of objects and persons and impaired orientation in surrounding and extended space.

vestibular system: an internal body sense that is composed of three structures in the inner ear that register the speed, force, and direction of movement; the effect of gravity on the body; and the position of one's head and body.

vision: the ability to interpret what is seen.

visual ability: a person's capacity to perform tasks that are dependent upon seeing.

visual acuity: the sharpness of vision with respect to the ability to distinguish detail, often measured as the eye's ability to distinguish the details and shapes of objects at a designated distance; involves central (macular) vision.

visual cortex: the primary cortical region of the brain that receives, integrates, and processes visual information relayed from the retinas.

visual field: the area that is visible without shifting the gaze; measured by the angle of the cone shape formed by the area that can be seen without shifting the gaze when looking at a point straight ahead.

visual impairment any degree of vision loss that affects an individual's ability to perform the tasks of daily life, caused by a visual system that is not working as typically expected or not formed correctly.

visual latency: the time taken to receive and process incoming visual information in the brain.

INDEX

Note: Page numbers followed by *f* indicate a figure on the corresponding page. Page numbers followed by *i* indicate a table on the corresponding page. Page numbers followed by *t* indicate a table on the corresponding page.

ABOUT THE AUTHOR

Anne V. McComiskey is a Teacher of the Visually Impaired who has been working in the field of visual impairments for over 47 years. She has founded three programs for families of very young children who are blind/visually impaired including the BEGIN program in Atlanta, Georgia. Anne received her Master's degree in education, specializing in visual impairment from Boston College and Perkins School for the Blind, where she taught 5th and 6th grades. She has extensive experience evaluating and working with children with multiple needs including cortical visual impairment. Family support and education is an integral part of her work. Anne designed the Braille Readiness Skills Grid published by *Journal of Visual Impairment & Blindness* in 1996 and included in *Foundations of Education*, volume 2, by Alan J. Koenig and M. Cay Holbrook. Anne lives in the Atlanta area with her husband, Frank. She has two children and two adorable grandchildren.

CPSIA information can be obtained
at www.ICGtesting.com
Printed in the USA
FSHW021212241121
86350FS